I0006892

PostgreSQL 9.6 Vol3: Client Interfaces

A catalogue record for this book is available from the Hong Kong Public Libraries.

Published in Hong Kong by Samurai Media Limited.

Email: info@samuraimedia.org

ISBN 978-988-8406-70-8

Copyright 1996 to 2016 The PostgreSQL Global Development Group

PostgreSQL is Copyright 1996 to 2016 by the PostgreSQL Global Development Group.
Postgres95 is Copyright 1994 to 1995 by the Regents of the University of California.
Permission to use, copy, modify, and distribute this software and its documentation for any purpose, without fee, and without a written agreement is hereby granted, provided that the above copyright notice and this paragraph and the following two paragraphs appear in all copies.

IN NO EVENT SHALL THE UNIVERSITY OF CALIFORNIA BE LIABLE TO ANY PARTY FOR DIRECT, INDIRECT, SPECIAL, INCIDENTAL, OR CONSEQUENTIAL DAMAGES, INCLUDING LOST PROFITS, ARISING OUT OF THE USE OF THIS SOFTWARE AND ITS DOCUMENTATION, EVEN IF THE UNIVERSITY OF CALIFORNIA HAS BEEN ADVISED OF THE POSSIBILITY OF SUCH DAMAGE.

THE UNIVERSITY OF CALIFORNIA SPECIFICALLY DISCLAIMS ANYWARRANTIES, INCLUDING, BUT NOT LIMITED TO, THE IMPLIED WARRANTIES OF MERCHANTABILITY AND FITNESS FOR A PARTICULAR PURPOSE. THE SOFTWARE PROVIDED HEREUNDER IS ON AN AS-IS BASIS, AND THE UNIVERSITY OF CALIFORNIA HAS NO OBLIGATIONS TO PROVIDE MAINTENANCE, SUPPORT, UPDATES, ENHANCEMENTS, OR MODIFICATIONS.

Minor modifications for publication Copyright 2016 Samurai Media Limited.

Background Cover Image by https://www.flickr.com/people/webtreatsetc/
The blue and white elephant logo is Copyright by Jeff MacDonald

Table of Contents

IV. Client Interfaces

This part describes the client programming interfaces distributed with PostgreSQL. Each of these chapters can be read independently. Note that there are many other programming interfaces for client programs that are distributed separately and contain their own documentation (Appendix H lists some of the more popular ones). Readers of this part should be familiar with using SQL commands to manipulate and query the database (see Part II) and of course with the programming language that the interface uses.

Chapter 32. libpq - C Library

libpq is the C application programmer's interface to PostgreSQL. libpq is a set of library functions that allow client programs to pass queries to the PostgreSQL backend server and to receive the results of these queries.

libpq is also the underlying engine for several other PostgreSQL application interfaces, including those written for C++, Perl, Python, Tcl and ECPG. So some aspects of libpq's behavior will be important to you if you use one of those packages. In particular, Section 32.14, Section 32.15 and Section 32.18 describe behavior that is visible to the user of any application that uses libpq.

Some short programs are included at the end of this chapter (Section 32.21) to show how to write programs that use libpq. There are also several complete examples of libpq applications in the directory `src/test/examples` in the source code distribution.

Client programs that use libpq must include the header file `libpq-fe.h` and must link with the libpq library.

32.1. Database Connection Control Functions

The following functions deal with making a connection to a PostgreSQL backend server. An application program can have several backend connections open at one time. (One reason to do that is to access more than one database.) Each connection is represented by a `PGconn` object, which is obtained from the function `PQconnectdb`, `PQconnectdbParams`, or `PQsetdbLogin`. Note that these functions will always return a non-null object pointer, unless perhaps there is too little memory even to allocate the `PGconn` object. The `PQstatus` function should be called to check the return value for a successful connection before queries are sent via the connection object.

Warning

On Unix, forking a process with open libpq connections can lead to unpredictable results because the parent and child processes share the same sockets and operating system resources. For this reason, such usage is not recommended, though doing an `exec` from the child process to load a new executable is safe.

Note: On Windows, there is a way to improve performance if a single database connection is repeatedly started and shutdown. Internally, libpq calls `WSAStartup()` and `WSACleanup()` for connection startup and shutdown, respectively. `WSAStartup()` increments an internal Windows library reference count which is decremented by `WSACleanup()`. When the reference count is just one, calling `WSACleanup()` frees all resources and all DLLs are unloaded. This is an expensive operation. To avoid this, an application can manually call `WSAStartup()` so resources will not be freed when the last database connection is closed.

`PQconnectdbParams`

Makes a new connection to the database server.

```
PGconn *PQconnectdbParams(const char * const *keywords,
```

```
const char * const *values,
int expand_dbname);
```

This function opens a new database connection using the parameters taken from two NULL-terminated arrays. The first, keywords, is defined as an array of strings, each one being a key word. The second, values, gives the value for each key word. Unlike PQsetdbLogin below, the parameter set can be extended without changing the function signature, so use of this function (or its nonblocking analogs PQconnectStartParams and PQconnectPoll) is preferred for new application programming.

The currently recognized parameter key words are listed in Section 32.1.2.

When expand_dbname is non-zero, the dbname key word value is allowed to be recognized as a connection string. Only the first occurrence of dbname is expanded this way, any subsequent dbname value is processed as plain database name. More details on the possible connection string formats appear in Section 32.1.1.

The passed arrays can be empty to use all default parameters, or can contain one or more parameter settings. They should be matched in length. Processing will stop at the first NULL element in the keywords array.

If any parameter is NULL or an empty string, the corresponding environment variable (see Section 32.14) is checked. If the environment variable is not set either, then the indicated built-in defaults are used.

In general key words are processed from the beginning of these arrays in index order. The effect of this is that when key words are repeated, the last processed value is retained. Therefore, through careful placement of the dbname key word, it is possible to determine what may be overridden by a conninfo string, and what may not.

PQconnectdb

Makes a new connection to the database server.

```
PGconn *PQconnectdb(const char *conninfo);
```

This function opens a new database connection using the parameters taken from the string conninfo.

The passed string can be empty to use all default parameters, or it can contain one or more parameter settings separated by whitespace, or it can contain a URI. See Section 32.1.1 for details.

PQsetdbLogin

Makes a new connection to the database server.

```
PGconn *PQsetdbLogin(const char *pghost,
                     const char *pgport,
                     const char *pgoptions,
                     const char *pgtty,
                     const char *dbName,
                     const char *login,
                     const char *pwd);
```

This is the predecessor of PQconnectdb with a fixed set of parameters. It has the same functionality except that the missing parameters will always take on default values. Write NULL or an empty string for any one of the fixed parameters that is to be defaulted.

If the `dbName` contains an = sign or has a valid connection URI prefix, it is taken as a `conninfo` string in exactly the same way as if it had been passed to `PQconnectdb`, and the remaining parameters are then applied as specified for `PQconnectdbParams`.

`PQsetdb`

Makes a new connection to the database server.

```
PGconn *PQsetdb(char *pghost,
                char *pgport,
                char *pgoptions,
                char *pgtty,
                char *dbName);
```

This is a macro that calls `PQsetdbLogin` with null pointers for the `login` and `pwd` parameters. It is provided for backward compatibility with very old programs.

`PQconnectStartParams`
`PQconnectStart`
`PQconnectPoll`

Make a connection to the database server in a nonblocking manner.

```
PGconn *PQconnectStartParams(const char * const *keywords,
                             const char * const *values,
                             int expand_dbname);
```

```
PGconn *PQconnectStart(const char *conninfo);
```

```
PostgresPollingStatusType PQconnectPoll(PGconn *conn);
```

These three functions are used to open a connection to a database server such that your application's thread of execution is not blocked on remote I/O whilst doing so. The point of this approach is that the waits for I/O to complete can occur in the application's main loop, rather than down inside `PQconnectdbParams` or `PQconnectdb`, and so the application can manage this operation in parallel with other activities.

With `PQconnectStartParams`, the database connection is made using the parameters taken from the `keywords` and `values` arrays, and controlled by `expand_dbname`, as described above for `PQconnectdbParams`.

With `PQconnectStart`, the database connection is made using the parameters taken from the string `conninfo` as described above for `PQconnectdb`.

Neither `PQconnectStartParams` nor `PQconnectStart` nor `PQconnectPoll` will block, so long as a number of restrictions are met:

- The `hostaddr` and `host` parameters are used appropriately to ensure that name and reverse name queries are not made. See the documentation of these parameters in Section 32.1.2 for details.

- If you call `PQtrace`, ensure that the stream object into which you trace will not block.

- You ensure that the socket is in the appropriate state before calling `PQconnectPoll`, as described below.

Note: use of `PQconnectStartParams` is analogous to `PQconnectStart` shown below.

To begin a nonblocking connection request, call `conn = PQconnectStart("connection_info_string")`. If `conn` is null, then libpq has been unable to allocate a new `PGconn` structure. Otherwise, a valid `PGconn` pointer is returned (though not yet representing a valid connection to the database). On return from `PQconnectStart`, call `status = PQstatus(conn)`. If `status` equals `CONNECTION_BAD`, `PQconnectStart` has failed.

If `PQconnectStart` succeeds, the next stage is to poll libpq so that it can proceed with the connection sequence. Use `PQsocket(conn)` to obtain the descriptor of the socket underlying the database connection. Loop thus: If `PQconnectPoll(conn)` last returned `PGRES_POLLING_READING`, wait until the socket is ready to read (as indicated by `select()`, `poll()`, or similar system function). Then call `PQconnectPoll(conn)` again. Conversely, if `PQconnectPoll(conn)` last returned `PGRES_POLLING_WRITING`, wait until the socket is ready to write, then call `PQconnectPoll(conn)` again. If you have yet to call `PQconnectPoll`, i.e., just after the call to `PQconnectStart`, behave as if it last returned `PGRES_POLLING_WRITING`. Continue this loop until `PQconnectPoll(conn)` returns `PGRES_POLLING_FAILED`, indicating the connection procedure has failed, or `PGRES_POLLING_OK`, indicating the connection has been successfully made.

At any time during connection, the status of the connection can be checked by calling `PQstatus`. If this call returns `CONNECTION_BAD`, then the connection procedure has failed; if the call returns `CONNECTION_OK`, then the connection is ready. Both of these states are equally detectable from the return value of `PQconnectPoll`, described above. Other states might also occur during (and only during) an asynchronous connection procedure. These indicate the current stage of the connection procedure and might be useful to provide feedback to the user for example. These statuses are:

`CONNECTION_STARTED`

Waiting for connection to be made.

`CONNECTION_MADE`

Connection OK; waiting to send.

`CONNECTION_AWAITING_RESPONSE`

Waiting for a response from the server.

`CONNECTION_AUTH_OK`

Received authentication; waiting for backend start-up to finish.

`CONNECTION_SSL_STARTUP`

Negotiating SSL encryption.

`CONNECTION_SETENV`

Negotiating environment-driven parameter settings.

Note that, although these constants will remain (in order to maintain compatibility), an application should never rely upon these occurring in a particular order, or at all, or on the status always being one of these documented values. An application might do something like this:

```
switch(PQstatus(conn))
{
        case CONNECTION_STARTED:
            feedback = "Connecting...";
```

```
            break;

        case CONNECTION_MADE:
            feedback = "Connected to server...";
            break;
        .
        .
        .

        default:
            feedback = "Connecting...";
}
```

The `connect_timeout` connection parameter is ignored when using `PQconnectPoll`; it is the application's responsibility to decide whether an excessive amount of time has elapsed. Otherwise, `PQconnectStart` followed by a `PQconnectPoll` loop is equivalent to `PQconnectdb`.

Note that if `PQconnectStart` returns a non-null pointer, you must call `PQfinish` when you are finished with it, in order to dispose of the structure and any associated memory blocks. This must be done even if the connection attempt fails or is abandoned.

PQconndefaults

Returns the default connection options.

```
PQconninfoOption *PQconndefaults(void);

typedef struct
{
    char    *keyword;   /* The keyword of the option */
    char    *envvar;    /* Fallback environment variable name */
    char    *compiled;  /* Fallback compiled in default value */
    char    *val;       /* Option's current value, or NULL */
    char    *label;     /* Label for field in connect dialog */
    char    *dispchar;  /* Indicates how to display this field
                           in a connect dialog. Values are:
                           ""        Display entered value as is
                           "*"       Password field - hide value
                           "D"       Debug option - don't show by default */
    int     dispsize;   /* Field size in characters for dialog */
} PQconninfoOption;
```

Returns a connection options array. This can be used to determine all possible `PQconnectdb` options and their current default values. The return value points to an array of `PQconninfoOption` structures, which ends with an entry having a null `keyword` pointer. The null pointer is returned if memory could not be allocated. Note that the current default values (`val` fields) will depend on environment variables and other context. A missing or invalid service file will be silently ignored. Callers must treat the connection options data as read-only.

After processing the options array, free it by passing it to `PQconninfoFree`. If this is not done, a small amount of memory is leaked for each call to `PQconndefaults`.

PQconninfo

Returns the connection options used by a live connection.

```
PQconninfoOption *PQconninfo(PGconn *conn);
```

Returns a connection options array. This can be used to determine all possible `PQconnectdb` options and the values that were used to connect to the server. The return value points to an array of `PQconninfoOption` structures, which ends with an entry having a null `keyword` pointer. All notes above for `PQconndefaults` also apply to the result of `PQconninfo`.

`PQconninfoParse`

Returns parsed connection options from the provided connection string.

`PQconninfoOption *PQconninfoParse(const char *conninfo, char **errmsg);`

Parses a connection string and returns the resulting options as an array; or returns `NULL` if there is a problem with the connection string. This function can be used to extract the `PQconnectdb` options in the provided connection string. The return value points to an array of `PQconninfoOption` structures, which ends with an entry having a null `keyword` pointer.

All legal options will be present in the result array, but the `PQconninfoOption` for any option not present in the connection string will have `val` set to `NULL`; default values are not inserted.

If `errmsg` is not `NULL`, then `*errmsg` is set to `NULL` on success, else to a `malloc`'d error string explaining the problem. (It is also possible for `*errmsg` to be set to `NULL` and the function to return `NULL`; this indicates an out-of-memory condition.)

After processing the options array, free it by passing it to `PQconninfoFree`. If this is not done, some memory is leaked for each call to `PQconninfoParse`. Conversely, if an error occurs and `errmsg` is not `NULL`, be sure to free the error string using `PQfreemem`.

`PQfinish`

Closes the connection to the server. Also frees memory used by the `PGconn` object.

`void PQfinish(PGconn *conn);`

Note that even if the server connection attempt fails (as indicated by `PQstatus`), the application should call `PQfinish` to free the memory used by the `PGconn` object. The `PGconn` pointer must not be used again after `PQfinish` has been called.

`PQreset`

Resets the communication channel to the server.

`void PQreset(PGconn *conn);`

This function will close the connection to the server and attempt to reestablish a new connection to the same server, using all the same parameters previously used. This might be useful for error recovery if a working connection is lost.

`PQresetStart`
`PQresetPoll`

Reset the communication channel to the server, in a nonblocking manner.

`int PQresetStart(PGconn *conn);`

`PostgresPollingStatusType PQresetPoll(PGconn *conn);`

These functions will close the connection to the server and attempt to reestablish a new connection to the same server, using all the same parameters previously used. This can be useful for error recovery if a working connection is lost. They differ from `PQreset` (above) in that they act in a nonblocking manner. These functions suffer from the same restrictions as PQconnectStartParams, PQconnectStart and PQconnectPoll.

To initiate a connection reset, call PQresetStart. If it returns 0, the reset has failed. If it returns 1, poll the reset using PQresetPoll in exactly the same way as you would create the connection using PQconnectPoll.

PQpingParams

PQpingParams reports the status of the server. It accepts connection parameters identical to those of PQconnectdbParams, described above. It is not necessary to supply correct user name, password, or database name values to obtain the server status; however, if incorrect values are provided, the server will log a failed connection attempt.

```
PGPing PQpingParams(const char * const *keywords,
                    const char * const *values,
                    int expand_dbname);
```
The function returns one of the following values:

PQPING_OK

The server is running and appears to be accepting connections.

PQPING_REJECT

The server is running but is in a state that disallows connections (startup, shutdown, or crash recovery).

PQPING_NO_RESPONSE

The server could not be contacted. This might indicate that the server is not running, or that there is something wrong with the given connection parameters (for example, wrong port number), or that there is a network connectivity problem (for example, a firewall blocking the connection request).

PQPING_NO_ATTEMPT

No attempt was made to contact the server, because the supplied parameters were obviously incorrect or there was some client-side problem (for example, out of memory).

PQping

PQping reports the status of the server. It accepts connection parameters identical to those of PQconnectdb, described above. It is not necessary to supply correct user name, password, or database name values to obtain the server status; however, if incorrect values are provided, the server will log a failed connection attempt.

```
PGPing PQping(const char *conninfo);
```
The return values are the same as for PQpingParams.

32.1.1. Connection Strings

Several libpq functions parse a user-specified string to obtain connection parameters. There are two accepted formats for these strings: plain `keyword = value` strings and RFC 3986[1] URIs.

32.1.1.1. Keyword/Value Connection Strings

In the first format, each parameter setting is in the form `keyword = value`. Spaces around the equal sign are optional. To write an empty value, or a value containing spaces, surround it with single quotes, e.g., `keyword = 'a value'`. Single quotes and backslashes within the value must be escaped with a backslash, i.e., `\'` and `\\`.

Example:

```
host=localhost port=5432 dbname=mydb connect_timeout=10
```

The recognized parameter key words are listed in Section 32.1.2.

32.1.1.2. Connection URIs

The general form for a connection URI is:

```
postgresql://[user[:password]@][netloc][:port][/dbname][?param1=value1&...]
```

The URI scheme designator can be either `postgresql://` or `postgres://`. Each of the URI parts is optional. The following examples illustrate valid URI syntax uses:

```
postgresql://
postgresql://localhost
postgresql://localhost:5433
postgresql://localhost/mydb
postgresql://user@localhost
postgresql://user:secret@localhost
postgresql://other@localhost/otherdb?connect_timeout=10&application_name=myapp
```

Components of the hierarchical part of the URI can also be given as parameters. For example:

```
postgresql:///mydb?host=localhost&port=5433
```

Percent-encoding may be used to include symbols with special meaning in any of the URI parts.

Any connection parameters not corresponding to key words listed in Section 32.1.2 are ignored and a warning message about them is sent to `stderr`.

For improved compatibility with JDBC connection URIs, instances of parameter `ssl=true` are translated into `sslmode=require`.

---

1. http://www.ietf.org/rfc/rfc3986.txt

The host part may be either host name or an IP address. To specify an IPv6 host address, enclose it in square brackets:

```
postgresql://[2001:db8::1234]/database
```

The host component is interpreted as described for the parameter host. In particular, a Unix-domain socket connection is chosen if the host part is either empty or starts with a slash, otherwise a TCP/IP connection is initiated. Note, however, that the slash is a reserved character in the hierarchical part of the URI. So, to specify a non-standard Unix-domain socket directory, either omit the host specification in the URI and specify the host as a parameter, or percent-encode the path in the host component of the URI:

```
postgresql:///dbname?host=/var/lib/postgresql
postgresql://%2Fvar%2Flib%2Fpostgresql/dbname
```

32.1.2. Parameter Key Words

The currently recognized parameter key words are:

host

> Name of host to connect to. If this begins with a slash, it specifies Unix-domain communication rather than TCP/IP communication; the value is the name of the directory in which the socket file is stored. The default behavior when host is not specified is to connect to a Unix-domain socket in /tmp (or whatever socket directory was specified when PostgreSQL was built). On machines without Unix-domain sockets, the default is to connect to localhost.

hostaddr

> Numeric IP address of host to connect to. This should be in the standard IPv4 address format, e.g., 172.28.40.9. If your machine supports IPv6, you can also use those addresses. TCP/IP communication is always used when a nonempty string is specified for this parameter.

> Using hostaddr instead of host allows the application to avoid a host name look-up, which might be important in applications with time constraints. However, a host name is required for GSSAPI or SSPI authentication methods, as well as for verify-full SSL certificate verification. The following rules are used:

> - If host is specified without hostaddr, a host name lookup occurs.

> - If hostaddr is specified without host, the value for hostaddr gives the server network address. The connection attempt will fail if the authentication method requires a host name.

> - If both host and hostaddr are specified, the value for hostaddr gives the server network address. The value for host is ignored unless the authentication method requires it, in which case it will be used as the host name.

> Note that authentication is likely to fail if host is not the name of the server at network address hostaddr. Also, note that host rather than hostaddr is used to identify the connection in ~/.pgpass (see Section 32.15).

Without either a host name or host address, libpq will connect using a local Unix-domain socket; or on machines without Unix-domain sockets, it will attempt to connect to `localhost`.

port

Port number to connect to at the server host, or socket file name extension for Unix-domain connections.

dbname

The database name. Defaults to be the same as the user name. In certain contexts, the value is checked for extended formats; see Section 32.1.1 for more details on those.

user

PostgreSQL user name to connect as. Defaults to be the same as the operating system name of the user running the application.

password

Password to be used if the server demands password authentication.

connect_timeout

Maximum wait for connection, in seconds (write as a decimal integer string). Zero or not specified means wait indefinitely. It is not recommended to use a timeout of less than 2 seconds.

client_encoding

This sets the `client_encoding` configuration parameter for this connection. In addition to the values accepted by the corresponding server option, you can use `auto` to determine the right encoding from the current locale in the client (`LC_CTYPE` environment variable on Unix systems).

options

Specifies command-line options to send to the server at connection start. For example, setting this to `-c geqo=off` sets the session's value of the `geqo` parameter to `off`. Spaces within this string are considered to separate command-line arguments, unless escaped with a backslash (\); write \\ to represent a literal backslash. For a detailed discussion of the available options, consult Chapter 19.

application_name

Specifies a value for the application_name configuration parameter.

fallback_application_name

Specifies a fallback value for the application_name configuration parameter. This value will be used if no value has been given for `application_name` via a connection parameter or the `PGAPPNAME` environment variable. Specifying a fallback name is useful in generic utility programs that wish to set a default application name but allow it to be overridden by the user.

keepalives

Controls whether client-side TCP keepalives are used. The default value is 1, meaning on, but you can change this to 0, meaning off, if keepalives are not wanted. This parameter is ignored for connections made via a Unix-domain socket.

keepalives_idle

Controls the number of seconds of inactivity after which TCP should send a keepalive message to the server. A value of zero uses the system default. This parameter is ignored for connections made via a Unix-domain socket, or if keepalives are disabled. It is only supported on systems where the `TCP_KEEPIDLE` or `TCP_KEEPALIVE` socket option is available, and on Windows; on other systems, it has no effect.

keepalives_interval

Controls the number of seconds after which a TCP keepalive message that is not acknowledged by the server should be retransmitted. A value of zero uses the system default. This parameter is ignored for connections made via a Unix-domain socket, or if keepalives are disabled. It is only supported on systems where the `TCP_KEEPINTVL` socket option is available, and on Windows; on other systems, it has no effect.

keepalives_count

Controls the number of TCP keepalives that can be lost before the client's connection to the server is considered dead. A value of zero uses the system default. This parameter is ignored for connections made via a Unix-domain socket, or if keepalives are disabled. It is only supported on systems where the `TCP_KEEPCNT` socket option is available; on other systems, it has no effect.

tty

Ignored (formerly, this specified where to send server debug output).

sslmode

This option determines whether or with what priority a secure SSL TCP/IP connection will be negotiated with the server. There are six modes:

disable

only try a non-SSL connection

allow

first try a non-SSL connection; if that fails, try an SSL connection

prefer (default)

first try an SSL connection; if that fails, try a non-SSL connection

require

only try an SSL connection. If a root CA file is present, verify the certificate in the same way as if `verify-ca` was specified

verify-ca

only try an SSL connection, and verify that the server certificate is issued by a trusted certificate authority (CA)

verify-full

only try an SSL connection, verify that the server certificate is issued by a trusted CA and that the requested server host name matches that in the certificate

See Section 32.18 for a detailed description of how these options work.

`sslmode` is ignored for Unix domain socket communication. If PostgreSQL is compiled without SSL support, using options `require`, `verify-ca`, or `verify-full` will cause an error, while options `allow` and `prefer` will be accepted but libpq will not actually attempt an SSL connection.

`requiressl`

> This option is deprecated in favor of the `sslmode` setting.
>
> If set to 1, an SSL connection to the server is required (this is equivalent to `sslmode require`). libpq will then refuse to connect if the server does not accept an SSL connection. If set to 0 (default), libpq will negotiate the connection type with the server (equivalent to `sslmode prefer`). This option is only available if PostgreSQL is compiled with SSL support.

`sslcompression`

> If set to 1 (default), data sent over SSL connections will be compressed (this requires OpenSSL version 0.9.8 or later). If set to 0, compression will be disabled (this requires OpenSSL 1.0.0 or later). This parameter is ignored if a connection without SSL is made, or if the version of OpenSSL used does not support it.
>
> Compression uses CPU time, but can improve throughput if the network is the bottleneck. Disabling compression can improve response time and throughput if CPU performance is the limiting factor.

`sslcert`

> This parameter specifies the file name of the client SSL certificate, replacing the default `~/.postgresql/postgresql.crt`. This parameter is ignored if an SSL connection is not made.

`sslkey`

> This parameter specifies the location for the secret key used for the client certificate. It can either specify a file name that will be used instead of the default `~/.postgresql/postgresql.key`, or it can specify a key obtained from an external "engine" (engines are OpenSSL loadable modules). An external engine specification should consist of a colon-separated engine name and an engine-specific key identifier. This parameter is ignored if an SSL connection is not made.

`sslrootcert`

> This parameter specifies the name of a file containing SSL certificate authority (CA) certificate(s). If the file exists, the server's certificate will be verified to be signed by one of these authorities. The default is `~/.postgresql/root.crt`.

`sslcrl`

> This parameter specifies the file name of the SSL certificate revocation list (CRL). Certificates listed in this file, if it exists, will be rejected while attempting to authenticate the server's certificate. The default is `~/.postgresql/root.crl`.

`requirepeer`

> This parameter specifies the operating-system user name of the server, for example `requirepeer=postgres`. When making a Unix-domain socket connection, if this parameter is set, the client checks at the beginning of the connection that the server process is running under the specified user name; if it is not, the connection is aborted with an error. This parameter can be used to provide server authentication similar to that available with SSL certificates on TCP/IP connections. (Note that if the Unix-domain socket is in `/tmp` or another publicly writable location, any user could start a server listening there. Use this parameter to ensure that you are connected to a server run by a trusted user.) This option is only supported on platforms for which the `peer` authentication method is implemented; see Section 20.3.6.

`krbsrvname`

> Kerberos service name to use when authenticating with GSSAPI. This must match the service name specified in the server configuration for Kerberos authentication to succeed. (See also Section 20.3.3.)

`gsslib`

> GSS library to use for GSSAPI authentication. Only used on Windows. Set to `gssapi` to force libpq to use the GSSAPI library for authentication instead of the default SSPI.

`service`

> Service name to use for additional parameters. It specifies a service name in `pg_service.conf` that holds additional connection parameters. This allows applications to specify only a service name so connection parameters can be centrally maintained. See Section 32.16.

32.2. Connection Status Functions

These functions can be used to interrogate the status of an existing database connection object.

> **Tip:** libpq application programmers should be careful to maintain the PGconn abstraction. Use the accessor functions described below to get at the contents of PGconn. Reference to internal PGconn fields using `libpq-int.h` is not recommended because they are subject to change in the future.

The following functions return parameter values established at connection. These values are fixed for the life of the PGconn object.

PQdb

> Returns the database name of the connection.
>
> ```
> char *PQdb(const PGconn *conn);
> ```

PQuser

> Returns the user name of the connection.
>
> ```
> char *PQuser(const PGconn *conn);
> ```

PQpass

> Returns the password of the connection.
>
> ```
> char *PQpass(const PGconn *conn);
> ```

PQhost

> Returns the server host name of the connection. This can be a host name, an IP address, or a directory path if the connection is via Unix socket. (The path case can be distinguished because it will always be an absolute path, beginning with /.)
>
> ```
> char *PQhost(const PGconn *conn);
> ```

PQport

Returns the port of the connection.

```
char *PQport(const PGconn *conn);
```

PQtty

Returns the debug TTY of the connection. (This is obsolete, since the server no longer pays attention to the TTY setting, but the function remains for backward compatibility.)

```
char *PQtty(const PGconn *conn);
```

PQoptions

Returns the command-line options passed in the connection request.

```
char *PQoptions(const PGconn *conn);
```

The following functions return status data that can change as operations are executed on the PGconn object.

PQstatus

Returns the status of the connection.

```
ConnStatusType PQstatus(const PGconn *conn);
```

The status can be one of a number of values. However, only two of these are seen outside of an asynchronous connection procedure: CONNECTION_OK and CONNECTION_BAD. A good connection to the database has the status CONNECTION_OK. A failed connection attempt is signaled by status CONNECTION_BAD. Ordinarily, an OK status will remain so until PQfinish, but a communications failure might result in the status changing to CONNECTION_BAD prematurely. In that case the application could try to recover by calling PQreset.

See the entry for PQconnectStartParams, PQconnectStart and PQconnectPoll with regards to other status codes that might be returned.

PQtransactionStatus

Returns the current in-transaction status of the server.

```
PGTransactionStatusType PQtransactionStatus(const PGconn *conn);
```
The status can be PQTRANS_IDLE (currently idle), PQTRANS_ACTIVE (a command is in progress), PQTRANS_INTRANS (idle, in a valid transaction block), or PQTRANS_INERROR (idle, in a failed transaction block). PQTRANS_UNKNOWN is reported if the connection is bad. PQTRANS_ACTIVE is reported only when a query has been sent to the server and not yet completed.

PQparameterStatus

Looks up a current parameter setting of the server.

```
const char *PQparameterStatus(const PGconn *conn, const char *paramName);
```
Certain parameter values are reported by the server automatically at connection startup or whenever their values change. PQparameterStatus can be used to interrogate these settings. It returns the current value of a parameter if known, or NULL if the parameter is not known.

Parameters reported as of the current release include server_version, server_encoding, client_encoding, application_name, is_superuser, session_authorization,

DateStyle, IntervalStyle, TimeZone, integer_datetimes, and standard_conforming_strings. (server_encoding, TimeZone, and integer_datetimes were not reported by releases before 8.0; standard_conforming_strings was not reported by releases before 8.1; IntervalStyle was not reported by releases before 8.4; application_name was not reported by releases before 9.0.) Note that server_version, server_encoding and integer_datetimes cannot change after startup.

Pre-3.0-protocol servers do not report parameter settings, but libpq includes logic to obtain values for server_version and client_encoding anyway. Applications are encouraged to use PQparameterStatus rather than *ad hoc* code to determine these values. (Beware however that on a pre-3.0 connection, changing client_encoding via SET after connection startup will not be reflected by PQparameterStatus.) For server_version, see also PQserverVersion, which returns the information in a numeric form that is much easier to compare against.

If no value for standard_conforming_strings is reported, applications can assume it is off, that is, backslashes are treated as escapes in string literals. Also, the presence of this parameter can be taken as an indication that the escape string syntax (E'...') is accepted.

Although the returned pointer is declared const, it in fact points to mutable storage associated with the PGconn structure. It is unwise to assume the pointer will remain valid across queries.

PQprotocolVersion

Interrogates the frontend/backend protocol being used.

```
int PQprotocolVersion(const PGconn *conn);
```

Applications might wish to use this function to determine whether certain features are supported. Currently, the possible values are 2 (2.0 protocol), 3 (3.0 protocol), or zero (connection bad). The protocol version will not change after connection startup is complete, but it could theoretically change during a connection reset. The 3.0 protocol will normally be used when communicating with PostgreSQL 7.4 or later servers; pre-7.4 servers support only protocol 2.0. (Protocol 1.0 is obsolete and not supported by libpq.)

PQserverVersion

Returns an integer representing the backend version.

```
int PQserverVersion(const PGconn *conn);
```

Applications might use this function to determine the version of the database server they are connected to. The number is formed by converting the major, minor, and revision numbers into two-decimal-digit numbers and appending them together. For example, version 8.1.5 will be returned as 80105, and version 8.2 will be returned as 80200 (leading zeroes are not shown). Zero is returned if the connection is bad.

PQerrorMessage

Returns the error message most recently generated by an operation on the connection.

```
char *PQerrorMessage(const PGconn *conn);
```

Nearly all libpq functions will set a message for PQerrorMessage if they fail. Note that by libpq convention, a nonempty PQerrorMessage result can consist of multiple lines, and will include a trailing newline. The caller should not free the result directly. It will be freed when the associated PGconn handle is passed to PQfinish. The result string should not be expected to remain the same across operations on the PGconn structure.

PQsocket

> Obtains the file descriptor number of the connection socket to the server. A valid descriptor will be greater than or equal to 0; a result of -1 indicates that no server connection is currently open. (This will not change during normal operation, but could change during connection setup or reset.)
>
> ```
> int PQsocket(const PGconn *conn);
> ```

PQbackendPID

> Returns the process ID (PID) of the backend process handling this connection.
>
> ```
> int PQbackendPID(const PGconn *conn);
> ```
>
> The backend PID is useful for debugging purposes and for comparison to NOTIFY messages (which include the PID of the notifying backend process). Note that the PID belongs to a process executing on the database server host, not the local host!

PQconnectionNeedsPassword

> Returns true (1) if the connection authentication method required a password, but none was available. Returns false (0) if not.
>
> ```
> int PQconnectionNeedsPassword(const PGconn *conn);
> ```
>
> This function can be applied after a failed connection attempt to decide whether to prompt the user for a password.

PQconnectionUsedPassword

> Returns true (1) if the connection authentication method used a password. Returns false (0) if not.
>
> ```
> int PQconnectionUsedPassword(const PGconn *conn);
> ```
>
> This function can be applied after either a failed or successful connection attempt to detect whether the server demanded a password.

The following functions return information related to SSL. This information usually doesn't change after a connection is established.

PQsslInUse

> Returns true (1) if the connection uses SSL, false (0) if not.
>
> ```
> int PQsslInUse(const PGconn *conn);
> ```

PQsslAttribute

> Returns SSL-related information about the connection.
>
> ```
> const char *PQsslAttribute(const PGconn *conn, const char *attribute_name);
> ```
>
> The list of available attributes varies depending on the SSL library being used, and the type of connection. If an attribute is not available, returns NULL.
>
> The following attributes are commonly available:
>
> library
>
> > Name of the SSL implementation in use. (Currently, only "OpenSSL" is implemented)

protocol

> SSL/TLS version in use. Common values are `"SSLv2"`, `"SSLv3"`, `"TLSv1"`, `"TLSv1.1"` and `"TLSv1.2"`, but an implementation may return other strings if some other protocol is used.

key_bits

> Number of key bits used by the encryption algorithm.

cipher

> A short name of the ciphersuite used, e.g. `"DHE-RSA-DES-CBC3-SHA"`. The names are specific to each SSL implementation.

compression

> If SSL compression is in use, returns the name of the compression algorithm, or "on" if compression is used but the algorithm is not known. If compression is not in use, returns "off".

PQsslAttributeNames

> Return an array of SSL attribute names available. The array is terminated by a NULL pointer.

```
const char * const * PQsslAttributeNames(const PGconn *conn);
```

PQsslStruct

> Return a pointer to an SSL-implementation-specific object describing the connection.

```
void *PQsslStruct(const PGconn *conn, const char *struct_name);
```

> The struct(s) available depend on the SSL implementation in use. For OpenSSL, there is one struct, available under the name "OpenSSL", and it returns a pointer to the OpenSSL `SSL` struct. To use this function, code along the following lines could be used:

```
#include <libpq-fe.h>
#include <openssl/ssl.h>

...

    SSL *ssl;

    dbconn = PQconnectdb(...);
    ...

    ssl = PQsslStruct(dbconn, "OpenSSL");
    if (ssl)
    {
        /* use OpenSSL functions to access ssl */
    }
```

> This structure can be used to verify encryption levels, check server certificates, and more. Refer to the OpenSSL documentation for information about this structure.

PQgetssl

> Returns the SSL structure used in the connection, or null if SSL is not in use.

```
void *PQgetssl(const PGconn *conn);
```

This function is equivalent to `PQsslStruct(conn, "OpenSSL")`. It should not be used in new applications, because the returned struct is specific to OpenSSL and will not be available if another SSL implementation is used. To check if a connection uses SSL, call `PQsslInUse` instead, and for more details about the connection, use `PQsslAttribute`.

32.3. Command Execution Functions

Once a connection to a database server has been successfully established, the functions described here are used to perform SQL queries and commands.

32.3.1. Main Functions

`PQexec`

Submits a command to the server and waits for the result.

```
PGresult *PQexec(PGconn *conn, const char *command);
```

Returns a `PGresult` pointer or possibly a null pointer. A non-null pointer will generally be returned except in out-of-memory conditions or serious errors such as inability to send the command to the server. The `PQresultStatus` function should be called to check the return value for any errors (including the value of a null pointer, in which case it will return `PGRES_FATAL_ERROR`). Use `PQerrorMessage` to get more information about such errors.

The command string can include multiple SQL commands (separated by semicolons). Multiple queries sent in a single `PQexec` call are processed in a single transaction, unless there are explicit `BEGIN`/`COMMIT` commands included in the query string to divide it into multiple transactions. Note however that the returned `PGresult` structure describes only the result of the last command executed from the string. Should one of the commands fail, processing of the string stops with it and the returned `PGresult` describes the error condition.

`PQexecParams`

Submits a command to the server and waits for the result, with the ability to pass parameters separately from the SQL command text.

```
PGresult *PQexecParams(PGconn *conn,
                       const char *command,
                       int nParams,
                       const Oid *paramTypes,
                       const char * const *paramValues,
                       const int *paramLengths,
                       const int *paramFormats,
                       int resultFormat);
```

`PQexecParams` is like `PQexec`, but offers additional functionality: parameter values can be specified separately from the command string proper, and query results can be requested in either text or binary format. PQexecParams is supported only in protocol 3.0 and later connections; it will fail when using protocol 2.0.

The function arguments are:

conn

> The connection object to send the command through.

command

> The SQL command string to be executed. If parameters are used, they are referred to in the command string as $1, $2, etc.

nParams

> The number of parameters supplied; it is the length of the arrays paramTypes[], paramValues[], paramLengths[], and paramFormats[]. (The array pointers can be NULL when nParams is zero.)

paramTypes[]

> Specifies, by OID, the data types to be assigned to the parameter symbols. If paramTypes is NULL, or any particular element in the array is zero, the server infers a data type for the parameter symbol in the same way it would do for an untyped literal string.

paramValues[]

> Specifies the actual values of the parameters. A null pointer in this array means the corresponding parameter is null; otherwise the pointer points to a zero-terminated text string (for text format) or binary data in the format expected by the server (for binary format).

paramLengths[]

> Specifies the actual data lengths of binary-format parameters. It is ignored for null parameters and text-format parameters. The array pointer can be null when there are no binary parameters.

paramFormats[]

> Specifies whether parameters are text (put a zero in the array entry for the corresponding parameter) or binary (put a one in the array entry for the corresponding parameter). If the array pointer is null then all parameters are presumed to be text strings.

> Values passed in binary format require knowledge of the internal representation expected by the backend. For example, integers must be passed in network byte order. Passing numeric values requires knowledge of the server storage format, as implemented in src/backend/utils/adt/numeric.c::numeric_send() and src/backend/utils/adt/numeric.c::numeric_recv().

resultFormat

> Specify zero to obtain results in text format, or one to obtain results in binary format. (There is not currently a provision to obtain different result columns in different formats, although that is possible in the underlying protocol.)

The primary advantage of PQexecParams over PQexec is that parameter values can be separated from the command string, thus avoiding the need for tedious and error-prone quoting and escaping.

Unlike PQexec, PQexecParams allows at most one SQL command in the given string. (There can be semicolons in it, but not more than one nonempty command.) This is a limitation of the underlying protocol, but has some usefulness as an extra defense against SQL-injection attacks.

> **Tip:** Specifying parameter types via OIDs is tedious, particularly if you prefer not to hard-wire particular OID values into your program. However, you can avoid doing so even in cases where the server by itself cannot determine the type of the parameter, or chooses a different type than you want. In the SQL command text, attach an explicit cast to the parameter symbol to show what data type you will send. For example:
>
> ```
> SELECT * FROM mytable WHERE x = $1::bigint;
> ```
>
> This forces parameter $1 to be treated as bigint, whereas by default it would be assigned the same type as x. Forcing the parameter type decision, either this way or by specifying a numeric type OID, is strongly recommended when sending parameter values in binary format, because binary format has less redundancy than text format and so there is less chance that the server will detect a type mismatch mistake for you.

PQprepare

Submits a request to create a prepared statement with the given parameters, and waits for completion.

```
PGresult *PQprepare(PGconn *conn,
                    const char *stmtName,
                    const char *query,
                    int nParams,
                    const Oid *paramTypes);
```

PQprepare creates a prepared statement for later execution with PQexecPrepared. This feature allows commands to be executed repeatedly without being parsed and planned each time; see PREPARE for details. PQprepare is supported only in protocol 3.0 and later connections; it will fail when using protocol 2.0.

The function creates a prepared statement named stmtName from the query string, which must contain a single SQL command. stmtName can be "" to create an unnamed statement, in which case any pre-existing unnamed statement is automatically replaced; otherwise it is an error if the statement name is already defined in the current session. If any parameters are used, they are referred to in the query as $1, $2, etc. nParams is the number of parameters for which types are pre-specified in the array paramTypes[]. (The array pointer can be NULL when nParams is zero.) paramTypes[] specifies, by OID, the data types to be assigned to the parameter symbols. If paramTypes is NULL, or any particular element in the array is zero, the server assigns a data type to the parameter symbol in the same way it would do for an untyped literal string. Also, the query can use parameter symbols with numbers higher than nParams; data types will be inferred for these symbols as well. (See PQdescribePrepared for a means to find out what data types were inferred.)

As with PQexec, the result is normally a PGresult object whose contents indicate server-side success or failure. A null result indicates out-of-memory or inability to send the command at all. Use PQerrorMessage to get more information about such errors.

Prepared statements for use with `PQexecPrepared` can also be created by executing SQL PREPARE statements. Also, although there is no libpq function for deleting a prepared statement, the SQL DEAL-LOCATE statement can be used for that purpose.

`PQexecPrepared`

Sends a request to execute a prepared statement with given parameters, and waits for the result.

```
PGresult *PQexecPrepared(PGconn *conn,
                         const char *stmtName,
                         int nParams,
                         const char * const *paramValues,
                         const int *paramLengths,
                         const int *paramFormats,
                         int resultFormat);
```

`PQexecPrepared` is like `PQexecParams`, but the command to be executed is specified by naming a previously-prepared statement, instead of giving a query string. This feature allows commands that will be used repeatedly to be parsed and planned just once, rather than each time they are executed. The statement must have been prepared previously in the current session. `PQexecPrepared` is supported only in protocol 3.0 and later connections; it will fail when using protocol 2.0.

The parameters are identical to `PQexecParams`, except that the name of a prepared statement is given instead of a query string, and the `paramTypes[]` parameter is not present (it is not needed since the prepared statement's parameter types were determined when it was created).

`PQdescribePrepared`

Submits a request to obtain information about the specified prepared statement, and waits for completion.

```
PGresult *PQdescribePrepared(PGconn *conn, const char *stmtName);
```

`PQdescribePrepared` allows an application to obtain information about a previously prepared statement. `PQdescribePrepared` is supported only in protocol 3.0 and later connections; it will fail when using protocol 2.0.

`stmtName` can be `""` or `NULL` to reference the unnamed statement, otherwise it must be the name of an existing prepared statement. On success, a `PGresult` with status `PGRES_COMMAND_OK` is returned. The functions `PQnparams` and `PQparamtype` can be applied to this `PGresult` to obtain information about the parameters of the prepared statement, and the functions `PQnfields`, `PQfname`, `PQftype`, etc provide information about the result columns (if any) of the statement.

`PQdescribePortal`

Submits a request to obtain information about the specified portal, and waits for completion.

```
PGresult *PQdescribePortal(PGconn *conn, const char *portalName);
```

`PQdescribePortal` allows an application to obtain information about a previously created portal. (libpq does not provide any direct access to portals, but you can use this function to inspect the properties of a cursor created with a `DECLARE CURSOR` SQL command.) `PQdescribePortal` is supported only in protocol 3.0 and later connections; it will fail when using protocol 2.0.

`portalName` can be `""` or `NULL` to reference the unnamed portal, otherwise it must be the name of an existing portal. On success, a `PGresult` with status `PGRES_COMMAND_OK` is returned. The functions

`PQnfields`, `PQfname`, `PQftype`, etc can be applied to the `PGresult` to obtain information about the result columns (if any) of the portal.

The `PGresult` structure encapsulates the result returned by the server. libpq application programmers should be careful to maintain the `PGresult` abstraction. Use the accessor functions below to get at the contents of `PGresult`. Avoid directly referencing the fields of the `PGresult` structure because they are subject to change in the future.

`PQresultStatus`

Returns the result status of the command.

`ExecStatusType PQresultStatus(const PGresult *res);`

`PQresultStatus` can return one of the following values:

`PGRES_EMPTY_QUERY`

The string sent to the server was empty.

`PGRES_COMMAND_OK`

Successful completion of a command returning no data.

`PGRES_TUPLES_OK`

Successful completion of a command returning data (such as a SELECT or SHOW).

`PGRES_COPY_OUT`

Copy Out (from server) data transfer started.

`PGRES_COPY_IN`

Copy In (to server) data transfer started.

`PGRES_BAD_RESPONSE`

The server's response was not understood.

`PGRES_NONFATAL_ERROR`

A nonfatal error (a notice or warning) occurred.

`PGRES_FATAL_ERROR`

A fatal error occurred.

`PGRES_COPY_BOTH`

Copy In/Out (to and from server) data transfer started. This feature is currently used only for streaming replication, so this status should not occur in ordinary applications.

`PGRES_SINGLE_TUPLE`

The `PGresult` contains a single result tuple from the current command. This status occurs only when single-row mode has been selected for the query (see Section 32.5).

If the result status is `PGRES_TUPLES_OK` or `PGRES_SINGLE_TUPLE`, then the functions described below can be used to retrieve the rows returned by the query. Note that a SELECT command that happens to retrieve zero rows still shows `PGRES_TUPLES_OK`. `PGRES_COMMAND_OK` is for commands that can never return rows (INSERT or UPDATE without a RETURNING clause, etc.). A response of PGRES_EMPTY_QUERY might indicate a bug in the client software.

A result of status PGRES_NONFATAL_ERROR will never be returned directly by PQexec or other query execution functions; results of this kind are instead passed to the notice processor (see Section 32.12).

PQresStatus

Converts the enumerated type returned by PQresultStatus into a string constant describing the status code. The caller should not free the result.

```
char *PQresStatus(ExecStatusType status);
```

PQresultErrorMessage

Returns the error message associated with the command, or an empty string if there was no error.

```
char *PQresultErrorMessage(const PGresult *res);
```
If there was an error, the returned string will include a trailing newline. The caller should not free the result directly. It will be freed when the associated PGresult handle is passed to PQclear.

Immediately following a PQexec or PQgetResult call, PQerrorMessage (on the connection) will return the same string as PQresultErrorMessage (on the result). However, a PGresult will retain its error message until destroyed, whereas the connection's error message will change when subsequent operations are done. Use PQresultErrorMessage when you want to know the status associated with a particular PGresult; use PQerrorMessage when you want to know the status from the latest operation on the connection.

PQresultVerboseErrorMessage

Returns a reformatted version of the error message associated with a PGresult object.

```
char *PQresultVerboseErrorMessage(const PGresult *res,
                                  PGVerbosity verbosity,
                                  PGContextVisibility show_context);
```
In some situations a client might wish to obtain a more detailed version of a previously-reported error. PQresultVerboseErrorMessage addresses this need by computing the message that would have been produced by PQresultErrorMessage if the specified verbosity settings had been in effect for the connection when the given PGresult was generated. If the PGresult is not an error result, "PGresult is not an error result" is reported instead. The returned string includes a trailing newline.

Unlike most other functions for extracting data from a PGresult, the result of this function is a freshly allocated string. The caller must free it using PQfreemem() when the string is no longer needed.

A NULL return is possible if there is insufficient memory.

PQresultErrorField

Returns an individual field of an error report.

```
char *PQresultErrorField(const PGresult *res, int fieldcode);
```
fieldcode is an error field identifier; see the symbols listed below. NULL is returned if the PGresult is not an error or warning result, or does not include the specified field. Field values will normally not include a trailing newline. The caller should not free the result directly. It will be freed when the associated PGresult handle is passed to PQclear.

The following field codes are available:

PG_DIAG_SEVERITY

> The severity; the field contents are ERROR, FATAL, or PANIC (in an error message), or WARNING, NOTICE, DEBUG, INFO, or LOG (in a notice message), or a localized translation of one of these. Always present.

PG_DIAG_SEVERITY_NONLOCALIZED

> The severity; the field contents are ERROR, FATAL, or PANIC (in an error message), or WARNING, NOTICE, DEBUG, INFO, or LOG (in a notice message). This is identical to the PG_DIAG_SEVERITY field except that the contents are never localized. This is present only in reports generated by PostgreSQL versions 9.6 and later.

PG_DIAG_SQLSTATE

> The SQLSTATE code for the error. The SQLSTATE code identifies the type of error that has occurred; it can be used by front-end applications to perform specific operations (such as error handling) in response to a particular database error. For a list of the possible SQLSTATE codes, see Appendix A. This field is not localizable, and is always present.

PG_DIAG_MESSAGE_PRIMARY

> The primary human-readable error message (typically one line). Always present.

PG_DIAG_MESSAGE_DETAIL

> Detail: an optional secondary error message carrying more detail about the problem. Might run to multiple lines.

PG_DIAG_MESSAGE_HINT

> Hint: an optional suggestion what to do about the problem. This is intended to differ from detail in that it offers advice (potentially inappropriate) rather than hard facts. Might run to multiple lines.

PG_DIAG_STATEMENT_POSITION

> A string containing a decimal integer indicating an error cursor position as an index into the original statement string. The first character has index 1, and positions are measured in characters not bytes.

PG_DIAG_INTERNAL_POSITION

> This is defined the same as the PG_DIAG_STATEMENT_POSITION field, but it is used when the cursor position refers to an internally generated command rather than the one submitted by the client. The PG_DIAG_INTERNAL_QUERY field will always appear when this field appears.

PG_DIAG_INTERNAL_QUERY

> The text of a failed internally-generated command. This could be, for example, a SQL query issued by a PL/pgSQL function.

PG_DIAG_CONTEXT

> An indication of the context in which the error occurred. Presently this includes a call stack traceback of active procedural language functions and internally-generated queries. The trace is one entry per line, most recent first.

PG_DIAG_SCHEMA_NAME

> If the error was associated with a specific database object, the name of the schema containing that object, if any.

PG_DIAG_TABLE_NAME

> If the error was associated with a specific table, the name of the table. (Refer to the schema name field for the name of the table's schema.)

PG_DIAG_COLUMN_NAME

> If the error was associated with a specific table column, the name of the column. (Refer to the schema and table name fields to identify the table.)

PG_DIAG_DATATYPE_NAME

> If the error was associated with a specific data type, the name of the data type. (Refer to the schema name field for the name of the data type's schema.)

PG_DIAG_CONSTRAINT_NAME

> If the error was associated with a specific constraint, the name of the constraint. Refer to fields listed above for the associated table or domain. (For this purpose, indexes are treated as constraints, even if they weren't created with constraint syntax.)

PG_DIAG_SOURCE_FILE

> The file name of the source-code location where the error was reported.

PG_DIAG_SOURCE_LINE

> The line number of the source-code location where the error was reported.

PG_DIAG_SOURCE_FUNCTION

> The name of the source-code function reporting the error.

> **Note:** The fields for schema name, table name, column name, data type name, and constraint name are supplied only for a limited number of error types; see Appendix A. Do not assume that the presence of any of these fields guarantees the presence of another field. Core error sources observe the interrelationships noted above, but user-defined functions may use these fields in other ways. In the same vein, do not assume that these fields denote contemporary objects in the current database.

The client is responsible for formatting displayed information to meet its needs; in particular it should break long lines as needed. Newline characters appearing in the error message fields should be treated as paragraph breaks, not line breaks.

Errors generated internally by libpq will have severity and primary message, but typically no other fields. Errors returned by a pre-3.0-protocol server will include severity and primary message, and sometimes a detail message, but no other fields.

Note that error fields are only available from PGresult objects, not PGconn objects; there is no PQerrorField function.

PQclear

> Frees the storage associated with a `PGresult`. Every command result should be freed via `PQclear` when it is no longer needed.
>
> ```
> void PQclear(PGresult *res);
> ```
>
> You can keep a `PGresult` object around for as long as you need it; it does not go away when you issue a new command, nor even if you close the connection. To get rid of it, you must call `PQclear`. Failure to do this will result in memory leaks in your application.

32.3.2. Retrieving Query Result Information

These functions are used to extract information from a `PGresult` object that represents a successful query result (that is, one that has status `PGRES_TUPLES_OK` or `PGRES_SINGLE_TUPLE`). They can also be used to extract information from a successful Describe operation: a Describe's result has all the same column information that actual execution of the query would provide, but it has zero rows. For objects with other status values, these functions will act as though the result has zero rows and zero columns.

PQntuples

> Returns the number of rows (tuples) in the query result. Because it returns an integer result, large result sets might overflow the return value on 32-bit operating systems.
>
> ```
> int PQntuples(const PGresult *res);
> ```

PQnfields

> Returns the number of columns (fields) in each row of the query result.
>
> ```
> int PQnfields(const PGresult *res);
> ```

PQfname

> Returns the column name associated with the given column number. Column numbers start at 0. The caller should not free the result directly. It will be freed when the associated `PGresult` handle is passed to `PQclear`.
>
> ```
> char *PQfname(const PGresult *res,
>               int column_number);
> ```
>
> `NULL` is returned if the column number is out of range.

PQfnumber

> Returns the column number associated with the given column name.
>
> ```
> int PQfnumber(const PGresult *res,
>               const char *column_name);
> ```
>
> -1 is returned if the given name does not match any column.
>
> The given name is treated like an identifier in an SQL command, that is, it is downcased unless double-quoted. For example, given a query result generated from the SQL command:
>
> ```
> SELECT 1 AS FOO, 2 AS "BAR";
> ```
> we would have the results:

```
PQfname(res, 0)                foo
PQfname(res, 1)                BAR
PQfnumber(res, "FOO")          0
PQfnumber(res, "foo")          0
PQfnumber(res, "BAR")          -1
PQfnumber(res, "\"BAR\"")      1
```

PQftable

> Returns the OID of the table from which the given column was fetched. Column numbers start at 0.
>
> ```
> Oid PQftable(const PGresult *res,
>              int column_number);
> ```
>
> InvalidOid is returned if the column number is out of range, or if the specified column is not a simple reference to a table column, or when using pre-3.0 protocol. You can query the system table pg_class to determine exactly which table is referenced.
>
> The type Oid and the constant InvalidOid will be defined when you include the libpq header file. They will both be some integer type.

PQftablecol

> Returns the column number (within its table) of the column making up the specified query result column. Query-result column numbers start at 0, but table columns have nonzero numbers.
>
> ```
> int PQftablecol(const PGresult *res,
>                 int column_number);
> ```
>
> Zero is returned if the column number is out of range, or if the specified column is not a simple reference to a table column, or when using pre-3.0 protocol.

PQfformat

> Returns the format code indicating the format of the given column. Column numbers start at 0.
>
> ```
> int PQfformat(const PGresult *res,
>               int column_number);
> ```
>
> Format code zero indicates textual data representation, while format code one indicates binary representation. (Other codes are reserved for future definition.)

PQftype

> Returns the data type associated with the given column number. The integer returned is the internal OID number of the type. Column numbers start at 0.
>
> ```
> Oid PQftype(const PGresult *res,
>             int column_number);
> ```
>
> You can query the system table pg_type to obtain the names and properties of the various data types. The OIDs of the built-in data types are defined in the file src/include/catalog/pg_type.h in the source tree.

PQfmod

> Returns the type modifier of the column associated with the given column number. Column numbers start at 0.
>
> ```
> int PQfmod(const PGresult *res,
>            int column_number);
> ```

The interpretation of modifier values is type-specific; they typically indicate precision or size limits. The value -1 is used to indicate "no information available". Most data types do not use modifiers, in which case the value is always -1.

PQfsize

Returns the size in bytes of the column associated with the given column number. Column numbers start at 0.

```
int PQfsize(const PGresult *res,
            int column_number);
```

PQfsize returns the space allocated for this column in a database row, in other words the size of the server's internal representation of the data type. (Accordingly, it is not really very useful to clients.) A negative value indicates the data type is variable-length.

PQbinaryTuples

Returns 1 if the PGresult contains binary data and 0 if it contains text data.

```
int PQbinaryTuples(const PGresult *res);
```

This function is deprecated (except for its use in connection with COPY), because it is possible for a single PGresult to contain text data in some columns and binary data in others. PQfformat is preferred. PQbinaryTuples returns 1 only if all columns of the result are binary (format 1).

PQgetvalue

Returns a single field value of one row of a PGresult. Row and column numbers start at 0. The caller should not free the result directly. It will be freed when the associated PGresult handle is passed to PQclear.

```
char *PQgetvalue(const PGresult *res,
                 int row_number,
                 int column_number);
```

For data in text format, the value returned by PQgetvalue is a null-terminated character string representation of the field value. For data in binary format, the value is in the binary representation determined by the data type's typsend and typreceive functions. (The value is actually followed by a zero byte in this case too, but that is not ordinarily useful, since the value is likely to contain embedded nulls.)

An empty string is returned if the field value is null. See PQgetisnull to distinguish null values from empty-string values.

The pointer returned by PQgetvalue points to storage that is part of the PGresult structure. One should not modify the data it points to, and one must explicitly copy the data into other storage if it is to be used past the lifetime of the PGresult structure itself.

PQgetisnull

Tests a field for a null value. Row and column numbers start at 0.

```
int PQgetisnull(const PGresult *res,
                int row_number,
                int column_number);
```

This function returns 1 if the field is null and 0 if it contains a non-null value. (Note that PQgetvalue will return an empty string, not a null pointer, for a null field.)

`PQgetlength`

Returns the actual length of a field value in bytes. Row and column numbers start at 0.

```
int PQgetlength(const PGresult *res,
                int row_number,
                int column_number);
```

This is the actual data length for the particular data value, that is, the size of the object pointed to by `PQgetvalue`. For text data format this is the same as `strlen()`. For binary format this is essential information. Note that one should *not* rely on `PQfsize` to obtain the actual data length.

`PQnparams`

Returns the number of parameters of a prepared statement.

```
int PQnparams(const PGresult *res);
```

This function is only useful when inspecting the result of `PQdescribePrepared`. For other types of queries it will return zero.

`PQparamtype`

Returns the data type of the indicated statement parameter. Parameter numbers start at 0.

```
Oid PQparamtype(const PGresult *res, int param_number);
```

This function is only useful when inspecting the result of `PQdescribePrepared`. For other types of queries it will return zero.

`PQprint`

Prints out all the rows and, optionally, the column names to the specified output stream.

```
void PQprint(FILE *fout,       /* output stream */
             const PGresult *res,
             const PQprintOpt *po);
typedef struct
{
    pqbool  header;      /* print output field headings and row count */
    pqbool  align;       /* fill align the fields */
    pqbool  standard;    /* old brain dead format */
    pqbool  html3;       /* output HTML tables */
    pqbool  expanded;    /* expand tables */
    pqbool  pager;       /* use pager for output if needed */
    char    *fieldSep;   /* field separator */
    char    *tableOpt;   /* attributes for HTML table element */
    char    *caption;    /* HTML table caption */
    char    **fieldName; /* null-terminated array of replacement field names */
} PQprintOpt;
```

This function was formerly used by psql to print query results, but this is no longer the case. Note that it assumes all the data is in text format.

32.3.3. Retrieving Other Result Information

These functions are used to extract other information from `PGresult` objects.

PQcmdStatus

> Returns the command status tag from the SQL command that generated the PGresult.
>
> `char *PQcmdStatus(PGresult *res);`
>
> Commonly this is just the name of the command, but it might include additional data such as the number of rows processed. The caller should not free the result directly. It will be freed when the associated PGresult handle is passed to PQclear.

PQcmdTuples

> Returns the number of rows affected by the SQL command.
>
> `char *PQcmdTuples(PGresult *res);`
>
> This function returns a string containing the number of rows affected by the SQL statement that generated the PGresult. This function can only be used following the execution of a SELECT, CREATE TABLE AS, INSERT, UPDATE, DELETE, MOVE, FETCH, or COPY statement, or an EXECUTE of a prepared query that contains an INSERT, UPDATE, or DELETE statement. If the command that generated the PGresult was anything else, PQcmdTuples returns an empty string. The caller should not free the return value directly. It will be freed when the associated PGresult handle is passed to PQclear.

PQoidValue

> Returns the OID of the inserted row, if the SQL command was an INSERT that inserted exactly one row into a table that has OIDs, or a EXECUTE of a prepared query containing a suitable INSERT statement. Otherwise, this function returns InvalidOid. This function will also return InvalidOid if the table affected by the INSERT statement does not contain OIDs.
>
> `Oid PQoidValue(const PGresult *res);`

PQoidStatus

> This function is deprecated in favor of PQoidValue and is not thread-safe. It returns a string with the OID of the inserted row, while PQoidValue returns the OID value.
>
> `char *PQoidStatus(const PGresult *res);`

32.3.4. Escaping Strings for Inclusion in SQL Commands

PQescapeLiteral

> `char *PQescapeLiteral(PGconn *conn, const char *str, size_t length);`
>
> PQescapeLiteral escapes a string for use within an SQL command. This is useful when inserting data values as literal constants in SQL commands. Certain characters (such as quotes and backslashes) must be escaped to prevent them from being interpreted specially by the SQL parser. PQescapeLiteral performs this operation.
>
> PQescapeLiteral returns an escaped version of the str parameter in memory allocated with malloc(). This memory should be freed using PQfreemem() when the result is no longer needed. A terminating zero byte is not required, and should not be counted in length. (If a terminating zero byte is found before length bytes are processed, PQescapeLiteral stops at the zero; the behavior is thus rather like strncpy.) The return string has all special characters replaced so that they can

be properly processed by the PostgreSQL string literal parser. A terminating zero byte is also added. The single quotes that must surround PostgreSQL string literals are included in the result string.

On error, PQescapeLiteral returns NULL and a suitable message is stored in the conn object.

> **Tip:** It is especially important to do proper escaping when handling strings that were received from an untrustworthy source. Otherwise there is a security risk: you are vulnerable to "SQL injection" attacks wherein unwanted SQL commands are fed to your database.

Note that it is not necessary nor correct to do escaping when a data value is passed as a separate parameter in PQexecParams or its sibling routines.

PQescapeIdentifier

```
char *PQescapeIdentifier(PGconn *conn, const char *str, size_t length);
```

PQescapeIdentifier escapes a string for use as an SQL identifier, such as a table, column, or function name. This is useful when a user-supplied identifier might contain special characters that would otherwise not be interpreted as part of the identifier by the SQL parser, or when the identifier might contain upper case characters whose case should be preserved.

PQescapeIdentifier returns a version of the str parameter escaped as an SQL identifier in memory allocated with malloc(). This memory must be freed using PQfreemem() when the result is no longer needed. A terminating zero byte is not required, and should not be counted in length. (If a terminating zero byte is found before length bytes are processed, PQescapeIdentifier stops at the zero; the behavior is thus rather like strncpy.) The return string has all special characters replaced so that it will be properly processed as an SQL identifier. A terminating zero byte is also added. The return string will also be surrounded by double quotes.

On error, PQescapeIdentifier returns NULL and a suitable message is stored in the conn object.

> **Tip:** As with string literals, to prevent SQL injection attacks, SQL identifiers must be escaped when they are received from an untrustworthy source.

PQescapeStringConn

```
size_t PQescapeStringConn(PGconn *conn,
                          char *to, const char *from, size_t length,
                          int *error);
```

PQescapeStringConn escapes string literals, much like PQescapeLiteral. Unlike PQescapeLiteral, the caller is responsible for providing an appropriately sized buffer. Furthermore, PQescapeStringConn does not generate the single quotes that must surround PostgreSQL string literals; they should be provided in the SQL command that the result is inserted into. The parameter from points to the first character of the string that is to be escaped, and the length parameter gives the number of bytes in this string. A terminating zero byte is not required, and should not be counted in length. (If a terminating zero byte is found before length bytes are processed, PQescapeStringConn stops at the zero; the behavior is thus rather like strncpy.) to shall point to a buffer that is able to hold at least one more byte than twice the value of length, otherwise the behavior is undefined. Behavior is likewise undefined if the `to` and `from` strings overlap.

If the `error` parameter is not `NULL`, then `*error` is set to zero on success, nonzero on error. Presently the only possible error conditions involve invalid multibyte encoding in the source string. The output string is still generated on error, but it can be expected that the server will reject it as malformed. On error, a suitable message is stored in the `conn` object, whether or not `error` is `NULL`.

`PQescapeStringConn` returns the number of bytes written to `to`, not including the terminating zero byte.

`PQescapeString`

> `PQescapeString` is an older, deprecated version of `PQescapeStringConn`.
>
> `size_t PQescapeString (char *to, const char *from, size_t length);`
>
> The only difference from `PQescapeStringConn` is that `PQescapeString` does not take `PGconn` or `error` parameters. Because of this, it cannot adjust its behavior depending on the connection properties (such as character encoding) and therefore *it might give the wrong results*. Also, it has no way to report error conditions.
>
> `PQescapeString` can be used safely in client programs that work with only one PostgreSQL connection at a time (in this case it can find out what it needs to know "behind the scenes"). In other contexts it is a security hazard and should be avoided in favor of `PQescapeStringConn`.

`PQescapeByteaConn`

> Escapes binary data for use within an SQL command with the type `bytea`. As with `PQescapeStringConn`, this is only used when inserting data directly into an SQL command string.
>
> ```
> unsigned char *PQescapeByteaConn(PGconn *conn,
>                                  const unsigned char *from,
>                                  size_t from_length,
>                                  size_t *to_length);
> ```
>
> Certain byte values must be escaped when used as part of a `bytea` literal in an SQL statement. `PQescapeByteaConn` escapes bytes using either hex encoding or backslash escaping. See Section 8.4 for more information.
>
> The `from` parameter points to the first byte of the string that is to be escaped, and the `from_length` parameter gives the number of bytes in this binary string. (A terminating zero byte is neither necessary nor counted.) The `to_length` parameter points to a variable that will hold the resultant escaped string length. This result string length includes the terminating zero byte of the result.
>
> `PQescapeByteaConn` returns an escaped version of the `from` parameter binary string in memory allocated with `malloc()`. This memory should be freed using `PQfreemem()` when the result is no longer needed. The return string has all special characters replaced so that they can be properly processed by the PostgreSQL string literal parser, and the `bytea` input function. A terminating zero byte is also added. The single quotes that must surround PostgreSQL string literals are not part of the result string.
>
> On error, a null pointer is returned, and a suitable error message is stored in the `conn` object. Currently, the only possible error is insufficient memory for the result string.

PQescapeBytea

> PQescapeBytea is an older, deprecated version of PQescapeByteaConn.
>
> ```
> unsigned char *PQescapeBytea(const unsigned char *from,
>                              size_t from_length,
>                              size_t *to_length);
> ```
>
> The only difference from PQescapeByteaConn is that PQescapeBytea does not take a PGconn parameter. Because of this, PQescapeBytea can only be used safely in client programs that use a single PostgreSQL connection at a time (in this case it can find out what it needs to know "behind the scenes"). It *might give the wrong results* if used in programs that use multiple database connections (use PQescapeByteaConn in such cases).

PQunescapeBytea

> Converts a string representation of binary data into binary data — the reverse of PQescapeBytea. This is needed when retrieving bytea data in text format, but not when retrieving it in binary format.
>
> ```
> unsigned char *PQunescapeBytea(const unsigned char *from, size_t *to_length);
> ```
>
> The from parameter points to a string such as might be returned by PQgetvalue when applied to a bytea column. PQunescapeBytea converts this string representation into its binary representation. It returns a pointer to a buffer allocated with malloc(), or NULL on error, and puts the size of the buffer in to_length. The result must be freed using PQfreemem when it is no longer needed.
>
> This conversion is not exactly the inverse of PQescapeBytea, because the string is not expected to be "escaped" when received from PQgetvalue. In particular this means there is no need for string quoting considerations, and so no need for a PGconn parameter.

32.4. Asynchronous Command Processing

The PQexec function is adequate for submitting commands in normal, synchronous applications. It has a few deficiencies, however, that can be of importance to some users:

- PQexec waits for the command to be completed. The application might have other work to do (such as maintaining a user interface), in which case it won't want to block waiting for the response.

- Since the execution of the client application is suspended while it waits for the result, it is hard for the application to decide that it would like to try to cancel the ongoing command. (It can be done from a signal handler, but not otherwise.)

- PQexec can return only one PGresult structure. If the submitted command string contains multiple SQL commands, all but the last PGresult are discarded by PQexec.

- PQexec always collects the command's entire result, buffering it in a single PGresult. While this simplifies error-handling logic for the application, it can be impractical for results containing many rows.

Applications that do not like these limitations can instead use the underlying functions that PQexec is built from: PQsendQuery and PQgetResult. There are also PQsendQueryParams, PQsendPrepare,

`PQsendQueryPrepared`, `PQsendDescribePrepared`, and `PQsendDescribePortal`, which can be used with `PQgetResult` to duplicate the functionality of `PQexecParams`, `PQprepare`, `PQexecPrepared`, `PQdescribePrepared`, and `PQdescribePortal` respectively.

`PQsendQuery`

> Submits a command to the server without waiting for the result(s). 1 is returned if the command was successfully dispatched and 0 if not (in which case, use `PQerrorMessage` to get more information about the failure).
>
> ```
> int PQsendQuery(PGconn *conn, const char *command);
> ```
> After successfully calling `PQsendQuery`, call `PQgetResult` one or more times to obtain the results. `PQsendQuery` cannot be called again (on the same connection) until `PQgetResult` has returned a null pointer, indicating that the command is done.

`PQsendQueryParams`

> Submits a command and separate parameters to the server without waiting for the result(s).
>
> ```
> int PQsendQueryParams(PGconn *conn,
>                       const char *command,
>                       int nParams,
>                       const Oid *paramTypes,
>                       const char * const *paramValues,
>                       const int *paramLengths,
>                       const int *paramFormats,
>                       int resultFormat);
> ```
> This is equivalent to `PQsendQuery` except that query parameters can be specified separately from the query string. The function's parameters are handled identically to `PQexecParams`. Like `PQexecParams`, it will not work on 2.0-protocol connections, and it allows only one command in the query string.

`PQsendPrepare`

> Sends a request to create a prepared statement with the given parameters, without waiting for completion.
>
> ```
> int PQsendPrepare(PGconn *conn,
>                   const char *stmtName,
>                   const char *query,
>                   int nParams,
>                   const Oid *paramTypes);
> ```
> This is an asynchronous version of `PQprepare`: it returns 1 if it was able to dispatch the request, and 0 if not. After a successful call, call `PQgetResult` to determine whether the server successfully created the prepared statement. The function's parameters are handled identically to `PQprepare`. Like `PQprepare`, it will not work on 2.0-protocol connections.

`PQsendQueryPrepared`

> Sends a request to execute a prepared statement with given parameters, without waiting for the result(s).
>
> ```
> int PQsendQueryPrepared(PGconn *conn,
>                         const char *stmtName,
>                         int nParams,
>                         const char * const *paramValues,
>                         const int *paramLengths,
> ```

```
                          const int *paramFormats,
                          int resultFormat);
```
This is similar to `PQsendQueryParams`, but the command to be executed is specified by naming a previously-prepared statement, instead of giving a query string. The function's parameters are handled identically to `PQexecPrepared`. Like `PQexecPrepared`, it will not work on 2.0-protocol connections.

`PQsendDescribePrepared`

Submits a request to obtain information about the specified prepared statement, without waiting for completion.

```
int PQsendDescribePrepared(PGconn *conn, const char *stmtName);
```
This is an asynchronous version of `PQdescribePrepared`: it returns 1 if it was able to dispatch the request, and 0 if not. After a successful call, call `PQgetResult` to obtain the results. The function's parameters are handled identically to `PQdescribePrepared`. Like `PQdescribePrepared`, it will not work on 2.0-protocol connections.

`PQsendDescribePortal`

Submits a request to obtain information about the specified portal, without waiting for completion.

```
int PQsendDescribePortal(PGconn *conn, const char *portalName);
```
This is an asynchronous version of `PQdescribePortal`: it returns 1 if it was able to dispatch the request, and 0 if not. After a successful call, call `PQgetResult` to obtain the results. The function's parameters are handled identically to `PQdescribePortal`. Like `PQdescribePortal`, it will not work on 2.0-protocol connections.

`PQgetResult`

Waits for the next result from a prior `PQsendQuery`, `PQsendQueryParams`, `PQsendPrepare`, `PQsendQueryPrepared`, `PQsendDescribePrepared`, or `PQsendDescribePortal` call, and returns it. A null pointer is returned when the command is complete and there will be no more results.

```
PGresult *PQgetResult(PGconn *conn);
```

`PQgetResult` must be called repeatedly until it returns a null pointer, indicating that the command is done. (If called when no command is active, `PQgetResult` will just return a null pointer at once.) Each non-null result from `PQgetResult` should be processed using the same `PGresult` accessor functions previously described. Don't forget to free each result object with `PQclear` when done with it. Note that `PQgetResult` will block only if a command is active and the necessary response data has not yet been read by `PQconsumeInput`.

> **Note:** Even when `PQresultStatus` indicates a fatal error, `PQgetResult` should be called until it returns a null pointer, to allow libpq to process the error information completely.

Using `PQsendQuery` and `PQgetResult` solves one of `PQexec`'s problems: If a command string contains multiple SQL commands, the results of those commands can be obtained individually. (This allows a simple form of overlapped processing, by the way: the client can be handling the results of one command while the server is still working on later queries in the same command string.)

Another frequently-desired feature that can be obtained with `PQsendQuery` and `PQgetResult` is retrieving large query results a row at a time. This is discussed in Section 32.5.

By itself, calling `PQgetResult` will still cause the client to block until the server completes the next SQL command. This can be avoided by proper use of two more functions:

`PQconsumeInput`

> If input is available from the server, consume it.
>
> ```
> int PQconsumeInput(PGconn *conn);
> ```
>
> `PQconsumeInput` normally returns 1 indicating "no error", but returns 0 if there was some kind of trouble (in which case `PQerrorMessage` can be consulted). Note that the result does not say whether any input data was actually collected. After calling `PQconsumeInput`, the application can check `PQisBusy` and/or `PQnotifies` to see if their state has changed.
>
> `PQconsumeInput` can be called even if the application is not prepared to deal with a result or notification just yet. The function will read available data and save it in a buffer, thereby causing a `select()` read-ready indication to go away. The application can thus use `PQconsumeInput` to clear the `select()` condition immediately, and then examine the results at leisure.

`PQisBusy`

> Returns 1 if a command is busy, that is, `PQgetResult` would block waiting for input. A 0 return indicates that `PQgetResult` can be called with assurance of not blocking.
>
> ```
> int PQisBusy(PGconn *conn);
> ```
>
> `PQisBusy` will not itself attempt to read data from the server; therefore `PQconsumeInput` must be invoked first, or the busy state will never end.

A typical application using these functions will have a main loop that uses `select()` or `poll()` to wait for all the conditions that it must respond to. One of the conditions will be input available from the server, which in terms of `select()` means readable data on the file descriptor identified by `PQsocket`. When the main loop detects input ready, it should call `PQconsumeInput` to read the input. It can then call `PQisBusy`, followed by `PQgetResult` if `PQisBusy` returns false (0). It can also call `PQnotifies` to detect NOTIFY messages (see Section 32.8).

A client that uses `PQsendQuery`/`PQgetResult` can also attempt to cancel a command that is still being processed by the server; see Section 32.6. But regardless of the return value of `PQcancel`, the application must continue with the normal result-reading sequence using `PQgetResult`. A successful cancellation will simply cause the command to terminate sooner than it would have otherwise.

By using the functions described above, it is possible to avoid blocking while waiting for input from the database server. However, it is still possible that the application will block waiting to send output to the server. This is relatively uncommon but can happen if very long SQL commands or data values are sent. (It is much more probable if the application sends data via COPY IN, however.) To prevent this possibility and achieve completely nonblocking database operation, the following additional functions can be used.

`PQsetnonblocking`

> Sets the nonblocking status of the connection.
>
> ```
> int PQsetnonblocking(PGconn *conn, int arg);
> ```

Sets the state of the connection to nonblocking if `arg` is 1, or blocking if `arg` is 0. Returns 0 if OK, -1 if error.

In the nonblocking state, calls to `PQsendQuery`, `PQputline`, `PQputnbytes`, `PQputCopyData`, and `PQendcopy` will not block but instead return an error if they need to be called again.

Note that `PQexec` does not honor nonblocking mode; if it is called, it will act in blocking fashion anyway.

`PQisnonblocking`

Returns the blocking status of the database connection.

```
int PQisnonblocking(const PGconn *conn);
```

Returns 1 if the connection is set to nonblocking mode and 0 if blocking.

`PQflush`

Attempts to flush any queued output data to the server. Returns 0 if successful (or if the send queue is empty), -1 if it failed for some reason, or 1 if it was unable to send all the data in the send queue yet (this case can only occur if the connection is nonblocking).

```
int PQflush(PGconn *conn);
```

After sending any command or data on a nonblocking connection, call `PQflush`. If it returns 1, wait for the socket to become read- or write-ready. If it becomes write-ready, call `PQflush` again. If it becomes read-ready, call `PQconsumeInput`, then call `PQflush` again. Repeat until `PQflush` returns 0. (It is necessary to check for read-ready and drain the input with `PQconsumeInput`, because the server can block trying to send us data, e.g. NOTICE messages, and won't read our data until we read its.) Once `PQflush` returns 0, wait for the socket to be read-ready and then read the response as described above.

32.5. Retrieving Query Results Row-By-Row

Ordinarily, libpq collects a SQL command's entire result and returns it to the application as a single `PGresult`. This can be unworkable for commands that return a large number of rows. For such cases, applications can use `PQsendQuery` and `PQgetResult` in *single-row mode*. In this mode, the result row(s) are returned to the application one at a time, as they are received from the server.

To enter single-row mode, call `PQsetSingleRowMode` immediately after a successful call of `PQsendQuery` (or a sibling function). This mode selection is effective only for the currently executing query. Then call `PQgetResult` repeatedly, until it returns null, as documented in Section 32.4. If the query returns any rows, they are returned as individual `PGresult` objects, which look like normal query results except for having status code `PGRES_SINGLE_TUPLE` instead of `PGRES_TUPLES_OK`. After the last row, or immediately if the query returns zero rows, a zero-row object with status `PGRES_TUPLES_OK` is returned; this is the signal that no more rows will arrive. (But note that it is still necessary to continue calling `PQgetResult` until it returns null.) All of these `PGresult` objects will contain the same row description data (column names, types, etc) that an ordinary `PGresult` object for the query would have. Each object should be freed with `PQclear` as usual.

`PQsetSingleRowMode`

Select single-row mode for the currently-executing query.

`int PQsetSingleRowMode(PGconn *conn);`

This function can only be called immediately after `PQsendQuery` or one of its sibling functions, before any other operation on the connection such as `PQconsumeInput` or `PQgetResult`. If called at the correct time, the function activates single-row mode for the current query and returns 1. Otherwise the mode stays unchanged and the function returns 0. In any case, the mode reverts to normal after completion of the current query.

Caution

While processing a query, the server may return some rows and then encounter an error, causing the query to be aborted. Ordinarily, libpq discards any such rows and reports only the error. But in single-row mode, those rows will have already been returned to the application. Hence, the application will see some `PGRES_SINGLE_TUPLE` `PGresult` objects followed by a `PGRES_FATAL_ERROR` object. For proper transactional behavior, the application must be designed to discard or undo whatever has been done with the previously-processed rows, if the query ultimately fails.

32.6. Canceling Queries in Progress

A client application can request cancellation of a command that is still being processed by the server, using the functions described in this section.

`PQgetCancel`

Creates a data structure containing the information needed to cancel a command issued through a particular database connection.

`PGcancel *PQgetCancel(PGconn *conn);`

`PQgetCancel` creates a `PGcancel` object given a `PGconn` connection object. It will return `NULL` if the given `conn` is `NULL` or an invalid connection. The `PGcancel` object is an opaque structure that is not meant to be accessed directly by the application; it can only be passed to `PQcancel` or `PQfreeCancel`.

`PQfreeCancel`

Frees a data structure created by `PQgetCancel`.

`void PQfreeCancel(PGcancel *cancel);`

`PQfreeCancel` frees a data object previously created by `PQgetCancel`.

`PQcancel`

Requests that the server abandon processing of the current command.

`int PQcancel(PGcancel *cancel, char *errbuf, int errbufsize);`

The return value is 1 if the cancel request was successfully dispatched and 0 if not. If not, `errbuf` is filled with an explanatory error message. `errbuf` must be a char array of size `errbufsize` (the recommended size is 256 bytes).

Successful dispatch is no guarantee that the request will have any effect, however. If the cancellation is effective, the current command will terminate early and return an error result. If the cancellation fails (say, because the server was already done processing the command), then there will be no visible result at all.

`PQcancel` can safely be invoked from a signal handler, if the `errbuf` is a local variable in the signal handler. The `PGcancel` object is read-only as far as `PQcancel` is concerned, so it can also be invoked from a thread that is separate from the one manipulating the `PGconn` object.

PQrequestCancel

PQrequestCancel is a deprecated variant of `PQcancel`.

```
int PQrequestCancel(PGconn *conn);
```

Requests that the server abandon processing of the current command. It operates directly on the `PGconn` object, and in case of failure stores the error message in the `PGconn` object (whence it can be retrieved by `PQerrorMessage`). Although the functionality is the same, this approach creates hazards for multiple-thread programs and signal handlers, since it is possible that overwriting the `PGconn`'s error message will mess up the operation currently in progress on the connection.

32.7. The Fast-Path Interface

PostgreSQL provides a fast-path interface to send simple function calls to the server.

> **Tip:** This interface is somewhat obsolete, as one can achieve similar performance and greater functionality by setting up a prepared statement to define the function call. Then, executing the statement with binary transmission of parameters and results substitutes for a fast-path function call.

The function `PQfn` requests execution of a server function via the fast-path interface:

```
PGresult *PQfn(PGconn *conn,
               int fnid,
               int *result_buf,
               int *result_len,
               int result_is_int,
               const PQArgBlock *args,
               int nargs);

typedef struct
{
    int len;
    int isint;
    union
    {
```

```
        int *ptr;
        int integer;
    } u;
} PQArgBlock;
```

The `fnid` argument is the OID of the function to be executed. `args` and `nargs` define the parameters to be passed to the function; they must match the declared function argument list. When the `isint` field of a parameter structure is true, the `u.integer` value is sent to the server as an integer of the indicated length (this must be 2 or 4 bytes); proper byte-swapping occurs. When `isint` is false, the indicated number of bytes at `*u.ptr` are sent with no processing; the data must be in the format expected by the server for binary transmission of the function's argument data type. (The declaration of `u.ptr` as being of type `int *` is historical; it would be better to consider it `void *`.) `result_buf` points to the buffer in which to place the function's return value. The caller must have allocated sufficient space to store the return value. (There is no check!) The actual result length in bytes will be returned in the integer pointed to by `result_len`. If a 2- or 4-byte integer result is expected, set `result_is_int` to 1, otherwise set it to 0. Setting `result_is_int` to 1 causes libpq to byte-swap the value if necessary, so that it is delivered as a proper `int` value for the client machine; note that a 4-byte integer is delivered into `*result_buf` for either allowed result size. When `result_is_int` is 0, the binary-format byte string sent by the server is returned unmodified. (In this case it's better to consider `result_buf` as being of type `void *`.)

`PQfn` always returns a valid `PGresult` pointer. The result status should be checked before the result is used. The caller is responsible for freeing the `PGresult` with `PQclear` when it is no longer needed.

Note that it is not possible to handle null arguments, null results, nor set-valued results when using this interface.

32.8. Asynchronous Notification

PostgreSQL offers asynchronous notification via the `LISTEN` and `NOTIFY` commands. A client session registers its interest in a particular notification channel with the `LISTEN` command (and can stop listening with the `UNLISTEN` command). All sessions listening on a particular channel will be notified asynchronously when a `NOTIFY` command with that channel name is executed by any session. A "payload" string can be passed to communicate additional data to the listeners.

libpq applications submit `LISTEN`, `UNLISTEN`, and `NOTIFY` commands as ordinary SQL commands. The arrival of `NOTIFY` messages can subsequently be detected by calling `PQnotifies`.

The function `PQnotifies` returns the next notification from a list of unhandled notification messages received from the server. It returns a null pointer if there are no pending notifications. Once a notification is returned from `PQnotifies`, it is considered handled and will be removed from the list of notifications.

```
PGnotify *PQnotifies(PGconn *conn);

typedef struct pgNotify
{
    char *relname;              /* notification channel name */
    int  be_pid;                /* process ID of notifying server process */
    char *extra;                /* notification payload string */
} PGnotify;
```

After processing a `PGnotify` object returned by `PQnotifies`, be sure to free it with `PQfreemem`. It is sufficient to free the `PGnotify` pointer; the `relname` and `extra` fields do not represent separate allocations. (The names of these fields are historical; in particular, channel names need not have anything to do with relation names.)

Example 32-2 gives a sample program that illustrates the use of asynchronous notification.

`PQnotifies` does not actually read data from the server; it just returns messages previously absorbed by another libpq function. In prior releases of libpq, the only way to ensure timely receipt of `NOTIFY` messages was to constantly submit commands, even empty ones, and then check `PQnotifies` after each `PQexec`. While this still works, it is deprecated as a waste of processing power.

A better way to check for `NOTIFY` messages when you have no useful commands to execute is to call `PQconsumeInput`, then check `PQnotifies`. You can use `select()` to wait for data to arrive from the server, thereby using no CPU power unless there is something to do. (See `PQsocket` to obtain the file descriptor number to use with `select()`.) Note that this will work OK whether you submit commands with `PQsendQuery`/`PQgetResult` or simply use `PQexec`. You should, however, remember to check `PQnotifies` after each `PQgetResult` or `PQexec`, to see if any notifications came in during the processing of the command.

32.9. Functions Associated with the `COPY` Command

The `COPY` command in PostgreSQL has options to read from or write to the network connection used by libpq. The functions described in this section allow applications to take advantage of this capability by supplying or consuming copied data.

The overall process is that the application first issues the SQL `COPY` command via `PQexec` or one of the equivalent functions. The response to this (if there is no error in the command) will be a `PGresult` object bearing a status code of `PGRES_COPY_OUT` or `PGRES_COPY_IN` (depending on the specified copy direction). The application should then use the functions of this section to receive or transmit data rows. When the data transfer is complete, another `PGresult` object is returned to indicate success or failure of the transfer. Its status will be `PGRES_COMMAND_OK` for success or `PGRES_FATAL_ERROR` if some problem was encountered. At this point further SQL commands can be issued via `PQexec`. (It is not possible to execute other SQL commands using the same connection while the `COPY` operation is in progress.)

If a `COPY` command is issued via `PQexec` in a string that could contain additional commands, the application must continue fetching results via `PQgetResult` after completing the `COPY` sequence. Only when `PQgetResult` returns `NULL` is it certain that the `PQexec` command string is done and it is safe to issue more commands.

The functions of this section should be executed only after obtaining a result status of `PGRES_COPY_OUT` or `PGRES_COPY_IN` from `PQexec` or `PQgetResult`.

A `PGresult` object bearing one of these status values carries some additional data about the `COPY` operation that is starting. This additional data is available using functions that are also used in connection with query results:

`PQnfields`

Returns the number of columns (fields) to be copied.

PQbinaryTuples

0 indicates the overall copy format is textual (rows separated by newlines, columns separated by separator characters, etc). 1 indicates the overall copy format is binary. See COPY for more information.

PQfformat

Returns the format code (0 for text, 1 for binary) associated with each column of the copy operation. The per-column format codes will always be zero when the overall copy format is textual, but the binary format can support both text and binary columns. (However, as of the current implementation of COPY, only binary columns appear in a binary copy; so the per-column formats always match the overall format at present.)

Note: These additional data values are only available when using protocol 3.0. When using protocol 2.0, all these functions will return 0.

32.9.1. Functions for Sending COPY Data

These functions are used to send data during COPY FROM STDIN. They will fail if called when the connection is not in COPY_IN state.

PQputCopyData

Sends data to the server during COPY_IN state.

```
int PQputCopyData(PGconn *conn,
                  const char *buffer,
                  int nbytes);
```

Transmits the COPY data in the specified buffer, of length nbytes, to the server. The result is 1 if the data was queued, zero if it was not queued because of full buffers (this will only happen in nonblocking mode), or -1 if an error occurred. (Use PQerrorMessage to retrieve details if the return value is -1. If the value is zero, wait for write-ready and try again.)

The application can divide the COPY data stream into buffer loads of any convenient size. Buffer-load boundaries have no semantic significance when sending. The contents of the data stream must match the data format expected by the COPY command; see COPY for details.

PQputCopyEnd

Sends end-of-data indication to the server during COPY_IN state.

```
int PQputCopyEnd(PGconn *conn,
                 const char *errormsg);
```

Ends the COPY_IN operation successfully if errormsg is NULL. If errormsg is not NULL then the COPY is forced to fail, with the string pointed to by errormsg used as the error message. (One should not assume that this exact error message will come back from the server, however, as the server might have already failed the COPY for its own reasons. Also note that the option to force failure does not work when using pre-3.0-protocol connections.)

The result is 1 if the termination message was sent; or in nonblocking mode, this may only indicate that the termination message was successfully queued. (In nonblocking mode, to be certain that the data has been sent, you should next wait for write-ready and call PQflush, repeating until it returns zero.) Zero indicates that the function could not queue the termination message because of full buffers; this will only happen in nonblocking mode. (In this case, wait for write-ready and try the PQputCopyEnd call again.) If a hard error occurs, -1 is returned; you can use PQerrorMessage to retrieve details.

After successfully calling PQputCopyEnd, call PQgetResult to obtain the final result status of the COPY command. One can wait for this result to be available in the usual way. Then return to normal operation.

32.9.2. Functions for Receiving COPY Data

These functions are used to receive data during COPY TO STDOUT. They will fail if called when the connection is not in COPY_OUT state.

PQgetCopyData

> Receives data from the server during COPY_OUT state.

```
int PQgetCopyData(PGconn *conn,
                  char **buffer,
                  int async);
```

Attempts to obtain another row of data from the server during a COPY. Data is always returned one data row at a time; if only a partial row is available, it is not returned. Successful return of a data row involves allocating a chunk of memory to hold the data. The buffer parameter must be non-NULL. *buffer is set to point to the allocated memory, or to NULL in cases where no buffer is returned. A non-NULL result buffer should be freed using PQfreemem when no longer needed.

When a row is successfully returned, the return value is the number of data bytes in the row (this will always be greater than zero). The returned string is always null-terminated, though this is probably only useful for textual COPY. A result of zero indicates that the COPY is still in progress, but no row is yet available (this is only possible when async is true). A result of -1 indicates that the COPY is done. A result of -2 indicates that an error occurred (consult PQerrorMessage for the reason).

When async is true (not zero), PQgetCopyData will not block waiting for input; it will return zero if the COPY is still in progress but no complete row is available. (In this case wait for read-ready and then call PQconsumeInput before calling PQgetCopyData again.) When async is false (zero), PQgetCopyData will block until data is available or the operation completes.

After PQgetCopyData returns -1, call PQgetResult to obtain the final result status of the COPY command. One can wait for this result to be available in the usual way. Then return to normal operation.

32.9.3. Obsolete Functions for COPY

These functions represent older methods of handling COPY. Although they still work, they are deprecated due to poor error handling, inconvenient methods of detecting end-of-data, and lack of support for binary or nonblocking transfers.

PQgetline

> Reads a newline-terminated line of characters (transmitted by the server) into a buffer string of size `length`.
>
> ```
> int PQgetline(PGconn *conn,
>               char *buffer,
>               int length);
> ```
>
> This function copies up to `length`-1 characters into the buffer and converts the terminating newline into a zero byte. PQgetline returns EOF at the end of input, 0 if the entire line has been read, and 1 if the buffer is full but the terminating newline has not yet been read.
>
> Note that the application must check to see if a new line consists of the two characters \ ., which indicates that the server has finished sending the results of the COPY command. If the application might receive lines that are more than `length`-1 characters long, care is needed to be sure it recognizes the \ . line correctly (and does not, for example, mistake the end of a long data line for a terminator line).

PQgetlineAsync

> Reads a row of COPY data (transmitted by the server) into a buffer without blocking.
>
> ```
> int PQgetlineAsync(PGconn *conn,
>                    char *buffer,
>                    int bufsize);
> ```
>
> This function is similar to PQgetline, but it can be used by applications that must read COPY data asynchronously, that is, without blocking. Having issued the COPY command and gotten a PGRES_COPY_OUT response, the application should call PQconsumeInput and PQgetlineAsync until the end-of-data signal is detected.
>
> Unlike PQgetline, this function takes responsibility for detecting end-of-data.
>
> On each call, PQgetlineAsync will return data if a complete data row is available in libpq's input buffer. Otherwise, no data is returned until the rest of the row arrives. The function returns -1 if the end-of-copy-data marker has been recognized, or 0 if no data is available, or a positive number giving the number of bytes of data returned. If -1 is returned, the caller must next call PQendcopy, and then return to normal processing.
>
> The data returned will not extend beyond a data-row boundary. If possible a whole row will be returned at one time. But if the buffer offered by the caller is too small to hold a row sent by the server, then a partial data row will be returned. With textual data this can be detected by testing whether the last returned byte is \n or not. (In a binary COPY, actual parsing of the COPY data format will be needed to make the equivalent determination.) The returned string is not null-terminated. (If you want to add a terminating null, be sure to pass a `bufsize` one smaller than the room actually available.)

PQputline

> Sends a null-terminated string to the server. Returns 0 if OK and EOF if unable to send the string.
>
> ```
> int PQputline(PGconn *conn,
>               const char *string);
> ```
>
> The COPY data stream sent by a series of calls to PQputline has the same format as that returned by PQgetlineAsync, except that applications are not obliged to send exactly one data row per PQputline call; it is okay to send a partial line or multiple lines per call.

Note: Before PostgreSQL protocol 3.0, it was necessary for the application to explicitly send the two characters \. as a final line to indicate to the server that it had finished sending COPY data. While this still works, it is deprecated and the special meaning of \. can be expected to be removed in a future release. It is sufficient to call PQendcopy after having sent the actual data.

PQputnbytes

Sends a non-null-terminated string to the server. Returns 0 if OK and EOF if unable to send the string.

```
int PQputnbytes(PGconn *conn,
                const char *buffer,
                int nbytes);
```

This is exactly like PQputline, except that the data buffer need not be null-terminated since the number of bytes to send is specified directly. Use this procedure when sending binary data.

PQendcopy

Synchronizes with the server.

```
int PQendcopy(PGconn *conn);
```

This function waits until the server has finished the copying. It should either be issued when the last string has been sent to the server using PQputline or when the last string has been received from the server using PGgetline. It must be issued or the server will get "out of sync" with the client. Upon return from this function, the server is ready to receive the next SQL command. The return value is 0 on successful completion, nonzero otherwise. (Use PQerrorMessage to retrieve details if the return value is nonzero.)

When using PQgetResult, the application should respond to a PGRES_COPY_OUT result by executing PQgetline repeatedly, followed by PQendcopy after the terminator line is seen. It should then return to the PQgetResult loop until PQgetResult returns a null pointer. Similarly a PGRES_COPY_IN result is processed by a series of PQputline calls followed by PQendcopy, then return to the PQgetResult loop. This arrangement will ensure that a COPY command embedded in a series of SQL commands will be executed correctly.

Older applications are likely to submit a COPY via PQexec and assume that the transaction is done after PQendcopy. This will work correctly only if the COPY is the only SQL command in the command string.

32.10. Control Functions

These functions control miscellaneous details of libpq's behavior.

PQclientEncoding

Returns the client encoding.

```
int PQclientEncoding(const PGconn *conn);
```

Note that it returns the encoding ID, not a symbolic string such as EUC_JP. If unsuccessful, it returns -1. To convert an encoding ID to an encoding name, you can use:

```
char *pg_encoding_to_char(int encoding_id);
```

`PQsetClientEncoding`

Sets the client encoding.

`int PQsetClientEncoding(PGconn *conn, const char *encoding);`
conn is a connection to the server, and *encoding* is the encoding you want to use. If the function successfully sets the encoding, it returns 0, otherwise -1. The current encoding for this connection can be determined by using `PQclientEncoding`.

`PQsetErrorVerbosity`

Determines the verbosity of messages returned by `PQerrorMessage` and `PQresultErrorMessage`.

```
typedef enum
{
    PQERRORS_TERSE,
    PQERRORS_DEFAULT,
    PQERRORS_VERBOSE
} PGVerbosity;
```

`PGVerbosity PQsetErrorVerbosity(PGconn *conn, PGVerbosity verbosity);`
`PQsetErrorVerbosity` sets the verbosity mode, returning the connection's previous setting. In *TERSE* mode, returned messages include severity, primary text, and position only; this will normally fit on a single line. The default mode produces messages that include the above plus any detail, hint, or context fields (these might span multiple lines). The *VERBOSE* mode includes all available fields. Changing the verbosity does not affect the messages available from already-existing `PGresult` objects, only subsequently-created ones. (But see `PQresultVerboseErrorMessage` if you want to print a previous error with a different verbosity.)

`PQsetErrorContextVisibility`

Determines the handling of CONTEXT fields in messages returned by `PQerrorMessage` and `PQresultErrorMessage`.

```
typedef enum
{
    PQSHOW_CONTEXT_NEVER,
    PQSHOW_CONTEXT_ERRORS,
    PQSHOW_CONTEXT_ALWAYS
} PGContextVisibility;
```

`PGContextVisibility PQsetErrorContextVisibility(PGconn *conn, PGContextVisibility`
`PQsetErrorContextVisibility` sets the context display mode, returning the connection's previous setting. This mode controls whether the CONTEXT field is included in messages (unless the verbosity setting is *TERSE*, in which case CONTEXT is never shown). The *NEVER* mode never includes CONTEXT, while *ALWAYS* always includes it if available. In *ERRORS* mode (the default), CONTEXT fields are included only for error messages, not for notices and warnings. Changing this mode does not affect the messages available from already-existing `PGresult` objects, only subsequently-created ones. (But see `PQresultVerboseErrorMessage` if you want to print a previous error with a different display mode.)

PQtrace

> Enables tracing of the client/server communication to a debugging file stream.
>
> ```
> void PQtrace(PGconn *conn, FILE *stream);
> ```
>
> > **Note:** On Windows, if the libpq library and an application are compiled with different flags, this function call will crash the application because the internal representation of the FILE pointers differ. Specifically, multithreaded/single-threaded, release/debug, and static/dynamic flags should be the same for the library and all applications using that library.

PQuntrace

> Disables tracing started by PQtrace.
>
> ```
> void PQuntrace(PGconn *conn);
> ```

32.11. Miscellaneous Functions

As always, there are some functions that just don't fit anywhere.

PQfreemem

> Frees memory allocated by libpq.
>
> ```
> void PQfreemem(void *ptr);
> ```
>
> Frees memory allocated by libpq, particularly PQescapeByteaConn, PQescapeBytea, PQunescapeBytea, and PQnotifies. It is particularly important that this function, rather than free(), be used on Microsoft Windows. This is because allocating memory in a DLL and releasing it in the application works only if multithreaded/single-threaded, release/debug, and static/dynamic flags are the same for the DLL and the application. On non-Microsoft Windows platforms, this function is the same as the standard library function free().

PQconninfoFree

> Frees the data structures allocated by PQconndefaults or PQconninfoParse.
>
> ```
> void PQconninfoFree(PQconninfoOption *connOptions);
> ```
>
> A simple PQfreemem will not do for this, since the array contains references to subsidiary strings.

PQencryptPassword

> Prepares the encrypted form of a PostgreSQL password.
>
> ```
> char * PQencryptPassword(const char *passwd, const char *user);
> ```
> This function is intended to be used by client applications that wish to send commands like ALTER USER joe PASSWORD 'pwd'. It is good practice not to send the original cleartext password in such a command, because it might be exposed in command logs, activity displays, and so on. Instead, use this function to convert the password to encrypted form before it is sent. The arguments are the cleartext password, and the SQL name of the user it is for. The return value is a string allocated by malloc, or NULL if out of memory. The caller can assume the string doesn't contain any special characters that would require escaping. Use PQfreemem to free the result when done with it.

PQmakeEmptyPGresult

Constructs an empty `PGresult` object with the given status.

`PGresult *PQmakeEmptyPGresult(PGconn *conn, ExecStatusType status);`

This is libpq's internal function to allocate and initialize an empty `PGresult` object. This function returns `NULL` if memory could not be allocated. It is exported because some applications find it useful to generate result objects (particularly objects with error status) themselves. If `conn` is not null and `status` indicates an error, the current error message of the specified connection is copied into the `PGresult`. Also, if `conn` is not null, any event procedures registered in the connection are copied into the `PGresult`. (They do not get `PGEVT_RESULTCREATE` calls, but see `PQfireResultCreateEvents`.) Note that `PQclear` should eventually be called on the object, just as with a `PGresult` returned by libpq itself.

PQfireResultCreateEvents

Fires a `PGEVT_RESULTCREATE` event (see Section 32.13) for each event procedure registered in the `PGresult` object. Returns non-zero for success, zero if any event procedure fails.

`int PQfireResultCreateEvents(PGconn *conn, PGresult *res);`

The `conn` argument is passed through to event procedures but not used directly. It can be `NULL` if the event procedures won't use it.

Event procedures that have already received a `PGEVT_RESULTCREATE` or `PGEVT_RESULTCOPY` event for this object are not fired again.

The main reason that this function is separate from `PQmakeEmptyPGresult` is that it is often appropriate to create a `PGresult` and fill it with data before invoking the event procedures.

PQcopyResult

Makes a copy of a `PGresult` object. The copy is not linked to the source result in any way and `PQclear` must be called when the copy is no longer needed. If the function fails, `NULL` is returned.

`PGresult *PQcopyResult(const PGresult *src, int flags);`

This is not intended to make an exact copy. The returned result is always put into `PGRES_TUPLES_OK` status, and does not copy any error message in the source. (It does copy the command status string, however.) The `flags` argument determines what else is copied. It is a bitwise OR of several flags. `PG_COPYRES_ATTRS` specifies copying the source result's attributes (column definitions). `PG_COPYRES_TUPLES` specifies copying the source result's tuples. (This implies copying the attributes, too.) `PG_COPYRES_NOTICEHOOKS` specifies copying the source result's notify hooks. `PG_COPYRES_EVENTS` specifies copying the source result's events. (But any instance data associated with the source is not copied.)

PQsetResultAttrs

Sets the attributes of a `PGresult` object.

`int PQsetResultAttrs(PGresult *res, int numAttributes, PGresAttDesc *attDescs);`

The provided `attDescs` are copied into the result. If the `attDescs` pointer is `NULL` or `numAttributes` is less than one, the request is ignored and the function succeeds. If `res` already contains attributes, the function will fail. If the function fails, the return value is zero. If the function succeeds, the return value is non-zero.

`PQsetvalue`

Sets a tuple field value of a `PGresult` object.

`int PQsetvalue(PGresult *res, int tup_num, int field_num, char *value, int len);`

The function will automatically grow the result's internal tuples array as needed. However, the `tup_num` argument must be less than or equal to `PQntuples`, meaning this function can only grow the tuples array one tuple at a time. But any field of any existing tuple can be modified in any order. If a value at `field_num` already exists, it will be overwritten. If `len` is -1 or `value` is `NULL`, the field value will be set to an SQL null value. The `value` is copied into the result's private storage, thus is no longer needed after the function returns. If the function fails, the return value is zero. If the function succeeds, the return value is non-zero.

`PQresultAlloc`

Allocate subsidiary storage for a `PGresult` object.

`void *PQresultAlloc(PGresult *res, size_t nBytes);`

Any memory allocated with this function will be freed when `res` is cleared. If the function fails, the return value is `NULL`. The result is guaranteed to be adequately aligned for any type of data, just as for `malloc`.

`PQlibVersion`

Return the version of libpq that is being used.

`int PQlibVersion(void);`

The result of this function can be used to determine, at run time, if specific functionality is available in the currently loaded version of libpq. The function can be used, for example, to determine which connection options are available for `PQconnectdb` or if the `hex bytea` output added in PostgreSQL 9.0 is supported.

The number is formed by converting the major, minor, and revision numbers into two-decimal-digit numbers and appending them together. For example, version 9.1 will be returned as 90100, and version 9.1.2 will be returned as 90102 (leading zeroes are not shown).

> **Note:** This function appeared in PostgreSQL version 9.1, so it cannot be used to detect required functionality in earlier versions, since linking to it will create a link dependency on version 9.1.

32.12. Notice Processing

Notice and warning messages generated by the server are not returned by the query execution functions, since they do not imply failure of the query. Instead they are passed to a notice handling function, and execution continues normally after the handler returns. The default notice handling function prints the message on `stderr`, but the application can override this behavior by supplying its own handling function.

For historical reasons, there are two levels of notice handling, called the notice receiver and notice processor. The default behavior is for the notice receiver to format the notice and pass a string to the notice processor for printing. However, an application that chooses to provide its own notice receiver will typically ignore the notice processor layer and just do all the work in the notice receiver.

The function `PQsetNoticeReceiver` sets or examines the current notice receiver for a connection object. Similarly, `PQsetNoticeProcessor` sets or examines the current notice processor.

```
typedef void (*PQnoticeReceiver) (void *arg, const PGresult *res);

PQnoticeReceiver
PQsetNoticeReceiver(PGconn *conn,
                    PQnoticeReceiver proc,
                    void *arg);

typedef void (*PQnoticeProcessor) (void *arg, const char *message);

PQnoticeProcessor
PQsetNoticeProcessor(PGconn *conn,
                     PQnoticeProcessor proc,
                     void *arg);
```

Each of these functions returns the previous notice receiver or processor function pointer, and sets the new value. If you supply a null function pointer, no action is taken, but the current pointer is returned.

When a notice or warning message is received from the server, or generated internally by libpq, the notice receiver function is called. It is passed the message in the form of a `PGRES_NONFATAL_ERROR` PGresult. (This allows the receiver to extract individual fields using `PQresultErrorField`, or obtain a complete preformatted message using `PQresultErrorMessage` or `PQresultVerboseErrorMessage`.) The same void pointer passed to `PQsetNoticeReceiver` is also passed. (This pointer can be used to access application-specific state if needed.)

The default notice receiver simply extracts the message (using `PQresultErrorMessage`) and passes it to the notice processor.

The notice processor is responsible for handling a notice or warning message given in text form. It is passed the string text of the message (including a trailing newline), plus a void pointer that is the same one passed to `PQsetNoticeProcessor`. (This pointer can be used to access application-specific state if needed.)

The default notice processor is simply:

```
static void
defaultNoticeProcessor(void *arg, const char *message)
{
    fprintf(stderr, "%s", message);
}
```

Once you have set a notice receiver or processor, you should expect that that function could be called as long as either the `PGconn` object or `PGresult` objects made from it exist. At creation of a `PGresult`, the `PGconn`'s current notice handling pointers are copied into the `PGresult` for possible use by functions like `PQgetvalue`.

32.13. Event System

libpq's event system is designed to notify registered event handlers about interesting libpq events, such as the creation or destruction of PGconn and PGresult objects. A principal use case is that this allows applications to associate their own data with a PGconn or PGresult and ensure that that data is freed at an appropriate time.

Each registered event handler is associated with two pieces of data, known to libpq only as opaque void * pointers. There is a *passthrough* pointer that is provided by the application when the event handler is registered with a PGconn. The passthrough pointer never changes for the life of the PGconn and all PGresults generated from it; so if used, it must point to long-lived data. In addition there is an *instance data* pointer, which starts out NULL in every PGconn and PGresult. This pointer can be manipulated using the PQinstanceData, PQsetInstanceData, PQresultInstanceData and PQsetResultInstanceData functions. Note that unlike the passthrough pointer, instance data of a PGconn is not automatically inherited by PGresults created from it. libpq does not know what passthrough and instance data pointers point to (if anything) and will never attempt to free them — that is the responsibility of the event handler.

32.13.1. Event Types

The enum PGEventId names the types of events handled by the event system. All its values have names beginning with PGEVT. For each event type, there is a corresponding event info structure that carries the parameters passed to the event handlers. The event types are:

PGEVT_REGISTER

> The register event occurs when PQregisterEventProc is called. It is the ideal time to initialize any instanceData an event procedure may need. Only one register event will be fired per event handler per connection. If the event procedure fails, the registration is aborted.
>
> ```
> typedef struct
> {
>     PGconn *conn;
> } PGEventRegister;
> ```
> When a PGEVT_REGISTER event is received, the evtInfo pointer should be cast to a PGEventRegister *. This structure contains a PGconn that should be in the CONNECTION_OK status; guaranteed if one calls PQregisterEventProc right after obtaining a good PGconn. When returning a failure code, all cleanup must be performed as no PGEVT_CONNDESTROY event will be sent.

PGEVT_CONNRESET

> The connection reset event is fired on completion of PQreset or PQresetPoll. In both cases, the event is only fired if the reset was successful. If the event procedure fails, the entire connection reset will fail; the PGconn is put into CONNECTION_BAD status and PQresetPoll will return PGRES_POLLING_FAILED.
>
> ```
> typedef struct
> {
>     PGconn *conn;
> } PGEventConnReset;
> ```

When a `PGEVT_CONNRESET` event is received, the `evtInfo` pointer should be cast to a `PGEventConnReset *`. Although the contained `PGconn` was just reset, all event data remains unchanged. This event should be used to reset/reload/requery any associated `instanceData`. Note that even if the event procedure fails to process `PGEVT_CONNRESET`, it will still receive a `PGEVT_CONNDESTROY` event when the connection is closed.

PGEVT_CONNDESTROY

The connection destroy event is fired in response to `PQfinish`. It is the event procedure's responsibility to properly clean up its event data as libpq has no ability to manage this memory. Failure to clean up will lead to memory leaks.

```
typedef struct
{
    PGconn *conn;
} PGEventConnDestroy;
```

When a `PGEVT_CONNDESTROY` event is received, the `evtInfo` pointer should be cast to a `PGEventConnDestroy *`. This event is fired prior to `PQfinish` performing any other cleanup. The return value of the event procedure is ignored since there is no way of indicating a failure from `PQfinish`. Also, an event procedure failure should not abort the process of cleaning up unwanted memory.

PGEVT_RESULTCREATE

The result creation event is fired in response to any query execution function that generates a result, including `PQgetResult`. This event will only be fired after the result has been created successfully.

```
typedef struct
{
    PGconn *conn;
    PGresult *result;
} PGEventResultCreate;
```

When a `PGEVT_RESULTCREATE` event is received, the `evtInfo` pointer should be cast to a `PGEventResultCreate *`. The `conn` is the connection used to generate the result. This is the ideal place to initialize any `instanceData` that needs to be associated with the result. If the event procedure fails, the result will be cleared and the failure will be propagated. The event procedure must not try to `PQclear` the result object for itself. When returning a failure code, all cleanup must be performed as no `PGEVT_RESULTDESTROY` event will be sent.

PGEVT_RESULTCOPY

The result copy event is fired in response to `PQcopyResult`. This event will only be fired after the copy is complete. Only event procedures that have successfully handled the `PGEVT_RESULTCREATE` or `PGEVT_RESULTCOPY` event for the source result will receive `PGEVT_RESULTCOPY` events.

```
typedef struct
{
    const PGresult *src;
    PGresult *dest;
} PGEventResultCopy;
```

When a `PGEVT_RESULTCOPY` event is received, the `evtInfo` pointer should be cast to a `PGEventResultCopy *`. The `src` result is what was copied while the `dest` result is the copy destination. This event can be used to provide a deep copy of `instanceData`, since `PQcopyResult` cannot do that. If the event procedure fails, the entire copy operation will fail and the `dest` result will be cleared. When returning a failure code, all cleanup must be performed as no `PGEVT_RESULTDESTROY` event will be sent for the destination result.

`PGEVT_RESULTDESTROY`

The result destroy event is fired in response to a `PQclear`. It is the event procedure's responsibility to properly clean up its event data as libpq has no ability to manage this memory. Failure to clean up will lead to memory leaks.

```
typedef struct
{
    PGresult *result;
} PGEventResultDestroy;
```

When a `PGEVT_RESULTDESTROY` event is received, the `evtInfo` pointer should be cast to a `PGEventResultDestroy *`. This event is fired prior to `PQclear` performing any other cleanup. The return value of the event procedure is ignored since there is no way of indicating a failure from `PQclear`. Also, an event procedure failure should not abort the process of cleaning up unwanted memory.

32.13.2. Event Callback Procedure

`PGEventProc`

`PGEventProc` is a typedef for a pointer to an event procedure, that is, the user callback function that receives events from libpq. The signature of an event procedure must be

```
int eventproc(PGEventId evtId, void *evtInfo, void *passThrough)
```

The `evtId` parameter indicates which `PGEVT` event occurred. The `evtInfo` pointer must be cast to the appropriate structure type to obtain further information about the event. The `passThrough` parameter is the pointer provided to `PQregisterEventProc` when the event procedure was registered. The function should return a non-zero value if it succeeds and zero if it fails.

A particular event procedure can be registered only once in any `PGconn`. This is because the address of the procedure is used as a lookup key to identify the associated instance data.

> ### Caution
> On Windows, functions can have two different addresses: one visible from outside a DLL and another visible from inside the DLL. One should be careful that only one of these addresses is used with libpq's event-procedure functions, else confusion will result. The simplest rule for writing code that will work is to ensure that event procedures are declared `static`. If the procedure's address must be available outside its own source file, expose a separate function to return the address.

32.13.3. Event Support Functions

PQregisterEventProc

> Registers an event callback procedure with libpq.
>
> ```
> int PQregisterEventProc(PGconn *conn, PGEventProc proc,
>                         const char *name, void *passThrough);
> ```
>
> An event procedure must be registered once on each `PGconn` you want to receive events about. There is no limit, other than memory, on the number of event procedures that can be registered with a connection. The function returns a non-zero value if it succeeds and zero if it fails.
>
> The `proc` argument will be called when a libpq event is fired. Its memory address is also used to lookup `instanceData`. The `name` argument is used to refer to the event procedure in error messages. This value cannot be `NULL` or a zero-length string. The name string is copied into the `PGconn`, so what is passed need not be long-lived. The `passThrough` pointer is passed to the `proc` whenever an event occurs. This argument can be `NULL`.

PQsetInstanceData

> Sets the connection `conn`'s `instanceData` for procedure `proc` to `data`. This returns non-zero for success and zero for failure. (Failure is only possible if `proc` has not been properly registered in conn.)
>
> ```
> int PQsetInstanceData(PGconn *conn, PGEventProc proc, void *data);
> ```

PQinstanceData

> Returns the connection `conn`'s `instanceData` associated with procedure `proc`, or `NULL` if there is none.
>
> ```
> void *PQinstanceData(const PGconn *conn, PGEventProc proc);
> ```

PQresultSetInstanceData

> Sets the result's `instanceData` for `proc` to `data`. This returns non-zero for success and zero for failure. (Failure is only possible if `proc` has not been properly registered in the result.)
>
> ```
> int PQresultSetInstanceData(PGresult *res, PGEventProc proc, void *data);
> ```

PQresultInstanceData

> Returns the result's `instanceData` associated with `proc`, or `NULL` if there is none.
>
> ```
> void *PQresultInstanceData(const PGresult *res, PGEventProc proc);
> ```

32.13.4. Event Example

Here is a skeleton example of managing private data associated with libpq connections and results.

```
/* required header for libpq events (note: includes libpq-fe.h) */
#include <libpq-events.h>

/* The instanceData */
typedef struct
{
    int n;
```

```
    char *str;
} mydata;

/* PGEventProc */
static int myEventProc(PGEventId evtId, void *evtInfo, void *passThrough);

int
main(void)
{
    mydata *data;
    PGresult *res;
    PGconn *conn = PQconnectdb("dbname = postgres");

    if (PQstatus(conn) != CONNECTION_OK)
    {
        fprintf(stderr, "Connection to database failed: %s",
                PQerrorMessage(conn));
        PQfinish(conn);
        return 1;
    }

    /* called once on any connection that should receive events.
     * Sends a PGEVT_REGISTER to myEventProc.
     */
    if (!PQregisterEventProc(conn, myEventProc, "mydata_proc", NULL))
    {
        fprintf(stderr, "Cannot register PGEventProc\n");
        PQfinish(conn);
        return 1;
    }

    /* conn instanceData is available */
    data = PQinstanceData(conn, myEventProc);

    /* Sends a PGEVT_RESULTCREATE to myEventProc */
    res = PQexec(conn, "SELECT 1 + 1");

    /* result instanceData is available */
    data = PQresultInstanceData(res, myEventProc);

    /* If PG_COPYRES_EVENTS is used, sends a PGEVT_RESULTCOPY to myEventProc */
    res_copy = PQcopyResult(res, PG_COPYRES_TUPLES | PG_COPYRES_EVENTS);

    /* result instanceData is available if PG_COPYRES_EVENTS was
     * used during the PQcopyResult call.
     */
    data = PQresultInstanceData(res_copy, myEventProc);

    /* Both clears send a PGEVT_RESULTDESTROY to myEventProc */
    PQclear(res);
    PQclear(res_copy);

    /* Sends a PGEVT_CONNDESTROY to myEventProc */
```

```
        PQfinish(conn);

        return 0;
}


static int
myEventProc(PGEventId evtId, void *evtInfo, void *passThrough)
{
    switch (evtId)
    {
        case PGEVT_REGISTER:
        {
            PGEventRegister *e = (PGEventRegister *)evtInfo;
            mydata *data = get_mydata(e->conn);

            /* associate app specific data with connection */
            PQsetInstanceData(e->conn, myEventProc, data);
            break;
        }

        case PGEVT_CONNRESET:
        {
            PGEventConnReset *e = (PGEventConnReset *)evtInfo;
            mydata *data = PQinstanceData(e->conn, myEventProc);

            if (data)
              memset(data, 0, sizeof(mydata));
            break;
        }

        case PGEVT_CONNDESTROY:
        {
            PGEventConnDestroy *e = (PGEventConnDestroy *)evtInfo;
            mydata *data = PQinstanceData(e->conn, myEventProc);

            /* free instance data because the conn is being destroyed */
            if (data)
              free_mydata(data);
            break;
        }

        case PGEVT_RESULTCREATE:
        {
            PGEventResultCreate *e = (PGEventResultCreate *)evtInfo;
            mydata *conn_data = PQinstanceData(e->conn, myEventProc);
            mydata *res_data = dup_mydata(conn_data);

            /* associate app specific data with result (copy it from conn) */
            PQsetResultInstanceData(e->result, myEventProc, res_data);
            break;
        }

        case PGEVT_RESULTCOPY:
```

```
    {
        PGEventResultCopy *e = (PGEventResultCopy *)evtInfo;
        mydata *src_data = PQresultInstanceData(e->src, myEventProc);
        mydata *dest_data = dup_mydata(src_data);

        /* associate app specific data with result (copy it from a result) */
        PQsetResultInstanceData(e->dest, myEventProc, dest_data);
        break;
    }

    case PGEVT_RESULTDESTROY:
    {
        PGEventResultDestroy *e = (PGEventResultDestroy *)evtInfo;
        mydata *data = PQresultInstanceData(e->result, myEventProc);

        /* free instance data because the result is being destroyed */
        if (data)
          free_mydata(data);
        break;
    }

    /* unknown event ID, just return TRUE. */
    default:
        break;
    }

    return TRUE; /* event processing succeeded */
}
```

32.14. Environment Variables

The following environment variables can be used to select default connection parameter values, which will be used by `PQconnectdb`, `PQsetdbLogin` and `PQsetdb` if no value is directly specified by the calling code. These are useful to avoid hard-coding database connection information into simple client applications, for example.

- `PGHOST` behaves the same as the host connection parameter.

- `PGHOSTADDR` behaves the same as the hostaddr connection parameter. This can be set instead of or in addition to `PGHOST` to avoid DNS lookup overhead.

- `PGPORT` behaves the same as the port connection parameter.

- `PGDATABASE` behaves the same as the dbname connection parameter.

- `PGUSER` behaves the same as the user connection parameter.

- `PGPASSWORD` behaves the same as the password connection parameter. Use of this environment variable is not recommended for security reasons, as some operating systems allow non-root users to see process environment variables via ps; instead consider using the `~/.pgpass` file (see Section 32.15).

- PGPASSFILE specifies the name of the password file to use for lookups. If not set, it defaults to ~/.pgpass (see Section 32.15).

- PGSERVICE behaves the same as the service connection parameter.

- PGSERVICEFILE specifies the name of the per-user connection service file. If not set, it defaults to ~/.pg_service.conf (see Section 32.16).

- PGREALM sets the Kerberos realm to use with PostgreSQL, if it is different from the local realm. If PGREALM is set, libpq applications will attempt authentication with servers for this realm and use separate ticket files to avoid conflicts with local ticket files. This environment variable is only used if GSSAPI authentication is selected by the server.

- PGOPTIONS behaves the same as the options connection parameter.

- PGAPPNAME behaves the same as the application_name connection parameter.

- PGSSLMODE behaves the same as the sslmode connection parameter.

- PGREQUIRESSL behaves the same as the requiressl connection parameter.

- PGSSLCOMPRESSION behaves the same as the sslcompression connection parameter.

- PGSSLCERT behaves the same as the sslcert connection parameter.

- PGSSLKEY behaves the same as the sslkey connection parameter.

- PGSSLROOTCERT behaves the same as the sslrootcert connection parameter.

- PGSSLCRL behaves the same as the sslcrl connection parameter.

- PGREQUIREPEER behaves the same as the requirepeer connection parameter.

- PGKRBSRVNAME behaves the same as the krbsrvname connection parameter.

- PGGSSLIB behaves the same as the gsslib connection parameter.

- PGCONNECT_TIMEOUT behaves the same as the connect_timeout connection parameter.

- PGCLIENTENCODING behaves the same as the client_encoding connection parameter.

The following environment variables can be used to specify default behavior for each PostgreSQL session. (See also the ALTER ROLE and ALTER DATABASE commands for ways to set default behavior on a per-user or per-database basis.)

- PGDATESTYLE sets the default style of date/time representation. (Equivalent to SET datestyle TO ....)

- PGTZ sets the default time zone. (Equivalent to SET timezone TO ....)

- PGGEQO sets the default mode for the genetic query optimizer. (Equivalent to SET geqo TO ....)

Refer to the SQL command SET for information on correct values for these environment variables.

The following environment variables determine internal behavior of libpq; they override compiled-in defaults.

- PGSYSCONFDIR sets the directory containing the pg_service.conf file and in a future version possibly other system-wide configuration files.

- PGLOCALEDIR sets the directory containing the locale files for message localization.

32.15. The Password File

The file .pgpass in a user's home directory or the file referenced by PGPASSFILE can contain passwords to be used if the connection requires a password (and no password has been specified otherwise). On Microsoft Windows the file is named %APPDATA%\postgresql\pgpass.conf (where %APPDATA% refers to the Application Data subdirectory in the user's profile).

This file should contain lines of the following format:

```
hostname:port:database:username:password
```

(You can add a reminder comment to the file by copying the line above and preceding it with #.) Each of the first four fields can be a literal value, or *, which matches anything. The password field from the first line that matches the current connection parameters will be used. (Therefore, put more-specific entries first when you are using wildcards.) If an entry needs to contain : or \, escape this character with \. A host name of localhost matches both TCP (host name localhost) and Unix domain socket (pghost empty or the default socket directory) connections coming from the local machine. In a standby server, a database name of replication matches streaming replication connections made to the master server. The database field is of limited usefulness because users have the same password for all databases in the same cluster.

On Unix systems, the permissions on .pgpass must disallow any access to world or group; achieve this by the command chmod 0600 ~/.pgpass. If the permissions are less strict than this, the file will be ignored. On Microsoft Windows, it is assumed that the file is stored in a directory that is secure, so no special permissions check is made.

32.16. The Connection Service File

The connection service file allows libpq connection parameters to be associated with a single service name. That service name can then be specified by a libpq connection, and the associated settings will be used. This allows connection parameters to be modified without requiring a recompile of the libpq application. The service name can also be specified using the PGSERVICE environment variable.

The connection service file can be a per-user service file at ~/.pg_service.conf or the location specified by the environment variable PGSERVICEFILE, or it can be a system-wide file at `pg_config --sysconfdir`/pg_service.conf or in the directory specified by the environment variable PGSYSCONFDIR. If service definitions with the same name exist in the user and the system file, the user file takes precedence.

The file uses an "INI file" format where the section name is the service name and the parameters are connection parameters; see Section 32.1.2 for a list. For example:

```
# comment
[mydb]
host=somehost
```

```
port=5433
user=admin
```

An example file is provided at `share/pg_service.conf.sample`.

32.17. LDAP Lookup of Connection Parameters

If libpq has been compiled with LDAP support (option `--with-ldap` for `configure`) it is possible to retrieve connection options like `host` or `dbname` via LDAP from a central server. The advantage is that if the connection parameters for a database change, the connection information doesn't have to be updated on all client machines.

LDAP connection parameter lookup uses the connection service file `pg_service.conf` (see Section 32.16). A line in a `pg_service.conf` stanza that starts with `ldap://` will be recognized as an LDAP URL and an LDAP query will be performed. The result must be a list of `keyword = value` pairs which will be used to set connection options. The URL must conform to RFC 1959 and be of the form

```
ldap://[hostname[:port]]/search_base?attribute?search_scope?filter
```

where *hostname* defaults to `localhost` and *port* defaults to 389.

Processing of `pg_service.conf` is terminated after a successful LDAP lookup, but is continued if the LDAP server cannot be contacted. This is to provide a fallback with further LDAP URL lines that point to different LDAP servers, classical `keyword = value` pairs, or default connection options. If you would rather get an error message in this case, add a syntactically incorrect line after the LDAP URL.

A sample LDAP entry that has been created with the LDIF file

```
version:1
dn:cn=mydatabase,dc=mycompany,dc=com
changetype:add
objectclass:top
objectclass:device
cn:mydatabase
description:host=dbserver.mycompany.com
description:port=5439
description:dbname=mydb
description:user=mydb_user
description:sslmode=require
```

might be queried with the following LDAP URL:

```
ldap://ldap.mycompany.com/dc=mycompany,dc=com?description?one?(cn=mydatabase)
```

You can also mix regular service file entries with LDAP lookups. A complete example for a stanza in `pg_service.conf` would be:

```
# only host and port are stored in LDAP, specify dbname and user explicitly
[customerdb]
dbname=customer
```

```
user=appuser
ldap://ldap.acme.com/cn=dbserver,cn=hosts?pgconnectinfo?base?(objectclass=*)
```

32.18. SSL Support

PostgreSQL has native support for using SSL connections to encrypt client/server communications for increased security. See Section 18.9 for details about the server-side SSL functionality.

libpq reads the system-wide OpenSSL configuration file. By default, this file is named `openssl.cnf` and is located in the directory reported by `openssl version -d`. This default can be overridden by setting environment variable `OPENSSL_CONF` to the name of the desired configuration file.

32.18.1. Client Verification of Server Certificates

By default, PostgreSQL will not perform any verification of the server certificate. This means that it is possible to spoof the server identity (for example by modifying a DNS record or by taking over the server IP address) without the client knowing. In order to prevent spoofing, SSL certificate verification must be used.

If the parameter `sslmode` is set to `verify-ca`, libpq will verify that the server is trustworthy by checking the certificate chain up to a trusted certificate authority (CA). If `sslmode` is set to `verify-full`, libpq will *also* verify that the server host name matches its certificate. The SSL connection will fail if the server certificate cannot be verified. `verify-full` is recommended in most security-sensitive environments.

In `verify-full` mode, the host name is matched against the certificate's Subject Alternative Name attribute(s), or against the Common Name attribute if no Subject Alternative Name of type `dNSName` is present. If the certificate's name attribute starts with an asterisk (`*`), the asterisk will be treated as a wildcard, which will match all characters *except* a dot (`.`). This means the certificate will not match subdomains. If the connection is made using an IP address instead of a host name, the IP address will be matched (without doing any DNS lookups).

To allow server certificate verification, the certificate(s) of one or more trusted CAs must be placed in the file `~/.postgresql/root.crt` in the user's home directory. If intermediate CAs appear in `root.crt`, the file must also contain certificate chains to their root CAs. (On Microsoft Windows the file is named `%APPDATA%\postgresql\root.crt`.)

Certificate Revocation List (CRL) entries are also checked if the file `~/.postgresql/root.crl` exists (`%APPDATA%\postgresql\root.crl` on Microsoft Windows).

The location of the root certificate file and the CRL can be changed by setting the connection parameters `sslrootcert` and `sslcrl` or the environment variables `PGSSLROOTCERT` and `PGSSLCRL`.

> **Note:** For backwards compatibility with earlier versions of PostgreSQL, if a root CA file exists, the behavior of `sslmode=require` will be the same as that of `verify-ca`, meaning the server certificate is validated against the CA. Relying on this behavior is discouraged, and applications that need certificate validation should always use `verify-ca` or `verify-full`.

32.18.2. Client Certificates

If the server requests a trusted client certificate, libpq will send the certificate stored in file ~/.postgresql/postgresql.crt in the user's home directory. The certificate must be signed by one of the certificate authorities (CA) trusted by the server. A matching private key file ~/.postgresql/postgresql.key must also be present. The private key file must not allow any access to world or group; achieve this by the command chmod 0600 ~/.postgresql/postgresql.key. On Microsoft Windows these files are named %APPDATA%\postgresql\postgresql.crt and %APPDATA%\postgresql\postgresql.key, and there is no special permissions check since the directory is presumed secure. The location of the certificate and key files can be overridden by the connection parameters sslcert and sslkey or the environment variables PGSSLCERT and PGSSLKEY.

In some cases, the client certificate might be signed by an "intermediate" certificate authority, rather than one that is directly trusted by the server. To use such a certificate, append the certificate of the signing authority to the postgresql.crt file, then its parent authority's certificate, and so on up to a certificate authority, "root" or "intermediate", that is trusted by the server, i.e. signed by a certificate in the server's root.crt file.

Note that the client's ~/.postgresql/root.crt lists the top-level CAs that are considered trusted for signing server certificates. In principle it need not list the CA that signed the client's certificate, though in most cases that CA would also be trusted for server certificates.

32.18.3. Protection Provided in Different Modes

The different values for the sslmode parameter provide different levels of protection. SSL can provide protection against three types of attacks:

Eavesdropping

> If a third party can examine the network traffic between the client and the server, it can read both connection information (including the user name and password) and the data that is passed. SSL uses encryption to prevent this.

Man in the middle (MITM)

> If a third party can modify the data while passing between the client and server, it can pretend to be the server and therefore see and modify data *even if it is encrypted*. The third party can then forward the connection information and data to the original server, making it impossible to detect this attack. Common vectors to do this include DNS poisoning and address hijacking, whereby the client is directed to a different server than intended. There are also several other attack methods that can accomplish this. SSL uses certificate verification to prevent this, by authenticating the server to the client.

Impersonation

> If a third party can pretend to be an authorized client, it can simply access data it should not have access to. Typically this can happen through insecure password management. SSL uses client certificates to prevent this, by making sure that only holders of valid certificates can access the server.

For a connection to be known secure, SSL usage must be configured on *both the client and the server* before the connection is made. If it is only configured on the server, the client may end up sending sensitive information (e.g. passwords) before it knows that the server requires high security. In libpq, secure connections can be ensured by setting the `sslmode` parameter to `verify-full` or `verify-ca`, and providing the system with a root certificate to verify against. This is analogous to using an `https` URL for encrypted web browsing.

Once the server has been authenticated, the client can pass sensitive data. This means that up until this point, the client does not need to know if certificates will be used for authentication, making it safe to specify that only in the server configuration.

All SSL options carry overhead in the form of encryption and key-exchange, so there is a trade-off that has to be made between performance and security. Table 32-1 illustrates the risks the different `sslmode` values protect against, and what statement they make about security and overhead.

Table 32-1. SSL Mode Descriptions

`sslmode`	Eavesdropping protection	MITM protection	Statement
`disable`	No	No	I don't care about security, and I don't want to pay the overhead of encryption.
`allow`	Maybe	No	I don't care about security, but I will pay the overhead of encryption if the server insists on it.
`prefer`	Maybe	No	I don't care about encryption, but I wish to pay the overhead of encryption if the server supports it.
`require`	Yes	No	I want my data to be encrypted, and I accept the overhead. I trust that the network will make sure I always connect to the server I want.
`verify-ca`	Yes	Depends on CA-policy	I want my data encrypted, and I accept the overhead. I want to be sure that I connect to a server that I trust.

sslmode	Eavesdropping protection	MITM protection	Statement
verify-full	Yes	Yes	I want my data encrypted, and I accept the overhead. I want to be sure that I connect to a server I trust, and that it's the one I specify.

The difference between verify-ca and verify-full depends on the policy of the root CA. If a public CA is used, verify-ca allows connections to a server that *somebody else* may have registered with the CA. In this case, verify-full should always be used. If a local CA is used, or even a self-signed certificate, using verify-ca often provides enough protection.

The default value for sslmode is prefer. As is shown in the table, this makes no sense from a security point of view, and it only promises performance overhead if possible. It is only provided as the default for backward compatibility, and is not recommended in secure deployments.

32.18.4. SSL Client File Usage

Table 32-2 summarizes the files that are relevant to the SSL setup on the client.

Table 32-2. Libpq/Client SSL File Usage

File	Contents	Effect
~/.postgresql/postgresql.crt	client certificate	requested by server
~/.postgresql/postgresql.key	client private key	proves client certificate sent by owner; does not indicate certificate owner is trustworthy
~/.postgresql/root.crt	trusted certificate authorities	checks that server certificate is signed by a trusted certificate authority
~/.postgresql/root.crl	certificates revoked by certificate authorities	server certificate must not be on this list

32.18.5. SSL Library Initialization

If your application initializes libssl and/or libcrypto libraries and libpq is built with SSL support, you should call PQinitOpenSSL to tell libpq that the libssl and/or libcrypto libraries have been initialized by your application, so that libpq will not also initialize those libraries. See http://h71000.www7.hp.com/doc/83final/ba554_90007/ch04.html for details on the SSL API.

PQinitOpenSSL

> Allows applications to select which security libraries to initialize.
>
> ```
> void PQinitOpenSSL(int do_ssl, int do_crypto);
> ```
>
> When `do_ssl` is non-zero, libpq will initialize the OpenSSL library before first opening a database connection. When `do_crypto` is non-zero, the `libcrypto` library will be initialized. By default (if `PQinitOpenSSL` is not called), both libraries are initialized. When SSL support is not compiled in, this function is present but does nothing.
>
> If your application uses and initializes either OpenSSL or its underlying `libcrypto` library, you *must* call this function with zeroes for the appropriate parameter(s) before first opening a database connection. Also be sure that you have done that initialization before opening a database connection.

PQinitSSL

> Allows applications to select which security libraries to initialize.
>
> ```
> void PQinitSSL(int do_ssl);
> ```
>
> This function is equivalent to `PQinitOpenSSL(do_ssl, do_ssl)`. It is sufficient for applications that initialize both or neither of OpenSSL and `libcrypto`.
>
> `PQinitSSL` has been present since PostgreSQL 8.0, while `PQinitOpenSSL` was added in PostgreSQL 8.4, so `PQinitSSL` might be preferable for applications that need to work with older versions of libpq.

32.19. Behavior in Threaded Programs

libpq is reentrant and thread-safe by default. You might need to use special compiler command-line options when you compile your application code. Refer to your system's documentation for information about how to build thread-enabled applications, or look in `src/Makefile.global` for `PTHREAD_CFLAGS` and `PTHREAD_LIBS`. This function allows the querying of libpq's thread-safe status:

PQisthreadsafe

> Returns the thread safety status of the libpq library.
>
> ```
> int PQisthreadsafe();
> ```
>
> Returns 1 if the libpq is thread-safe and 0 if it is not.

One thread restriction is that no two threads attempt to manipulate the same `PGconn` object at the same time. In particular, you cannot issue concurrent commands from different threads through the same connection object. (If you need to run concurrent commands, use multiple connections.)

`PGresult` objects are normally read-only after creation, and so can be passed around freely between threads. However, if you use any of the `PGresult`-modifying functions described in Section 32.11 or Section 32.13, it's up to you to avoid concurrent operations on the same `PGresult`, too.

The deprecated functions `PQrequestCancel` and `PQoidStatus` are not thread-safe and should not be used in multithread programs. `PQrequestCancel` can be replaced by `PQcancel`. `PQoidStatus` can be replaced by `PQoidValue`.

If you are using Kerberos inside your application (in addition to inside libpq), you will need to do locking around Kerberos calls because Kerberos functions are not thread-safe. See function `PQregisterThreadLock` in the libpq source code for a way to do cooperative locking between libpq and your application.

If you experience problems with threaded applications, run the program in `src/tools/thread` to see if your platform has thread-unsafe functions. This program is run by `configure`, but for binary distributions your library might not match the library used to build the binaries.

32.20. Building libpq Programs

To build (i.e., compile and link) a program using libpq you need to do all of the following things:

- Include the `libpq-fe.h` header file:

  ```
  #include <libpq-fe.h>
  ```
  If you failed to do that then you will normally get error messages from your compiler similar to:

  ```
  foo.c: In function 'main':
  foo.c:34: 'PGconn' undeclared (first use in this function)
  foo.c:35: 'PGresult' undeclared (first use in this function)
  foo.c:54: 'CONNECTION_BAD' undeclared (first use in this function)
  foo.c:68: 'PGRES_COMMAND_OK' undeclared (first use in this function)
  foo.c:95: 'PGRES_TUPLES_OK' undeclared (first use in this function)
  ```

- Point your compiler to the directory where the PostgreSQL header files were installed, by supplying the `-Idirectory` option to your compiler. (In some cases the compiler will look into the directory in question by default, so you can omit this option.) For instance, your compile command line could look like:

  ```
  cc -c -I/usr/local/pgsql/include testprog.c
  ```
  If you are using makefiles then add the option to the `CPPFLAGS` variable:

  ```
  CPPFLAGS += -I/usr/local/pgsql/include
  ```

  If there is any chance that your program might be compiled by other users then you should not hardcode the directory location like that. Instead, you can run the utility `pg_config` to find out where the header files are on the local system:

  ```
  $ pg_config --includedir
  /usr/local/include
  ```

  If you have `pkg-config` installed, you can run instead:

  ```
  $ pkg-config --cflags libpq
  -I/usr/local/include
  ```
  Note that this will already include the `-I` in front of the path.

  Failure to specify the correct option to the compiler will result in an error message such as:

  ```
  testlibpq.c:8:22: libpq-fe.h: No such file or directory
  ```

- When linking the final program, specify the option `-lpq` so that the libpq library gets pulled in, as well as the option `-Ldirectory` to point the compiler to the directory where the libpq library resides.

(Again, the compiler will search some directories by default.) For maximum portability, put the `-L` option before the `-lpq` option. For example:

```
cc -o testprog testprog1.o testprog2.o -L/usr/local/pgsql/lib -lpq
```

You can find out the library directory using `pg_config` as well:

```
$ pg_config --libdir
/usr/local/pgsql/lib
```

Or again use `pkg-config`:

```
$ pkg-config --libs libpq
-L/usr/local/pgsql/lib -lpq
```

Note again that this prints the full options, not only the path.

Error messages that point to problems in this area could look like the following:

```
testlibpq.o: In function 'main':
testlibpq.o(.text+0x60): undefined reference to 'PQsetdbLogin'
testlibpq.o(.text+0x71): undefined reference to 'PQstatus'
testlibpq.o(.text+0xa4): undefined reference to 'PQerrorMessage'
```

This means you forgot `-lpq`.

```
/usr/bin/ld: cannot find -lpq
```

This means you forgot the `-L` option or did not specify the right directory.

32.21. Example Programs

These examples and others can be found in the directory `src/test/examples` in the source code distribution.

Example 32-1. libpq Example Program 1

```
/*
 * testlibpq.c
 *
 *      Test the C version of libpq, the PostgreSQL frontend library.
 */
#include <stdio.h>
#include <stdlib.h>
#include <libpq-fe.h>

static void
exit_nicely(PGconn *conn)
{
    PQfinish(conn);
    exit(1);
}


int
main(int argc, char **argv)
{
```

```
const char *conninfo;
PGconn     *conn;
PGresult   *res;
int         nFields;
int         i,
            j;

/*
 * If the user supplies a parameter on the command line, use it as the
 * conninfo string; otherwise default to setting dbname=postgres and using
 * environment variables or defaults for all other connection parameters.
 */
if (argc > 1)
    conninfo = argv[1];
else
    conninfo = "dbname = postgres";

/* Make a connection to the database */
conn = PQconnectdb(conninfo);

/* Check to see that the backend connection was successfully made */
if (PQstatus(conn) != CONNECTION_OK)
{
    fprintf(stderr, "Connection to database failed: %s",
            PQerrorMessage(conn));
    exit_nicely(conn);
}

/*
 * Our test case here involves using a cursor, for which we must be inside
 * a transaction block.  We could do the whole thing with a single
 * PQexec() of "select * from pg_database", but that's too trivial to make
 * a good example.
 */

/* Start a transaction block */
res = PQexec(conn, "BEGIN");
if (PQresultStatus(res) != PGRES_COMMAND_OK)
{
    fprintf(stderr, "BEGIN command failed: %s", PQerrorMessage(conn));
    PQclear(res);
    exit_nicely(conn);
}

/*
 * Should PQclear PGresult whenever it is no longer needed to avoid memory
 * leaks
 */
PQclear(res);

/*
 * Fetch rows from pg_database, the system catalog of databases
 */
```

```
res = PQexec(conn, "DECLARE myportal CURSOR FOR select * from pg_database");
if (PQresultStatus(res) != PGRES_COMMAND_OK)
{
    fprintf(stderr, "DECLARE CURSOR failed: %s", PQerrorMessage(conn));
    PQclear(res);
    exit_nicely(conn);
}
PQclear(res);

res = PQexec(conn, "FETCH ALL in myportal");
if (PQresultStatus(res) != PGRES_TUPLES_OK)
{
    fprintf(stderr, "FETCH ALL failed: %s", PQerrorMessage(conn));
    PQclear(res);
    exit_nicely(conn);
}

/* first, print out the attribute names */
nFields = PQnfields(res);
for (i = 0; i < nFields; i++)
    printf("%-15s", PQfname(res, i));
printf("\n\n");

/* next, print out the rows */
for (i = 0; i < PQntuples(res); i++)
{
    for (j = 0; j < nFields; j++)
        printf("%-15s", PQgetvalue(res, i, j));
    printf("\n");
}

PQclear(res);

/* close the portal ... we don't bother to check for errors ... */
res = PQexec(conn, "CLOSE myportal");
PQclear(res);

/* end the transaction */
res = PQexec(conn, "END");
PQclear(res);

/* close the connection to the database and cleanup */
PQfinish(conn);

return 0;
}
```

Example 32-2. libpq Example Program 2

```
/*
 * testlibpq2.c
 *      Test of the asynchronous notification interface
 *
 * Start this program, then from psql in another window do
 *   NOTIFY TBL2;
 * Repeat four times to get this program to exit.
 *
 * Or, if you want to get fancy, try this:
 * populate a database with the following commands
 * (provided in src/test/examples/testlibpq2.sql):
 *
 *   CREATE TABLE TBL1 (i int4);
 *
 *   CREATE TABLE TBL2 (i int4);
 *
 *   CREATE RULE r1 AS ON INSERT TO TBL1 DO
 *      (INSERT INTO TBL2 VALUES (new.i); NOTIFY TBL2);
 *
 * and do this four times:
 *
 *   INSERT INTO TBL1 VALUES (10);
 */

#ifdef WIN32
#include <windows.h>
#endif
#include <stdio.h>
#include <stdlib.h>
#include <string.h>
#include <errno.h>
#include <sys/time.h>
#include <sys/types.h>
#include "libpq-fe.h"

static void
exit_nicely(PGconn *conn)
{
    PQfinish(conn);
    exit(1);
}

int
main(int argc, char **argv)
{
    const char *conninfo;
    PGconn      *conn;
    PGresult    *res;
    PGnotify    *notify;
    int          nnotifies;
```

```
/*
 * If the user supplies a parameter on the command line, use it as the
 * conninfo string; otherwise default to setting dbname=postgres and using
 * environment variables or defaults for all other connection parameters.
 */
if (argc > 1)
    conninfo = argv[1];
else
    conninfo = "dbname = postgres";

/* Make a connection to the database */
conn = PQconnectdb(conninfo);

/* Check to see that the backend connection was successfully made */
if (PQstatus(conn) != CONNECTION_OK)
{
    fprintf(stderr, "Connection to database failed: %s",
            PQerrorMessage(conn));
    exit_nicely(conn);
}


/*
 * Issue LISTEN command to enable notifications from the rule's NOTIFY.
 */
res = PQexec(conn, "LISTEN TBL2");
if (PQresultStatus(res) != PGRES_COMMAND_OK)
{
    fprintf(stderr, "LISTEN command failed: %s", PQerrorMessage(conn));
    PQclear(res);
    exit_nicely(conn);
}

/*
 * should PQclear PGresult whenever it is no longer needed to avoid memory
 * leaks
 */
PQclear(res);

/* Quit after four notifies are received. */
nnotifies = 0;
while (nnotifies < 4)
{
    /*
     * Sleep until something happens on the connection.  We use select(2)
     * to wait for input, but you could also use poll() or similar
     * facilities.
     */
    int         sock;
    fd_set      input_mask;

    sock = PQsocket(conn);

    if (sock < 0)
```

```
            break;                    /* shouldn't happen */

        FD_ZERO(&input_mask);
        FD_SET(sock, &input_mask);

        if (select(sock + 1, &input_mask, NULL, NULL, NULL) < 0)
        {
            fprintf(stderr, "select() failed: %s\n", strerror(errno));
            exit_nicely(conn);
        }

        /* Now check for input */
        PQconsumeInput(conn);
        while ((notify = PQnotifies(conn)) != NULL)
        {
            fprintf(stderr,
                    "ASYNC NOTIFY of '%s' received from backend PID %d\n",
                    notify->relname, notify->be_pid);
            PQfreemem(notify);
            nnotifies++;
        }
    }

    fprintf(stderr, "Done.\n");

    /* close the connection to the database and cleanup */
    PQfinish(conn);

    return 0;
}
```

Example 32-3. libpq Example Program 3

```
/*
 * testlibpq3.c
 *      Test out-of-line parameters and binary I/O.
 *
 * Before running this, populate a database with the following commands
 * (provided in src/test/examples/testlibpq3.sql):
 *
 * CREATE TABLE test1 (i int4, t text, b bytea);
 *
 * INSERT INTO test1 values (1, 'joe''s place', '\\000\\001\\002\\003\\004');
 * INSERT INTO test1 values (2, 'ho there', '\\004\\003\\002\\001\\000');
 *
 * The expected output is:
 *
 * tuple 0: got
 *  i = (4 bytes) 1
 *  t = (11 bytes) 'joe's place'
 *  b = (5 bytes) \000\001\002\003\004
 *
```

```
 * tuple 0: got
 *   i = (4 bytes) 2
 *   t = (8 bytes) 'ho there'
 *   b = (5 bytes) \004\003\002\001\000
 */

#ifdef WIN32
#include <windows.h>
#endif

#include <stdio.h>
#include <stdlib.h>
#include <stdint.h>
#include <string.h>
#include <sys/types.h>
#include "libpq-fe.h"

/* for ntohl/htonl */
#include <netinet/in.h>
#include <arpa/inet.h>


static void
exit_nicely(PGconn *conn)
{
    PQfinish(conn);
    exit(1);
}


/*
 * This function prints a query result that is a binary-format fetch from
 * a table defined as in the comment above.  We split it out because the
 * main() function uses it twice.
 */
static void
show_binary_results(PGresult *res)
{
    int         i,
                j;
    int         i_fnum,
                t_fnum,
                b_fnum;

    /* Use PQfnumber to avoid assumptions about field order in result */
    i_fnum = PQfnumber(res, "i");
    t_fnum = PQfnumber(res, "t");
    b_fnum = PQfnumber(res, "b");

    for (i = 0; i < PQntuples(res); i++)
    {
        char        *iptr;
        char        *tptr;
        char        *bptr;
```

```
        int         blen;
        int         ival;

        /* Get the field values (we ignore possibility they are null!) */
        iptr = PQgetvalue(res, i, i_fnum);
        tptr = PQgetvalue(res, i, t_fnum);
        bptr = PQgetvalue(res, i, b_fnum);

        /*
         * The binary representation of INT4 is in network byte order, which
         * we'd better coerce to the local byte order.
         */
        ival = ntohl(*((uint32_t *) iptr));

        /*
         * The binary representation of TEXT is, well, text, and since libpq
         * was nice enough to append a zero byte to it, it'll work just fine
         * as a C string.
         *
         * The binary representation of BYTEA is a bunch of bytes, which could
         * include embedded nulls so we have to pay attention to field length.
         */
        blen = PQgetlength(res, i, b_fnum);

        printf("tuple %d: got\n", i);
        printf(" i = (%d bytes) %d\n",
               PQgetlength(res, i, i_fnum), ival);
        printf(" t = (%d bytes) '%s'\n",
               PQgetlength(res, i, t_fnum), tptr);
        printf(" b = (%d bytes) ", blen);
        for (j = 0; j < blen; j++)
            printf("\\%03o", bptr[j]);
        printf("\n\n");
    }
}

int
main(int argc, char **argv)
{
    const char *conninfo;
    PGconn      *conn;
    PGresult    *res;
    const char *paramValues[1];
    int         paramLengths[1];
    int         paramFormats[1];
    uint32_t    binaryIntVal;

    /*
     * If the user supplies a parameter on the command line, use it as the
     * conninfo string; otherwise default to setting dbname=postgres and using
     * environment variables or defaults for all other connection parameters.
     */
    if (argc > 1)
```

```
        conninfo = argv[1];
else
        conninfo = "dbname = postgres";

/* Make a connection to the database */
conn = PQconnectdb(conninfo);

/* Check to see that the backend connection was successfully made */
if (PQstatus(conn) != CONNECTION_OK)
{
    fprintf(stderr, "Connection to database failed: %s",
            PQerrorMessage(conn));
    exit_nicely(conn);
}

/*
 * The point of this program is to illustrate use of PQexecParams() with
 * out-of-line parameters, as well as binary transmission of data.
 *
 * This first example transmits the parameters as text, but receives the
 * results in binary format.  By using out-of-line parameters we can avoid
 * a lot of tedious mucking about with quoting and escaping, even though
 * the data is text.  Notice how we don't have to do anything special with
 * the quote mark in the parameter value.
 */

/* Here is our out-of-line parameter value */
paramValues[0] = "joe's place";

res = PQexecParams(conn,
                   "SELECT * FROM test1 WHERE t = $1",
                   1,       /* one param */
                   NULL,    /* let the backend deduce param type */
                   paramValues,
                   NULL,    /* don't need param lengths since text */
                   NULL,    /* default to all text params */
                   1);      /* ask for binary results */

if (PQresultStatus(res) != PGRES_TUPLES_OK)
{
    fprintf(stderr, "SELECT failed: %s", PQerrorMessage(conn));
    PQclear(res);
    exit_nicely(conn);
}

show_binary_results(res);

PQclear(res);

/*
 * In this second example we transmit an integer parameter in binary form,
 * and again retrieve the results in binary form.
 *
```

```
 * Although we tell PQexecParams we are letting the backend deduce
 * parameter type, we really force the decision by casting the parameter
 * symbol in the query text.  This is a good safety measure when sending
 * binary parameters.
 */

/* Convert integer value "2" to network byte order */
binaryIntVal = htonl((uint32_t) 2);

/* Set up parameter arrays for PQexecParams */
paramValues[0] = (char *) &binaryIntVal;
paramLengths[0] = sizeof(binaryIntVal);
paramFormats[0] = 1;           /* binary */

res = PQexecParams(conn,
                   "SELECT * FROM test1 WHERE i = $1::int4",
                   1,        /* one param */
                   NULL,     /* let the backend deduce param type */
                   paramValues,
                   paramLengths,
                   paramFormats,
                   1);       /* ask for binary results */

if (PQresultStatus(res) != PGRES_TUPLES_OK)
{
    fprintf(stderr, "SELECT failed: %s", PQerrorMessage(conn));
    PQclear(res);
    exit_nicely(conn);
}

show_binary_results(res);

PQclear(res);

/* close the connection to the database and cleanup */
PQfinish(conn);

return 0;
}
```

Chapter 33. Large Objects

PostgreSQL has a *large object* facility, which provides stream-style access to user data that is stored in a special large-object structure. Streaming access is useful when working with data values that are too large to manipulate conveniently as a whole.

This chapter describes the implementation and the programming and query language interfaces to PostgreSQL large object data. We use the libpq C library for the examples in this chapter, but most programming interfaces native to PostgreSQL support equivalent functionality. Other interfaces might use the large object interface internally to provide generic support for large values. This is not described here.

33.1. Introduction

All large objects are stored in a single system table named `pg_largeobject`. Each large object also has an entry in the system table `pg_largeobject_metadata`. Large objects can be created, modified, and deleted using a read/write API that is similar to standard operations on files.

PostgreSQL also supports a storage system called "TOAST", which automatically stores values larger than a single database page into a secondary storage area per table. This makes the large object facility partially obsolete. One remaining advantage of the large object facility is that it allows values up to 4 TB in size, whereas TOASTed fields can be at most 1 GB. Also, reading and updating portions of a large object can be done efficiently, while most operations on a TOASTed field will read or write the whole value as a unit.

33.2. Implementation Features

The large object implementation breaks large objects up into "chunks" and stores the chunks in rows in the database. A B-tree index guarantees fast searches for the correct chunk number when doing random access reads and writes.

The chunks stored for a large object do not have to be contiguous. For example, if an application opens a new large object, seeks to offset 1000000, and writes a few bytes there, this does not result in allocation of 1000000 bytes worth of storage; only of chunks covering the range of data bytes actually written. A read operation will, however, read out zeroes for any unallocated locations preceding the last existing chunk. This corresponds to the common behavior of "sparsely allocated" files in Unix file systems.

As of PostgreSQL 9.0, large objects have an owner and a set of access permissions, which can be managed using GRANT and REVOKE. SELECT privileges are required to read a large object, and UPDATE privileges are required to write or truncate it. Only the large object's owner (or a database superuser) can delete, comment on, or change the owner of a large object. To adjust this behavior for compatibility with prior releases, see the lo_compat_privileges run-time parameter.

33.3. Client Interfaces

This section describes the facilities that PostgreSQL's libpq client interface library provides for accessing large objects. The PostgreSQL large object interface is modeled after the Unix file-system interface, with analogues of `open`, `read`, `write`, `lseek`, etc.

All large object manipulation using these functions *must* take place within an SQL transaction block, since large object file descriptors are only valid for the duration of a transaction.

If an error occurs while executing any one of these functions, the function will return an otherwise-impossible value, typically 0 or -1. A message describing the error is stored in the connection object and can be retrieved with `PQerrorMessage`.

Client applications that use these functions should include the header file `libpq/libpq-fs.h` and link with the libpq library.

33.3.1. Creating a Large Object

The function

```
Oid lo_creat(PGconn *conn, int mode);
```

creates a new large object. The return value is the OID that was assigned to the new large object, or `InvalidOid` (zero) on failure. *mode* is unused and ignored as of PostgreSQL 8.1; however, for backward compatibility with earlier releases it is best to set it to `INV_READ`, `INV_WRITE`, or `INV_READ | INV_WRITE`. (These symbolic constants are defined in the header file `libpq/libpq-fs.h`.)

An example:

```
inv_oid = lo_creat(conn, INV_READ|INV_WRITE);
```

The function

```
Oid lo_create(PGconn *conn, Oid lobjId);
```

also creates a new large object. The OID to be assigned can be specified by *lobjId*; if so, failure occurs if that OID is already in use for some large object. If *lobjId* is `InvalidOid` (zero) then `lo_create` assigns an unused OID (this is the same behavior as `lo_creat`). The return value is the OID that was assigned to the new large object, or `InvalidOid` (zero) on failure.

`lo_create` is new as of PostgreSQL 8.1; if this function is run against an older server version, it will fail and return `InvalidOid`.

An example:

```
inv_oid = lo_create(conn, desired_oid);
```

33.3.2. Importing a Large Object

To import an operating system file as a large object, call

```
Oid lo_import(PGconn *conn, const char *filename);
```

`filename` specifies the operating system name of the file to be imported as a large object. The return value is the OID that was assigned to the new large object, or `InvalidOid` (zero) on failure. Note that the file is read by the client interface library, not by the server; so it must exist in the client file system and be readable by the client application.

The function

```
Oid lo_import_with_oid(PGconn *conn, const char *filename, Oid lobjId);
```

also imports a new large object. The OID to be assigned can be specified by `lobjId`; if so, failure occurs if that OID is already in use for some large object. If `lobjId` is `InvalidOid` (zero) then `lo_import_with_oid` assigns an unused OID (this is the same behavior as `lo_import`). The return value is the OID that was assigned to the new large object, or `InvalidOid` (zero) on failure.

`lo_import_with_oid` is new as of PostgreSQL 8.4 and uses `lo_create` internally which is new in 8.1; if this function is run against 8.0 or before, it will fail and return `InvalidOid`.

33.3.3. Exporting a Large Object

To export a large object into an operating system file, call

```
int lo_export(PGconn *conn, Oid lobjId, const char *filename);
```

The `lobjId` argument specifies the OID of the large object to export and the `filename` argument specifies the operating system name of the file. Note that the file is written by the client interface library, not by the server. Returns 1 on success, -1 on failure.

33.3.4. Opening an Existing Large Object

To open an existing large object for reading or writing, call

```
int lo_open(PGconn *conn, Oid lobjId, int mode);
```

The `lobjId` argument specifies the OID of the large object to open. The `mode` bits control whether the object is opened for reading (`INV_READ`), writing (`INV_WRITE`), or both. (These symbolic constants are defined in the header file `libpq/libpq-fs.h`.) `lo_open` returns a (non-negative) large object descriptor for later use in `lo_read`, `lo_write`, `lo_lseek`, `lo_lseek64`, `lo_tell`, `lo_tell64`, `lo_truncate`, `lo_truncate64`, and `lo_close`. The descriptor is only valid for the duration of the current transaction. On failure, -1 is returned.

The server currently does not distinguish between modes `INV_WRITE` and `INV_READ | INV_WRITE`: you are allowed to read from the descriptor in either case. However there is a significant difference between these modes and `INV_READ` alone: with `INV_READ` you cannot write on the descriptor, and the data read from it will reflect the contents of the large object at the time of the transaction snapshot that was active when `lo_open` was executed, regardless of later writes by this or other transactions. Reading from a descriptor opened with `INV_WRITE` returns data that reflects all writes of other committed transactions as well as writes of the current transaction. This is similar to the behavior of `REPEATABLE READ` versus `READ COMMITTED` transaction modes for ordinary SQL `SELECT` commands.

An example:

```
inv_fd = lo_open(conn, inv_oid, INV_READ|INV_WRITE);
```

33.3.5. Writing Data to a Large Object

The function

```
int lo_write(PGconn *conn, int fd, const char *buf, size_t len);
```

writes `len` bytes from `buf` (which must be of size `len`) to large object descriptor `fd`. The `fd` argument must have been returned by a previous `lo_open`. The number of bytes actually written is returned (in the current implementation, this will always equal `len` unless there is an error). In the event of an error, the return value is -1.

Although the `len` parameter is declared as `size_t`, this function will reject length values larger than `INT_MAX`. In practice, it's best to transfer data in chunks of at most a few megabytes anyway.

33.3.6. Reading Data from a Large Object

The function

```
int lo_read(PGconn *conn, int fd, char *buf, size_t len);
```

reads up to `len` bytes from large object descriptor `fd` into `buf` (which must be of size `len`). The `fd` argument must have been returned by a previous `lo_open`. The number of bytes actually read is returned; this will be less than `len` if the end of the large object is reached first. In the event of an error, the return value is -1.

Although the `len` parameter is declared as `size_t`, this function will reject length values larger than `INT_MAX`. In practice, it's best to transfer data in chunks of at most a few megabytes anyway.

33.3.7. Seeking in a Large Object

To change the current read or write location associated with a large object descriptor, call

```
int lo_lseek(PGconn *conn, int fd, int offset, int whence);
```

This function moves the current location pointer for the large object descriptor identified by `fd` to the new location specified by `offset`. The valid values for `whence` are `SEEK_SET` (seek from object start), `SEEK_CUR` (seek from current position), and `SEEK_END` (seek from object end). The return value is the new location pointer, or -1 on error.

When dealing with large objects that might exceed 2GB in size, instead use

```
pg_int64 lo_lseek64(PGconn *conn, int fd, pg_int64 offset, int whence);
```

This function has the same behavior as `lo_lseek`, but it can accept an `offset` larger than 2GB and/or deliver a result larger than 2GB. Note that `lo_lseek` will fail if the new location pointer would be greater than 2GB.

`lo_lseek64` is new as of PostgreSQL 9.3. If this function is run against an older server version, it will fail and return -1.

33.3.8. Obtaining the Seek Position of a Large Object

To obtain the current read or write location of a large object descriptor, call

```
int lo_tell(PGconn *conn, int fd);
```

If there is an error, the return value is -1.

When dealing with large objects that might exceed 2GB in size, instead use

```
pg_int64 lo_tell64(PGconn *conn, int fd);
```

This function has the same behavior as `lo_tell`, but it can deliver a result larger than 2GB. Note that `lo_tell` will fail if the current read/write location is greater than 2GB.

`lo_tell64` is new as of PostgreSQL 9.3. If this function is run against an older server version, it will fail and return -1.

33.3.9. Truncating a Large Object

To truncate a large object to a given length, call

```
int lo_truncate(PGcon *conn, int fd, size_t len);
```

This function truncates the large object descriptor `fd` to length `len`. The `fd` argument must have been returned by a previous `lo_open`. If `len` is greater than the large object's current length, the large object is extended to the specified length with null bytes ('\0'). On success, `lo_truncate` returns zero. On error, the return value is -1.

The read/write location associated with the descriptor `fd` is not changed.

Although the `len` parameter is declared as `size_t`, `lo_truncate` will reject length values larger than `INT_MAX`.

When dealing with large objects that might exceed 2GB in size, instead use

```
int lo_truncate64(PGcon *conn, int fd, pg_int64 len);
```

This function has the same behavior as `lo_truncate`, but it can accept a `len` value exceeding 2GB.

`lo_truncate` is new as of PostgreSQL 8.3; if this function is run against an older server version, it will fail and return -1.

`lo_truncate64` is new as of PostgreSQL 9.3; if this function is run against an older server version, it will fail and return -1.

33.3.10. Closing a Large Object Descriptor

A large object descriptor can be closed by calling

```
int lo_close(PGconn *conn, int fd);
```

where `fd` is a large object descriptor returned by `lo_open`. On success, `lo_close` returns zero. On error, the return value is -1.

Any large object descriptors that remain open at the end of a transaction will be closed automatically.

33.3.11. Removing a Large Object

To remove a large object from the database, call

```
int lo_unlink(PGconn *conn, Oid lobjId);
```

The `lobjId` argument specifies the OID of the large object to remove. Returns 1 if successful, -1 on failure.

33.4. Server-side Functions

Server-side functions tailored for manipulating large objects from SQL are listed in Table 33-1.

Table 33-1. SQL-oriented Large Object Functions

Function	Return Type	Description	Example	Result
`lo_from_bytea(loid oid, string bytea)`	oid	Create a large object and store data there, returning its OID. Pass 0 to have the system choose an OID.	`lo_from_bytea(0, E'\\xffffff00')`	24528
`lo_put(loid oid, offset bigint, str bytea)`	void	Write data at the given offset.	`lo_put(24528, 1, E'\\xaa')`	
`lo_get(loid oid [, from bigint, for int])`	bytea	Extract contents or a substring thereof.	`lo_get(24528, 0, 3)`	\xffaaff

There are additional server-side functions corresponding to each of the client-side functions described earlier; indeed, for the most part the client-side functions are simply interfaces to the equivalent server-side functions. The ones just as convenient to call via SQL commands are `lo_creat`, `lo_create`, `lo_unlink`, `lo_import`, and `lo_export`. Here are examples of their use:

```
CREATE TABLE image (
    name            text,
    raster          oid
);

SELECT lo_creat(-1);        -- returns OID of new, empty large object

SELECT lo_create(43213);    -- attempts to create large object with OID 43213

SELECT lo_unlink(173454);   -- deletes large object with OID 173454

INSERT INTO image (name, raster)
    VALUES ('beautiful image', lo_import('/etc/motd'));

INSERT INTO image (name, raster)   -- same as above, but specify OID to use
    VALUES ('beautiful image', lo_import('/etc/motd', 68583));

SELECT lo_export(image.raster, '/tmp/motd') FROM image
    WHERE name = 'beautiful image';
```

The server-side `lo_import` and `lo_export` functions behave considerably differently from their client-side analogs. These two functions read and write files in the server's file system, using the permissions of the database's owning user. Therefore, their use is restricted to superusers. In contrast, the client-side import and export functions read and write files in the client's file system, using the permissions of the client program. The client-side functions do not require superuser privilege.

The functionality of `lo_read` and `lo_write` is also available via server-side calls, but the names of the server-side functions differ from the client side interfaces in that they do not contain underscores. You must call these functions as `loread` and `lowrite`.

33.5. Example Program

Example 33-1 is a sample program which shows how the large object interface in libpq can be used. Parts of the program are commented out but are left in the source for the reader's benefit. This program can also be found in `src/test/examples/testlo.c` in the source distribution.

Example 33-1. Large Objects with libpq Example Program

```
/*-------------------------------------------------------------------------
 *
 * testlo.c
 *    test using large objects with libpq
 *
 * Portions Copyright (c) 1996-2016, PostgreSQL Global Development Group
 * Portions Copyright (c) 1994, Regents of the University of California
 *
 *
 * IDENTIFICATION
 *    src/test/examples/testlo.c
```

```
 *
 *-------------------------------------------------------------------------
 */
#include <stdio.h>
#include <stdlib.h>

#include <sys/types.h>
#include <sys/stat.h>
#include <fcntl.h>
#include <unistd.h>

#include "libpq-fe.h"
#include "libpq/libpq-fs.h"

#define BUFSIZE          1024

/*
 * importFile -
 *    import file "in_filename" into database as large object "lobjOid"
 *
 */
static Oid
importFile(PGconn *conn, char *filename)
{
    Oid         lobjId;
    int         lobj_fd;
    char        buf[BUFSIZE];
    int         nbytes,
                tmp;
    int         fd;

    /*
     * open the file to be read in
     */
    fd = open(filename, O_RDONLY, 0666);
    if (fd < 0)
    {                             /* error */
        fprintf(stderr, "cannot open unix file\"%s\"\n", filename);
    }

    /*
     * create the large object
     */
    lobjId = lo_creat(conn, INV_READ | INV_WRITE);
    if (lobjId == 0)
        fprintf(stderr, "cannot create large object");

    lobj_fd = lo_open(conn, lobjId, INV_WRITE);

    /*
     * read in from the Unix file and write to the inversion file
     */
    while ((nbytes = read(fd, buf, BUFSIZE)) > 0)
```

```
        {
            tmp = lo_write(conn, lobj_fd, buf, nbytes);
            if (tmp < nbytes)
                fprintf(stderr, "error while reading \"%s\"", filename);
        }

        close(fd);
        lo_close(conn, lobj_fd);

        return lobjId;
    }

    static void
    pickout(PGconn *conn, Oid lobjId, int start, int len)
    {
        int         lobj_fd;
        char        *buf;
        int         nbytes;
        int         nread;

        lobj_fd = lo_open(conn, lobjId, INV_READ);
        if (lobj_fd < 0)
            fprintf(stderr, "cannot open large object %u", lobjId);

        lo_lseek(conn, lobj_fd, start, SEEK_SET);
        buf = malloc(len + 1);

        nread = 0;
        while (len - nread > 0)
        {
            nbytes = lo_read(conn, lobj_fd, buf, len - nread);
            buf[nbytes] = '\0';
            fprintf(stderr, ">>> %s", buf);
            nread += nbytes;
            if (nbytes <= 0)
                break;              /* no more data? */
        }
        free(buf);
        fprintf(stderr, "\n");
        lo_close(conn, lobj_fd);
    }

    static void
    overwrite(PGconn *conn, Oid lobjId, int start, int len)
    {
        int         lobj_fd;
        char        *buf;
        int         nbytes;
        int         nwritten;
        int         i;

        lobj_fd = lo_open(conn, lobjId, INV_WRITE);
        if (lobj_fd < 0)
```

```
        fprintf(stderr, "cannot open large object %u", lobjId);

    lo_lseek(conn, lobj_fd, start, SEEK_SET);
    buf = malloc(len + 1);

    for (i = 0; i < len; i++)
        buf[i] = 'X';
    buf[i] = '\0';

    nwritten = 0;
    while (len - nwritten > 0)
    {
        nbytes = lo_write(conn, lobj_fd, buf + nwritten, len - nwritten);
        nwritten += nbytes;
        if (nbytes <= 0)
        {
            fprintf(stderr, "\nWRITE FAILED!\n");
            break;
        }
    }
    free(buf);
    fprintf(stderr, "\n");
    lo_close(conn, lobj_fd);
}


/*
 * exportFile -
 *    export large object "lobjOid" to file "out_filename"
 *
 */
static void
exportFile(PGconn *conn, Oid lobjId, char *filename)
{
    int        lobj_fd;
    char       buf[BUFSIZE];
    int        nbytes,
               tmp;
    int        fd;

    /*
     * open the large object
     */
    lobj_fd = lo_open(conn, lobjId, INV_READ);
    if (lobj_fd < 0)
        fprintf(stderr, "cannot open large object %u", lobjId);

    /*
     * open the file to be written to
     */
    fd = open(filename, O_CREAT | O_WRONLY | O_TRUNC, 0666);
    if (fd < 0)
    {                               /* error */
```

```
            fprintf(stderr, "cannot open unix file\"%s\"",
                    filename);
        }

        /*
         * read in from the inversion file and write to the Unix file
         */
        while ((nbytes = lo_read(conn, lobj_fd, buf, BUFSIZE)) > 0)
        {
            tmp = write(fd, buf, nbytes);
            if (tmp < nbytes)
            {
                fprintf(stderr, "error while writing \"%s\"",
                        filename);
            }
        }

        lo_close(conn, lobj_fd);
        close(fd);

        return;
    }

    static void
    exit_nicely(PGconn *conn)
    {
        PQfinish(conn);
        exit(1);
    }

    int
    main(int argc, char **argv)
    {
        char        *in_filename,
                    *out_filename;
        char        *database;
        Oid          lobjOid;
        PGconn      *conn;
        PGresult    *res;

        if (argc != 4)
        {
            fprintf(stderr, "Usage: %s database_name in_filename out_filename\n",
                    argv[0]);
            exit(1);
        }

        database = argv[1];
        in_filename = argv[2];
        out_filename = argv[3];

        /*
         * set up the connection
```

```
    */
    conn = PQsetdb(NULL, NULL, NULL, NULL, database);

    /* check to see that the backend connection was successfully made */
    if (PQstatus(conn) != CONNECTION_OK)
    {
        fprintf(stderr, "Connection to database failed: %s",
                PQerrorMessage(conn));
        exit_nicely(conn);
    }

    res = PQexec(conn, "begin");
    PQclear(res);
    printf("importing file \"%s\" ...\n", in_filename);
/*  lobjOid = importFile(conn, in_filename); */
    lobjOid = lo_import(conn, in_filename);
    if (lobjOid == 0)
        fprintf(stderr, "%s\n", PQerrorMessage(conn));
    else
    {
        printf("\tas large object %u.\n", lobjOid);

        printf("picking out bytes 1000-2000 of the large object\n");
        pickout(conn, lobjOid, 1000, 1000);

        printf("overwriting bytes 1000-2000 of the large object with X's\n");
        overwrite(conn, lobjOid, 1000, 1000);

        printf("exporting large object to file \"%s\" ...\n", out_filename);
/*      exportFile(conn, lobjOid, out_filename); */
        if (lo_export(conn, lobjOid, out_filename) < 0)
            fprintf(stderr, "%s\n", PQerrorMessage(conn));
    }

    res = PQexec(conn, "end");
    PQclear(res);
    PQfinish(conn);
    return 0;
}
```

Chapter 34. ECPG - Embedded SQL in C

This chapter describes the embedded SQL package for PostgreSQL. It was written by Linus Tolke (`<linus@epact.se>`) and Michael Meskes (`<meskes@postgresql.org>`). Originally it was written to work with C. It also works with C++, but it does not recognize all C++ constructs yet.

This documentation is quite incomplete. But since this interface is standardized, additional information can be found in many resources about SQL.

34.1. The Concept

An embedded SQL program consists of code written in an ordinary programming language, in this case C, mixed with SQL commands in specially marked sections. To build the program, the source code (`*.pgc`) is first passed through the embedded SQL preprocessor, which converts it to an ordinary C program (`*.c`), and afterwards it can be processed by a C compiler. (For details about the compiling and linking see Section 34.10). Converted ECPG applications call functions in the libpq library through the embedded SQL library (ecpglib), and communicate with the PostgreSQL server using the normal frontend-backend protocol.

Embedded SQL has advantages over other methods for handling SQL commands from C code. First, it takes care of the tedious passing of information to and from variables in your C program. Second, the SQL code in the program is checked at build time for syntactical correctness. Third, embedded SQL in C is specified in the SQL standard and supported by many other SQL database systems. The PostgreSQL implementation is designed to match this standard as much as possible, and it is usually possible to port embedded SQL programs written for other SQL databases to PostgreSQL with relative ease.

As already stated, programs written for the embedded SQL interface are normal C programs with special code inserted to perform database-related actions. This special code always has the form:

```
EXEC SQL ...;
```

These statements syntactically take the place of a C statement. Depending on the particular statement, they can appear at the global level or within a function. Embedded SQL statements follow the case-sensitivity rules of normal SQL code, and not those of C. Also they allow nested C-style comments that are part of the SQL standard. The C part of the program, however, follows the C standard of not accepting nested comments.

The following sections explain all the embedded SQL statements.

34.2. Managing Database Connections

This section describes how to open, close, and switch database connections.

34.2.1. Connecting to the Database Server

One connects to a database using the following statement:

```
EXEC SQL CONNECT TO target [AS connection-name] [USER user-name];
```

The `target` can be specified in the following ways:

- `dbname[@hostname][:port]`
- `tcp:postgresql://hostname[:port][/dbname][?options]`
- `unix:postgresql://hostname[:port][/dbname][?options]`
- an SQL string literal containing one of the above forms
- a reference to a character variable containing one of the above forms (see examples)
- `DEFAULT`

If you specify the connection target literally (that is, not through a variable reference) and you don't quote the value, then the case-insensitivity rules of normal SQL are applied. In that case you can also double-quote the individual parameters separately as needed. In practice, it is probably less error-prone to use a (single-quoted) string literal or a variable reference. The connection target `DEFAULT` initiates a connection to the default database under the default user name. No separate user name or connection name can be specified in that case.

There are also different ways to specify the user name:

- `username`
- `username/password`
- `username IDENTIFIED BY password`
- `username USING password`

As above, the parameters `username` and `password` can be an SQL identifier, an SQL string literal, or a reference to a character variable.

The `connection-name` is used to handle multiple connections in one program. It can be omitted if a program uses only one connection. The most recently opened connection becomes the current connection, which is used by default when an SQL statement is to be executed (see later in this chapter).

Here are some examples of CONNECT statements:

```
EXEC SQL CONNECT TO mydb@sql.mydomain.com;

EXEC SQL CONNECT TO unix:postgresql://sql.mydomain.com/mydb AS myconnection USER joh

EXEC SQL BEGIN DECLARE SECTION;
const char *target = "mydb@sql.mydomain.com";
const char *user = "john";
const char *passwd = "secret";
EXEC SQL END DECLARE SECTION;
 ...
EXEC SQL CONNECT TO :target USER :user USING :passwd;
```

```
/* or EXEC SQL CONNECT TO :target USER :user/:passwd; */
```

The last form makes use of the variant referred to above as character variable reference. You will see in later sections how C variables can be used in SQL statements when you prefix them with a colon.

Be advised that the format of the connection target is not specified in the SQL standard. So if you want to develop portable applications, you might want to use something based on the last example above to encapsulate the connection target string somewhere.

34.2.2. Choosing a Connection

SQL statements in embedded SQL programs are by default executed on the current connection, that is, the most recently opened one. If an application needs to manage multiple connections, then there are two ways to handle this.

The first option is to explicitly choose a connection for each SQL statement, for example:

```
EXEC SQL AT connection-name SELECT ...;
```

This option is particularly suitable if the application needs to use several connections in mixed order.

If your application uses multiple threads of execution, they cannot share a connection concurrently. You must either explicitly control access to the connection (using mutexes) or use a connection for each thread. If each thread uses its own connection, you will need to use the AT clause to specify which connection the thread will use.

The second option is to execute a statement to switch the current connection. That statement is:

```
EXEC SQL SET CONNECTION connection-name;
```

This option is particularly convenient if many statements are to be executed on the same connection. It is not thread-aware.

Here is an example program managing multiple database connections:

```
#include <stdio.h>

EXEC SQL BEGIN DECLARE SECTION;
    char dbname[1024];
EXEC SQL END DECLARE SECTION;

int
main()
{
    EXEC SQL CONNECT TO testdb1 AS con1 USER testuser;
    EXEC SQL CONNECT TO testdb2 AS con2 USER testuser;
    EXEC SQL CONNECT TO testdb3 AS con3 USER testuser;

    /* This query would be executed in the last opened database "testdb3". */
    EXEC SQL SELECT current_database() INTO :dbname;
    printf("current=%s (should be testdb3)\n", dbname);

    /* Using "AT" to run a query in "testdb2" */
```

```
    EXEC SQL AT con2 SELECT current_database() INTO :dbname;
    printf("current=%s (should be testdb2)\n", dbname);

    /* Switch the current connection to "testdb1". */
    EXEC SQL SET CONNECTION con1;

    EXEC SQL SELECT current_database() INTO :dbname;
    printf("current=%s (should be testdb1)\n", dbname);

    EXEC SQL DISCONNECT ALL;
    return 0;
}
```

This example would produce this output:

```
current=testdb3 (should be testdb3)
current=testdb2 (should be testdb2)
current=testdb1 (should be testdb1)
```

34.2.3. Closing a Connection

To close a connection, use the following statement:

```
EXEC SQL DISCONNECT [connection];
```

The `connection` can be specified in the following ways:

- `connection-name`

- `DEFAULT`

- `CURRENT`

- `ALL`

If no connection name is specified, the current connection is closed.

It is good style that an application always explicitly disconnect from every connection it opened.

34.3. Running SQL Commands

Any SQL command can be run from within an embedded SQL application. Below are some examples of how to do that.

34.3.1. Executing SQL Statements

Creating a table:

```
EXEC SQL CREATE TABLE foo (number integer, ascii char(16));
EXEC SQL CREATE UNIQUE INDEX num1 ON foo(number);
EXEC SQL COMMIT;
```

Inserting rows:

```
EXEC SQL INSERT INTO foo (number, ascii) VALUES (9999, 'doodad');
EXEC SQL COMMIT;
```

Deleting rows:

```
EXEC SQL DELETE FROM foo WHERE number = 9999;
EXEC SQL COMMIT;
```

Updates:

```
EXEC SQL UPDATE foo
    SET ascii = 'foobar'
    WHERE number = 9999;
EXEC SQL COMMIT;
```

SELECT statements that return a single result row can also be executed using EXEC SQL directly. To handle result sets with multiple rows, an application has to use a cursor; see Section 34.3.2 below. (As a special case, an application can fetch multiple rows at once into an array host variable; see Section 34.4.4.3.1.)

Single-row select:

```
EXEC SQL SELECT foo INTO :FooBar FROM table1 WHERE ascii = 'doodad';
```

Also, a configuration parameter can be retrieved with the SHOW command:

```
EXEC SQL SHOW search_path INTO :var;
```

The tokens of the form :*something* are *host variables*, that is, they refer to variables in the C program. They are explained in Section 34.4.

34.3.2. Using Cursors

To retrieve a result set holding multiple rows, an application has to declare a cursor and fetch each row from the cursor. The steps to use a cursor are the following: declare a cursor, open it, fetch a row from the cursor, repeat, and finally close it.

Select using cursors:

```
EXEC SQL DECLARE foo_bar CURSOR FOR
    SELECT number, ascii FROM foo
    ORDER BY ascii;
EXEC SQL OPEN foo_bar;
EXEC SQL FETCH foo_bar INTO :FooBar, DooDad;
...
EXEC SQL CLOSE foo_bar;
EXEC SQL COMMIT;
```

For more details about declaration of the cursor, see DECLARE, and see FETCH for `FETCH` command details.

> **Note:** The ECPG `DECLARE` command does not actually cause a statement to be sent to the PostgreSQL backend. The cursor is opened in the backend (using the backend's `DECLARE` command) at the point when the `OPEN` command is executed.

34.3.3. Managing Transactions

In the default mode, statements are committed only when `EXEC SQL COMMIT` is issued. The embedded SQL interface also supports autocommit of transactions (similar to psql's default behavior) via the `-t` command-line option to `ecpg` (see ecpg) or via the `EXEC SQL SET AUTOCOMMIT TO ON` statement. In autocommit mode, each command is automatically committed unless it is inside an explicit transaction block. This mode can be explicitly turned off using `EXEC SQL SET AUTOCOMMIT TO OFF`.

The following transaction management commands are available:

`EXEC SQL COMMIT`

Commit an in-progress transaction.

`EXEC SQL ROLLBACK`

Roll back an in-progress transaction.

`EXEC SQL SET AUTOCOMMIT TO ON`

Enable autocommit mode.

`SET AUTOCOMMIT TO OFF`

Disable autocommit mode. This is the default.

34.3.4. Prepared Statements

When the values to be passed to an SQL statement are not known at compile time, or the same statement is going to be used many times, then prepared statements can be useful.

The statement is prepared using the command PREPARE. For the values that are not known yet, use the placeholder "?":

```
EXEC SQL PREPARE stmt1 FROM "SELECT oid, datname FROM pg_database WHERE oid = ?";
```

If a statement returns a single row, the application can call EXECUTE after PREPARE to execute the statement, supplying the actual values for the placeholders with a USING clause:

```
EXEC SQL EXECUTE stmt1 INTO :dboid, :dbname USING 1;
```

If a statement returns multiple rows, the application can use a cursor declared based on the prepared statement. To bind input parameters, the cursor must be opened with a USING clause:

```
EXEC SQL PREPARE stmt1 FROM "SELECT oid,datname FROM pg_database WHERE oid > ?";
EXEC SQL DECLARE foo_bar CURSOR FOR stmt1;

/* when end of result set reached, break out of while loop */
EXEC SQL WHENEVER NOT FOUND DO BREAK;

EXEC SQL OPEN foo_bar USING 100;
...
while (1)
{
    EXEC SQL FETCH NEXT FROM foo_bar INTO :dboid, :dbname;
    ...
}
EXEC SQL CLOSE foo_bar;
```

When you don't need the prepared statement anymore, you should deallocate it:

```
EXEC SQL DEALLOCATE PREPARE name;
```

For more details about PREPARE, see PREPARE. Also see Section 34.5 for more details about using placeholders and input parameters.

34.4. Using Host Variables

In Section 34.3 you saw how you can execute SQL statements from an embedded SQL program. Some of those statements only used fixed values and did not provide a way to insert user-supplied values into statements or have the program process the values returned by the query. Those kinds of statements are not really useful in real applications. This section explains in detail how you can pass data between your C program and the embedded SQL statements using a simple mechanism called *host variables*. In an embedded SQL program we consider the SQL statements to be *guests* in the C program code which is the *host language*. Therefore the variables of the C program are called *host variables*.

Another way to exchange values between PostgreSQL backends and ECPG applications is the use of SQL descriptors, described in Section 34.7.

34.4.1. Overview

Passing data between the C program and the SQL statements is particularly simple in embedded SQL. Instead of having the program paste the data into the statement, which entails various complications, such as properly quoting the value, you can simply write the name of a C variable into the SQL statement, prefixed by a colon. For example:

```
EXEC SQL INSERT INTO sometable VALUES (:v1, 'foo', :v2);
```

This statement refers to two C variables named v1 and v2 and also uses a regular SQL string literal, to illustrate that you are not restricted to use one kind of data or the other.

This style of inserting C variables in SQL statements works anywhere a value expression is expected in an SQL statement.

34.4.2. Declare Sections

To pass data from the program to the database, for example as parameters in a query, or to pass data from the database back to the program, the C variables that are intended to contain this data need to be declared in specially marked sections, so the embedded SQL preprocessor is made aware of them.

This section starts with:

```
EXEC SQL BEGIN DECLARE SECTION;
```

and ends with:

```
EXEC SQL END DECLARE SECTION;
```

Between those lines, there must be normal C variable declarations, such as:

```
int    x = 4;
char   foo[16], bar[16];
```

As you can see, you can optionally assign an initial value to the variable. The variable's scope is determined by the location of its declaring section within the program. You can also declare variables with the following syntax which implicitly creates a declare section:

```
EXEC SQL int i = 4;
```

You can have as many declare sections in a program as you like.

The declarations are also echoed to the output file as normal C variables, so there's no need to declare them again. Variables that are not intended to be used in SQL commands can be declared normally outside these special sections.

The definition of a structure or union also must be listed inside a DECLARE section. Otherwise the preprocessor cannot handle these types since it does not know the definition.

34.4.3. Retrieving Query Results

Now you should be able to pass data generated by your program into an SQL command. But how do you retrieve the results of a query? For that purpose, embedded SQL provides special variants of the usual commands SELECT and FETCH. These commands have a special INTO clause that specifies which host variables the retrieved values are to be stored in. SELECT is used for a query that returns only single row, and FETCH is used for a query that returns multiple rows, using a cursor.

Here is an example:

```
/*
 * assume this table:
 * CREATE TABLE test1 (a int, b varchar(50));
 */

EXEC SQL BEGIN DECLARE SECTION;
int v1;
VARCHAR v2;
EXEC SQL END DECLARE SECTION;

    ...

EXEC SQL SELECT a, b INTO :v1, :v2 FROM test;
```

So the INTO clause appears between the select list and the FROM clause. The number of elements in the select list and the list after INTO (also called the target list) must be equal.

Here is an example using the command FETCH:

```
EXEC SQL BEGIN DECLARE SECTION;
int v1;
VARCHAR v2;
EXEC SQL END DECLARE SECTION;

    ...

EXEC SQL DECLARE foo CURSOR FOR SELECT a, b FROM test;

    ...

do
{
    ...
    EXEC SQL FETCH NEXT FROM foo INTO :v1, :v2;
    ...
```

```
} while (...);
```

Here the INTO clause appears after all the normal clauses.

34.4.4. Type Mapping

When ECPG applications exchange values between the PostgreSQL server and the C application, such as when retrieving query results from the server or executing SQL statements with input parameters, the values need to be converted between PostgreSQL data types and host language variable types (C language data types, concretely). One of the main points of ECPG is that it takes care of this automatically in most cases.

In this respect, there are two kinds of data types: Some simple PostgreSQL data types, such as integer and text, can be read and written by the application directly. Other PostgreSQL data types, such as timestamp and numeric can only be accessed through special library functions; see Section 34.4.4.2.

Table 34-1 shows which PostgreSQL data types correspond to which C data types. When you wish to send or receive a value of a given PostgreSQL data type, you should declare a C variable of the corresponding C data type in the declare section.

Table 34-1. Mapping Between PostgreSQL Data Types and C Variable Types

PostgreSQL data type	Host variable type
smallint	short
integer	int
bigint	long long int
decimal	decimala
numeric	numerica
real	float
double precision	double
smallserial	short
serial	int
bigserial	long long int
oid	unsigned int
character(n), varchar(n), text	char[n+1], VARCHAR[n+1]b
name	char[NAMEDATALEN]
timestamp	timestampa
interval	intervala
date	datea
boolean	boolc

Notes:
a. This type can only be accessed through special library functions; see Section 34.4.4.2.
b. declared in ecpglib.h
c. declared in ecpglib.h if not native

34.4.4.1. Handling Character Strings

To handle SQL character string data types, such as `varchar` and `text`, there are two possible ways to declare the host variables.

One way is using `char[]`, an array of `char`, which is the most common way to handle character data in C.

```
EXEC SQL BEGIN DECLARE SECTION;
    char str[50];
EXEC SQL END DECLARE SECTION;
```

Note that you have to take care of the length yourself. If you use this host variable as the target variable of a query which returns a string with more than 49 characters, a buffer overflow occurs.

The other way is using the `VARCHAR` type, which is a special type provided by ECPG. The definition on an array of type `VARCHAR` is converted into a named `struct` for every variable. A declaration like:

```
VARCHAR var[180];
```

is converted into:

```
struct varchar_var { int len; char arr[180]; } var;
```

The member `arr` hosts the string including a terminating zero byte. Thus, to store a string in a `VARCHAR` host variable, the host variable has to be declared with the length including the zero byte terminator. The member `len` holds the length of the string stored in the `arr` without the terminating zero byte. When a host variable is used as input for a query, if `strlen(arr)` and `len` are different, the shorter one is used.

`VARCHAR` can be written in upper or lower case, but not in mixed case.

`char` and `VARCHAR` host variables can also hold values of other SQL types, which will be stored in their string forms.

34.4.4.2. Accessing Special Data Types

ECPG contains some special types that help you to interact easily with some special data types from the PostgreSQL server. In particular, it has implemented support for the `numeric`, `decimal`, `date`, `timestamp`, and `interval` types. These data types cannot usefully be mapped to primitive host variable types (such as `int`, `long long int`, or `char[]`), because they have a complex internal structure. Applications deal with these types by declaring host variables in special types and accessing them using functions in the pgtypes library. The pgtypes library, described in detail in Section 34.6 contains basic functions to deal with those types, such that you do not need to send a query to the SQL server just for adding an interval to a time stamp for example.

The follow subsections describe these special data types. For more details about pgtypes library functions, see Section 34.6.

34.4.4.2.1. timestamp, date

Here is a pattern for handling `timestamp` variables in the ECPG host application.

First, the program has to include the header file for the `timestamp` type:

```
#include <pgtypes_timestamp.h>
```

Next, declare a host variable as type `timestamp` in the declare section:

```
EXEC SQL BEGIN DECLARE SECTION;
timestamp ts;
EXEC SQL END DECLARE SECTION;
```

And after reading a value into the host variable, process it using pgtypes library functions. In following example, the `timestamp` value is converted into text (ASCII) form with the `PGTYPEStimestamp_to_asc()` function:

```
EXEC SQL SELECT now()::timestamp INTO :ts;

printf("ts = %s\n", PGTYPEStimestamp_to_asc(ts));
```

This example will show some result like following:

```
ts = 2010-06-27 18:03:56.949343
```

In addition, the DATE type can be handled in the same way. The program has to include `pgtypes_date.h`, declare a host variable as the date type and convert a DATE value into a text form using `PGTYPESdate_to_asc()` function. For more details about the pgtypes library functions, see Section 34.6.

34.4.4.2.2. interval

The handling of the `interval` type is also similar to the `timestamp` and `date` types. It is required, however, to allocate memory for an `interval` type value explicitly. In other words, the memory space for the variable has to be allocated in the heap memory, not in the stack memory.

Here is an example program:

```
#include <stdio.h>
#include <stdlib.h>
#include <pgtypes_interval.h>

int
main(void)
{
EXEC SQL BEGIN DECLARE SECTION;
    interval *in;
EXEC SQL END DECLARE SECTION;

    EXEC SQL CONNECT TO testdb;

    in = PGTYPESinterval_new();
    EXEC SQL SELECT '1 min'::interval INTO :in;
```

```
    printf("interval = %s\n", PGTYPESinterval_to_asc(in));
    PGTYPESinterval_free(in);

    EXEC SQL COMMIT;
    EXEC SQL DISCONNECT ALL;
    return 0;
}
```

34.4.4.2.3. numeric, decimal

The handling of the numeric and decimal types is similar to the interval type: It requires defining a pointer, allocating some memory space on the heap, and accessing the variable using the pgtypes library functions. For more details about the pgtypes library functions, see Section 34.6.

No functions are provided specifically for the decimal type. An application has to convert it to a numeric variable using a pgtypes library function to do further processing.

Here is an example program handling numeric and decimal type variables.

```
#include <stdio.h>
#include <stdlib.h>
#include <pgtypes_numeric.h>

EXEC SQL WHENEVER SQLERROR STOP;

int
main(void)
{
EXEC SQL BEGIN DECLARE SECTION;
    numeric *num;
    numeric *num2;
    decimal *dec;
EXEC SQL END DECLARE SECTION;

    EXEC SQL CONNECT TO testdb;

    num = PGTYPESnumeric_new();
    dec = PGTYPESdecimal_new();

    EXEC SQL SELECT 12.345::numeric(4,2), 23.456::decimal(4,2) INTO :num, :dec;

    printf("numeric = %s\n", PGTYPESnumeric_to_asc(num, 0));
    printf("numeric = %s\n", PGTYPESnumeric_to_asc(num, 1));
    printf("numeric = %s\n", PGTYPESnumeric_to_asc(num, 2));

    /* Convert decimal to numeric to show a decimal value. */
    num2 = PGTYPESnumeric_new();
    PGTYPESnumeric_from_decimal(dec, num2);

    printf("decimal = %s\n", PGTYPESnumeric_to_asc(num2, 0));
    printf("decimal = %s\n", PGTYPESnumeric_to_asc(num2, 1));
```

```
printf("decimal = %s\n", PGTYPESnumeric_to_asc(num2, 2));

PGTYPESnumeric_free(num2);
PGTYPESdecimal_free(dec);
PGTYPESnumeric_free(num);

EXEC SQL COMMIT;
EXEC SQL DISCONNECT ALL;
return 0;
}
```

34.4.4.3. Host Variables with Nonprimitive Types

As a host variable you can also use arrays, typedefs, structs, and pointers.

34.4.4.3.1. Arrays

There are two use cases for arrays as host variables. The first is a way to store some text string in char[] or VARCHAR[], as explained Section 34.4.4.1. The second use case is to retrieve multiple rows from a query result without using a cursor. Without an array, to process a query result consisting of multiple rows, it is required to use a cursor and the FETCH command. But with array host variables, multiple rows can be received at once. The length of the array has to be defined to be able to accommodate all rows, otherwise a buffer overflow will likely occur.

Following example scans the pg_database system table and shows all OIDs and names of the available databases:

```
int
main(void)
{
EXEC SQL BEGIN DECLARE SECTION;
    int dbid[8];
    char dbname[8][16];
    int i;
EXEC SQL END DECLARE SECTION;

    memset(dbname, 0, sizeof(char) * 16 * 8);
    memset(dbid, 0, sizeof(int) * 8);

    EXEC SQL CONNECT TO testdb;

    /* Retrieve multiple rows into arrays at once. */
    EXEC SQL SELECT oid,datname INTO :dbid, :dbname FROM pg_database;

    for (i = 0; i < 8; i++)
        printf("oid=%d, dbname=%s\n", dbid[i], dbname[i]);

    EXEC SQL COMMIT;
    EXEC SQL DISCONNECT ALL;
```

```
    return 0;
}
```

This example shows following result. (The exact values depend on local circumstances.)

```
oid=1, dbname=template1
oid=11510, dbname=template0
oid=11511, dbname=postgres
oid=313780, dbname=testdb
oid=0, dbname=
oid=0, dbname=
oid=0, dbname=
```

34.4.4.3.2. Structures

A structure whose member names match the column names of a query result, can be used to retrieve multiple columns at once. The structure enables handling multiple column values in a single host variable.

The following example retrieves OIDs, names, and sizes of the available databases from the `pg_database` system table and using the `pg_database_size()` function. In this example, a structure variable `dbinfo_t` with members whose names match each column in the `SELECT` result is used to retrieve one result row without putting multiple host variables in the `FETCH` statement.

```
EXEC SQL BEGIN DECLARE SECTION;
    typedef struct
    {
        int oid;
        char datname[65];
        long long int size;
    } dbinfo_t;

    dbinfo_t dbval;
EXEC SQL END DECLARE SECTION;

    memset(&dbval, 0, sizeof(dbinfo_t));

    EXEC SQL DECLARE cur1 CURSOR FOR SELECT oid, datname, pg_database_size(oid) AS s
    EXEC SQL OPEN cur1;

    /* when end of result set reached, break out of while loop */
    EXEC SQL WHENEVER NOT FOUND DO BREAK;

    while (1)
    {
        /* Fetch multiple columns into one structure. */
        EXEC SQL FETCH FROM cur1 INTO :dbval;

        /* Print members of the structure. */
        printf("oid=%d, datname=%s, size=%lld\n", dbval.oid, dbval.datname, dbval.si
    }
```

```
EXEC SQL CLOSE cur1;
```

This example shows following result. (The exact values depend on local circumstances.)

```
oid=1, datname=template1, size=4324580
oid=11510, datname=template0, size=4243460
oid=11511, datname=postgres, size=4324580
oid=313780, datname=testdb, size=8183012
```

Structure host variables "absorb" as many columns as the structure as fields. Additional columns can be assigned to other host variables. For example, the above program could also be restructured like this, with the size variable outside the structure:

```
EXEC SQL BEGIN DECLARE SECTION;
    typedef struct
    {
       int oid;
       char datname[65];
    } dbinfo_t;

    dbinfo_t dbval;
    long long int size;
EXEC SQL END DECLARE SECTION;

    memset(&dbval, 0, sizeof(dbinfo_t));

    EXEC SQL DECLARE cur1 CURSOR FOR SELECT oid, datname, pg_database_size(oid) AS s
    EXEC SQL OPEN cur1;

    /* when end of result set reached, break out of while loop */
    EXEC SQL WHENEVER NOT FOUND DO BREAK;

    while (1)
    {
        /* Fetch multiple columns into one structure. */
        EXEC SQL FETCH FROM cur1 INTO :dbval, :size;

        /* Print members of the structure. */
        printf("oid=%d, datname=%s, size=%lld\n", dbval.oid, dbval.datname, size);
    }

    EXEC SQL CLOSE cur1;
```

34.4.4.3.3. Typedefs

Use the `typedef` keyword to map new types to already existing types.

```
EXEC SQL BEGIN DECLARE SECTION;
    typedef char mychartype[40];
    typedef long serial_t;
EXEC SQL END DECLARE SECTION;
```

Note that you could also use:

```
EXEC SQL TYPE serial_t IS long;
```

This declaration does not need to be part of a declare section.

34.4.4.3.4. Pointers

You can declare pointers to the most common types. Note however that you cannot use pointers as target variables of queries without auto-allocation. See Section 34.7 for more information on auto-allocation.

```
EXEC SQL BEGIN DECLARE SECTION;
    int    *intp;
    char **charp;
EXEC SQL END DECLARE SECTION;
```

34.4.5. Handling Nonprimitive SQL Data Types

This section contains information on how to handle nonscalar and user-defined SQL-level data types in ECPG applications. Note that this is distinct from the handling of host variables of nonprimitive types, described in the previous section.

34.4.5.1. Arrays

Multi-dimensional SQL-level arrays are not directly supported in ECPG. One-dimensional SQL-level arrays can be mapped into C array host variables and vice-versa. However, when creating a statement ecpg does not know the types of the columns, so that it cannot check if a C array is input into a corresponding SQL-level array. When processing the output of a SQL statement, ecpg has the necessary information and thus checks if both are arrays.

If a query accesses *elements* of an array separately, then this avoids the use of arrays in ECPG. Then, a host variable with a type that can be mapped to the element type should be used. For example, if a column type is array of `integer`, a host variable of type `int` can be used. Also if the element type is `varchar` or `text`, a host variable of type `char[]` or `VARCHAR[]` can be used.

Here is an example. Assume the following table:

```
CREATE TABLE t3 (
```

```
    ii integer[]
);

testdb=> SELECT * FROM t3;
      ii
-------------
 {1,2,3,4,5}
(1 row)
```

The following example program retrieves the 4th element of the array and stores it into a host variable of type int:

```
EXEC SQL BEGIN DECLARE SECTION;
int ii;
EXEC SQL END DECLARE SECTION;

EXEC SQL DECLARE cur1 CURSOR FOR SELECT ii[4] FROM t3;
EXEC SQL OPEN cur1;

EXEC SQL WHENEVER NOT FOUND DO BREAK;

while (1)
{
    EXEC SQL FETCH FROM cur1 INTO :ii ;
    printf("ii=%d\n", ii);
}

EXEC SQL CLOSE cur1;
```

This example shows the following result:

```
ii=4
```

To map multiple array elements to the multiple elements in an array type host variables each element of array column and each element of the host variable array have to be managed separately, for example:

```
EXEC SQL BEGIN DECLARE SECTION;
int ii_a[8];
EXEC SQL END DECLARE SECTION;

EXEC SQL DECLARE cur1 CURSOR FOR SELECT ii[1], ii[2], ii[3], ii[4] FROM t3;
EXEC SQL OPEN cur1;

EXEC SQL WHENEVER NOT FOUND DO BREAK;

while (1)
{
    EXEC SQL FETCH FROM cur1 INTO :ii_a[0], :ii_a[1], :ii_a[2], :ii_a[3];
    ...
}
```

Note again that

```
EXEC SQL BEGIN DECLARE SECTION;
int ii_a[8];
EXEC SQL END DECLARE SECTION;

EXEC SQL DECLARE cur1 CURSOR FOR SELECT ii FROM t3;
EXEC SQL OPEN cur1;

EXEC SQL WHENEVER NOT FOUND DO BREAK;

while (1)
{
    /* WRONG */
    EXEC SQL FETCH FROM cur1 INTO :ii_a;
    ...
}
```

would not work correctly in this case, because you cannot map an array type column to an array host variable directly.

Another workaround is to store arrays in their external string representation in host variables of type `char[]` or `VARCHAR[]`. For more details about this representation, see Section 8.15.2. Note that this means that the array cannot be accessed naturally as an array in the host program (without further processing that parses the text representation).

34.4.5.2. Composite Types

Composite types are not directly supported in ECPG, but an easy workaround is possible. The available workarounds are similar to the ones described for arrays above: Either access each attribute separately or use the external string representation.

For the following examples, assume the following type and table:

```
CREATE TYPE comp_t AS (intval integer, textval varchar(32));
CREATE TABLE t4 (compval comp_t);
INSERT INTO t4 VALUES ( (256, 'PostgreSQL') );
```

The most obvious solution is to access each attribute separately. The following program retrieves data from the example table by selecting each attribute of the type `comp_t` separately:

```
EXEC SQL BEGIN DECLARE SECTION;
int intval;
varchar textval[33];
EXEC SQL END DECLARE SECTION;

/* Put each element of the composite type column in the SELECT list. */
EXEC SQL DECLARE cur1 CURSOR FOR SELECT (compval).intval, (compval).textval FROM t4;
EXEC SQL OPEN cur1;

EXEC SQL WHENEVER NOT FOUND DO BREAK;

while (1)
```

```
{
    /* Fetch each element of the composite type column into host variables. */
    EXEC SQL FETCH FROM cur1 INTO :intval, :textval;

    printf("intval=%d, textval=%s\n", intval, textval.arr);
}

EXEC SQL CLOSE cur1;
```

To enhance this example, the host variables to store values in the FETCH command can be gathered into one structure. For more details about the host variable in the structure form, see Section 34.4.4.3.2. To switch to the structure, the example can be modified as below. The two host variables, intval and textval, become members of the comp_t structure, and the structure is specified on the FETCH command.

```
EXEC SQL BEGIN DECLARE SECTION;
typedef struct
{
    int intval;
    varchar textval[33];
} comp_t;

comp_t compval;
EXEC SQL END DECLARE SECTION;

/* Put each element of the composite type column in the SELECT list. */
EXEC SQL DECLARE cur1 CURSOR FOR SELECT (compval).intval, (compval).textval FROM t4;
EXEC SQL OPEN cur1;

EXEC SQL WHENEVER NOT FOUND DO BREAK;

while (1)
{
    /* Put all values in the SELECT list into one structure. */
    EXEC SQL FETCH FROM cur1 INTO :compval;

    printf("intval=%d, textval=%s\n", compval.intval, compval.textval.arr);
}

EXEC SQL CLOSE cur1;
```

Although a structure is used in the FETCH command, the attribute names in the SELECT clause are specified one by one. This can be enhanced by using a * to ask for all attributes of the composite type value.

```
...
EXEC SQL DECLARE cur1 CURSOR FOR SELECT (compval).* FROM t4;
EXEC SQL OPEN cur1;

EXEC SQL WHENEVER NOT FOUND DO BREAK;

while (1)
{
```

```
/* Put all values in the SELECT list into one structure. */
EXEC SQL FETCH FROM cur1 INTO :compval;

printf("intval=%d, textval=%s\n", compval.intval, compval.textval.arr);
}
...
```

This way, composite types can be mapped into structures almost seamlessly, even though ECPG does not understand the composite type itself.

Finally, it is also possible to store composite type values in their external string representation in host variables of type `char[]` or `VARCHAR[]`. But that way, it is not easily possible to access the fields of the value from the host program.

34.4.5.3. User-defined Base Types

New user-defined base types are not directly supported by ECPG. You can use the external string representation and host variables of type `char[]` or `VARCHAR[]`, and this solution is indeed appropriate and sufficient for many types.

Here is an example using the data type `complex` from the example in Section 36.11. The external string representation of that type is `(%lf,%lf)`, which is defined in the functions `complex_in()` and `complex_out()` functions in Section 36.11. The following example inserts the complex type values `(1,1)` and `(3,3)` into the columns a and b, and select them from the table after that.

```
EXEC SQL BEGIN DECLARE SECTION;
    varchar a[64];
    varchar b[64];
EXEC SQL END DECLARE SECTION;

    EXEC SQL INSERT INTO test_complex VALUES ('(1,1)', '(3,3)');

    EXEC SQL DECLARE cur1 CURSOR FOR SELECT a, b FROM test_complex;
    EXEC SQL OPEN cur1;

    EXEC SQL WHENEVER NOT FOUND DO BREAK;

    while (1)
    {
        EXEC SQL FETCH FROM cur1 INTO :a, :b;
        printf("a=%s, b=%s\n", a.arr, b.arr);
    }

    EXEC SQL CLOSE cur1;
```

This example shows following result:

```
a=(1,1), b=(3,3)
```

Another workaround is avoiding the direct use of the user-defined types in ECPG and instead create a function or cast that converts between the user-defined type and a primitive type that ECPG can handle.

Note, however, that type casts, especially implicit ones, should be introduced into the type system very carefully.

For example,

```
CREATE FUNCTION create_complex(r double, i double) RETURNS complex
LANGUAGE SQL
IMMUTABLE
AS $$ SELECT $1 * complex '(1,0')' + $2 * complex '(0,1)' $$;
```

After this definition, the following

```
EXEC SQL BEGIN DECLARE SECTION;
double a, b, c, d;
EXEC SQL END DECLARE SECTION;

a = 1;
b = 2;
c = 3;
d = 4;

EXEC SQL INSERT INTO test_complex VALUES (create_complex(:a, :b), create_complex(:c,
```

has the same effect as

```
EXEC SQL INSERT INTO test_complex VALUES ('(1,2)', '(3,4)');
```

34.4.6. Indicators

The examples above do not handle null values. In fact, the retrieval examples will raise an error if they fetch a null value from the database. To be able to pass null values to the database or retrieve null values from the database, you need to append a second host variable specification to each host variable that contains data. This second host variable is called the *indicator* and contains a flag that tells whether the datum is null, in which case the value of the real host variable is ignored. Here is an example that handles the retrieval of null values correctly:

```
EXEC SQL BEGIN DECLARE SECTION;
VARCHAR val;
int val_ind;
EXEC SQL END DECLARE SECTION:

    ...

EXEC SQL SELECT b INTO :val :val_ind FROM test1;
```

The indicator variable `val_ind` will be zero if the value was not null, and it will be negative if the value was null.

The indicator has another function: if the indicator value is positive, it means that the value is not null, but it was truncated when it was stored in the host variable.

If the argument −r no_indicator is passed to the preprocessor ecpg, it works in "no-indicator" mode. In no-indicator mode, if no indicator variable is specified, null values are signaled (on input and output) for character string types as empty string and for integer types as the lowest possible value for type (for example, INT_MIN for int).

34.5. Dynamic SQL

In many cases, the particular SQL statements that an application has to execute are known at the time the application is written. In some cases, however, the SQL statements are composed at run time or provided by an external source. In these cases you cannot embed the SQL statements directly into the C source code, but there is a facility that allows you to call arbitrary SQL statements that you provide in a string variable.

34.5.1. Executing Statements without a Result Set

The simplest way to execute an arbitrary SQL statement is to use the command EXECUTE IMMEDIATE. For example:

```
EXEC SQL BEGIN DECLARE SECTION;
const char *stmt = "CREATE TABLE test1 (...);";
EXEC SQL END DECLARE SECTION;

EXEC SQL EXECUTE IMMEDIATE :stmt;
```

EXECUTE IMMEDIATE can be used for SQL statements that do not return a result set (e.g., DDL, INSERT, UPDATE, DELETE). You cannot execute statements that retrieve data (e.g., SELECT) this way. The next section describes how to do that.

34.5.2. Executing a Statement with Input Parameters

A more powerful way to execute arbitrary SQL statements is to prepare them once and execute the prepared statement as often as you like. It is also possible to prepare a generalized version of a statement and then execute specific versions of it by substituting parameters. When preparing the statement, write question marks where you want to substitute parameters later. For example:

```
EXEC SQL BEGIN DECLARE SECTION;
const char *stmt = "INSERT INTO test1 VALUES(?, ?);";
EXEC SQL END DECLARE SECTION;

EXEC SQL PREPARE mystmt FROM :stmt;
 ...
EXEC SQL EXECUTE mystmt USING 42, 'foobar';
```

When you don't need the prepared statement anymore, you should deallocate it:

```
EXEC SQL DEALLOCATE PREPARE name;
```

34.5.3. Executing a Statement with a Result Set

To execute an SQL statement with a single result row, EXECUTE can be used. To save the result, add an INTO clause.

```
EXEC SQL BEGIN DECLARE SECTION;
const char *stmt = "SELECT a, b, c FROM test1 WHERE a > ?";
int v1, v2;
VARCHAR v3[50];
EXEC SQL END DECLARE SECTION;

EXEC SQL PREPARE mystmt FROM :stmt;
 ...
EXEC SQL EXECUTE mystmt INTO :v1, :v2, :v3 USING 37;
```

An EXECUTE command can have an INTO clause, a USING clause, both, or neither.

If a query is expected to return more than one result row, a cursor should be used, as in the following example. (See Section 34.3.2 for more details about the cursor.)

```
EXEC SQL BEGIN DECLARE SECTION;
char dbaname[128];
char datname[128];
char *stmt = "SELECT u.usename as dbaname, d.datname "
             "  FROM pg_database d, pg_user u "
             "  WHERE d.datdba = u.usesysid";
EXEC SQL END DECLARE SECTION;

EXEC SQL CONNECT TO testdb AS con1 USER testuser;

EXEC SQL PREPARE stmt1 FROM :stmt;

EXEC SQL DECLARE cursor1 CURSOR FOR stmt1;
EXEC SQL OPEN cursor1;

EXEC SQL WHENEVER NOT FOUND DO BREAK;

while (1)
{
    EXEC SQL FETCH cursor1 INTO :dbaname,:datname;
    printf("dbaname=%s, datname=%s\n", dbaname, datname);
}

EXEC SQL CLOSE cursor1;

EXEC SQL COMMIT;
```

```
EXEC SQL DISCONNECT ALL;
```

34.6. pgtypes Library

The pgtypes library maps PostgreSQL database types to C equivalents that can be used in C programs. It also offers functions to do basic calculations with those types within C, i.e., without the help of the PostgreSQL server. See the following example:

```
EXEC SQL BEGIN DECLARE SECTION;
    date date1;
    timestamp ts1, tsout;
    interval iv1;
    char *out;
EXEC SQL END DECLARE SECTION;

PGTYPESdate_today(&date1);
EXEC SQL SELECT started, duration INTO :ts1, :iv1 FROM datetbl WHERE d=:date1;
PGTYPEStimestamp_add_interval(&ts1, &iv1, &tsout);
out = PGTYPEStimestamp_to_asc(&tsout);
printf("Started + duration: %s\n", out);
free(out);
```

34.6.1. The numeric Type

The numeric type offers to do calculations with arbitrary precision. See Section 8.1 for the equivalent type in the PostgreSQL server. Because of the arbitrary precision this variable needs to be able to expand and shrink dynamically. That's why you can only create numeric variables on the heap, by means of the PGTYPESnumeric_new and PGTYPESnumeric_free functions. The decimal type, which is similar but limited in precision, can be created on the stack as well as on the heap.

The following functions can be used to work with the numeric type:

PGTYPESnumeric_new

Request a pointer to a newly allocated numeric variable.

```
numeric *PGTYPESnumeric_new(void);
```

PGTYPESnumeric_free

Free a numeric type, release all of its memory.

```
void PGTYPESnumeric_free(numeric *var);
```

`PGTYPESnumeric_from_asc`

Parse a numeric type from its string notation.

`numeric *PGTYPESnumeric_from_asc(char *str, char **endptr);`
Valid formats are for example: `-2`, `.794`, `+3.44`, `592.49E07` or `-32.84e-4`. If the value could be parsed successfully, a valid pointer is returned, else the NULL pointer. At the moment ECPG always parses the complete string and so it currently does not support to store the address of the first invalid character in `*endptr`. You can safely set `endptr` to NULL.

`PGTYPESnumeric_to_asc`

Returns a pointer to a string allocated by `malloc` that contains the string representation of the numeric type `num`.

`char *PGTYPESnumeric_to_asc(numeric *num, int dscale);`
The numeric value will be printed with `dscale` decimal digits, with rounding applied if necessary.

`PGTYPESnumeric_add`

Add two numeric variables into a third one.

`int PGTYPESnumeric_add(numeric *var1, numeric *var2, numeric *result);`
The function adds the variables `var1` and `var2` into the result variable `result`. The function returns 0 on success and -1 in case of error.

`PGTYPESnumeric_sub`

Subtract two numeric variables and return the result in a third one.

`int PGTYPESnumeric_sub(numeric *var1, numeric *var2, numeric *result);`
The function subtracts the variable `var2` from the variable `var1`. The result of the operation is stored in the variable `result`. The function returns 0 on success and -1 in case of error.

`PGTYPESnumeric_mul`

Multiply two numeric variables and return the result in a third one.

`int PGTYPESnumeric_mul(numeric *var1, numeric *var2, numeric *result);`
The function multiplies the variables `var1` and `var2`. The result of the operation is stored in the variable `result`. The function returns 0 on success and -1 in case of error.

`PGTYPESnumeric_div`

Divide two numeric variables and return the result in a third one.

`int PGTYPESnumeric_div(numeric *var1, numeric *var2, numeric *result);`
The function divides the variables `var1` by `var2`. The result of the operation is stored in the variable `result`. The function returns 0 on success and -1 in case of error.

`PGTYPESnumeric_cmp`

Compare two numeric variables.

`int PGTYPESnumeric_cmp(numeric *var1, numeric *var2)`
This function compares two numeric variables. In case of error, `INT_MAX` is returned. On success, the function returns one of three possible results:

- 1, if `var1` is bigger than `var2`
- -1, if `var1` is smaller than `var2`
- 0, if `var1` and `var2` are equal

`PGTYPESnumeric_from_int`

Convert an int variable to a numeric variable.

`int PGTYPESnumeric_from_int(signed int int_val, numeric *var);`
This function accepts a variable of type signed int and stores it in the numeric variable `var`. Upon success, 0 is returned and -1 in case of a failure.

`PGTYPESnumeric_from_long`

Convert a long int variable to a numeric variable.

`int PGTYPESnumeric_from_long(signed long int long_val, numeric *var);`
This function accepts a variable of type signed long int and stores it in the numeric variable `var`. Upon success, 0 is returned and -1 in case of a failure.

`PGTYPESnumeric_copy`

Copy over one numeric variable into another one.

`int PGTYPESnumeric_copy(numeric *src, numeric *dst);`
This function copies over the value of the variable that `src` points to into the variable that `dst` points to. It returns 0 on success and -1 if an error occurs.

`PGTYPESnumeric_from_double`

Convert a variable of type double to a numeric.

`int  PGTYPESnumeric_from_double(double d, numeric *dst);`
This function accepts a variable of type double and stores the result in the variable that `dst` points to. It returns 0 on success and -1 if an error occurs.

`PGTYPESnumeric_to_double`

Convert a variable of type numeric to double.

`int PGTYPESnumeric_to_double(numeric *nv, double *dp)`
The function converts the numeric value from the variable that `nv` points to into the double variable that `dp` points to. It returns 0 on success and -1 if an error occurs, including overflow. On overflow, the global variable `errno` will be set to `PGTYPES_NUM_OVERFLOW` additionally.

`PGTYPESnumeric_to_int`

Convert a variable of type numeric to int.

`int PGTYPESnumeric_to_int(numeric *nv, int *ip);`
The function converts the numeric value from the variable that `nv` points to into the integer variable that `ip` points to. It returns 0 on success and -1 if an error occurs, including overflow. On overflow, the global variable `errno` will be set to `PGTYPES_NUM_OVERFLOW` additionally.

`PGTYPESnumeric_to_long`

Convert a variable of type numeric to long.

`int PGTYPESnumeric_to_long(numeric *nv, long *lp);`
The function converts the numeric value from the variable that `nv` points to into the long integer variable that `lp` points to. It returns 0 on success and -1 if an error occurs, including overflow. On overflow, the global variable `errno` will be set to `PGTYPES_NUM_OVERFLOW` additionally.

PGTYPESnumeric_to_decimal

> Convert a variable of type numeric to decimal.
>
> int PGTYPESnumeric_to_decimal(numeric *src, decimal *dst);
> The function converts the numeric value from the variable that src points to into the decimal variable that dst points to. It returns 0 on success and -1 if an error occurs, including overflow. On overflow, the global variable errno will be set to PGTYPES_NUM_OVERFLOW additionally.

PGTYPESnumeric_from_decimal

> Convert a variable of type decimal to numeric.
>
> int PGTYPESnumeric_from_decimal(decimal *src, numeric *dst);
> The function converts the decimal value from the variable that src points to into the numeric variable that dst points to. It returns 0 on success and -1 if an error occurs. Since the decimal type is implemented as a limited version of the numeric type, overflow cannot occur with this conversion.

34.6.2. The date Type

The date type in C enables your programs to deal with data of the SQL type date. See Section 8.5 for the equivalent type in the PostgreSQL server.

The following functions can be used to work with the date type:

PGTYPESdate_from_timestamp

> Extract the date part from a timestamp.
>
> date PGTYPESdate_from_timestamp(timestamp dt);
> The function receives a timestamp as its only argument and returns the extracted date part from this timestamp.

PGTYPESdate_from_asc

> Parse a date from its textual representation.
>
> date PGTYPESdate_from_asc(char *str, char **endptr);
> The function receives a C char* string str and a pointer to a C char* string endptr. At the moment ECPG always parses the complete string and so it currently does not support to store the address of the first invalid character in *endptr. You can safely set endptr to NULL.
>
> Note that the function always assumes MDY-formatted dates and there is currently no variable to change that within ECPG.
>
> Table 34-2 shows the allowed input formats.
>
> **Table 34-2. Valid Input Formats for PGTYPESdate_from_asc**
>
> | Input | Result |
> |---|---|
> | January 8, 1999 | January 8, 1999 |
> | 1999-01-08 | January 8, 1999 |
> | 1/8/1999 | January 8, 1999 |

Input	Result
1/18/1999	January 18, 1999
01/02/03	February 1, 2003
1999-Jan-08	January 8, 1999
Jan-08-1999	January 8, 1999
08-Jan-1999	January 8, 1999
99-Jan-08	January 8, 1999
08-Jan-99	January 8, 1999
08-Jan-06	January 8, 2006
Jan-08-99	January 8, 1999
19990108	ISO 8601; January 8, 1999
990108	ISO 8601; January 8, 1999
1999.008	year and day of year
J2451187	Julian day
January 8, 99 BC	year 99 before the Common Era

`PGTYPESdate_to_asc`

Return the textual representation of a date variable.

`char *PGTYPESdate_to_asc(date dDate);`

The function receives the date `dDate` as its only parameter. It will output the date in the form `1999-01-18`, i.e., in the `YYYY-MM-DD` format.

`PGTYPESdate_julmdy`

Extract the values for the day, the month and the year from a variable of type date.

`void PGTYPESdate_julmdy(date d, int *mdy);`

The function receives the date `d` and a pointer to an array of 3 integer values `mdy`. The variable name indicates the sequential order: `mdy[0]` will be set to contain the number of the month, `mdy[1]` will be set to the value of the day and `mdy[2]` will contain the year.

`PGTYPESdate_mdyjul`

Create a date value from an array of 3 integers that specify the day, the month and the year of the date.

`void PGTYPESdate_mdyjul(int *mdy, date *jdate);`

The function receives the array of the 3 integers (`mdy`) as its first argument and as its second argument a pointer to a variable of type date that should hold the result of the operation.

`PGTYPESdate_dayofweek`

Return a number representing the day of the week for a date value.

`int PGTYPESdate_dayofweek(date d);`

The function receives the date variable `d` as its only argument and returns an integer that indicates the day of the week for this date.

- 0 - Sunday

- 1 - Monday

- 2 - Tuesday
- 3 - Wednesday
- 4 - Thursday
- 5 - Friday
- 6 - Saturday

`PGTYPESdate_today`

Get the current date.

`void PGTYPESdate_today(date *d);`
The function receives a pointer to a date variable (d) that it sets to the current date.

`PGTYPESdate_fmt_asc`

Convert a variable of type date to its textual representation using a format mask.

`int PGTYPESdate_fmt_asc(date dDate, char *fmtstring, char *outbuf);`
The function receives the date to convert (dDate), the format mask (fmtstring) and the string that will hold the textual representation of the date (outbuf).

On success, 0 is returned and a negative value if an error occurred.

The following literals are the field specifiers you can use:

- dd - The number of the day of the month.
- mm - The number of the month of the year.
- yy - The number of the year as a two digit number.
- yyyy - The number of the year as a four digit number.
- ddd - The name of the day (abbreviated).
- mmm - The name of the month (abbreviated).

All other characters are copied 1:1 to the output string.

Table 34-3 indicates a few possible formats. This will give you an idea of how to use this function. All output lines are based on the same date: November 23, 1959.

Table 34-3. Valid Input Formats for `PGTYPESdate_fmt_asc`

Format	Result
mmddyy	112359
ddmmyy	231159
yymmdd	591123
yy/mm/dd	59/11/23
yy mm dd	59 11 23
yy.mm.dd	59.11.23
.mm.yyyy.dd.	.11.1959.23.
mmm. dd, yyyy	Nov. 23, 1959

Format	Result
mmm dd yyyy	Nov 23 1959
yyyy dd mm	1959 23 11
ddd, mmm. dd, yyyy	Mon, Nov. 23, 1959
(ddd) mmm. dd, yyyy	(Mon) Nov. 23, 1959

`PGTYPESdate_defmt_asc`

Use a format mask to convert a C char* string to a value of type date.

`int PGTYPESdate_defmt_asc(date *d, char *fmt, char *str);`

The function receives a pointer to the date value that should hold the result of the operation (d), the format mask to use for parsing the date (fmt) and the C char* string containing the textual representation of the date (str). The textual representation is expected to match the format mask. However you do not need to have a 1:1 mapping of the string to the format mask. The function only analyzes the sequential order and looks for the literals yy or yyyy that indicate the position of the year, mm to indicate the position of the month and dd to indicate the position of the day.

Table 34-4 indicates a few possible formats. This will give you an idea of how to use this function.

Table 34-4. Valid Input Formats for `rdefmtdate`

Format	String	Result
ddmmyy	21-2-54	1954-02-21
ddmmyy	2-12-54	1954-12-02
ddmmyy	20111954	1954-11-20
ddmmyy	130464	1964-04-13
mmm.dd.yyyy	MAR-12-1967	1967-03-12
yy/mm/dd	1954, February 3rd	1954-02-03
mmm.dd.yyyy	041269	1969-04-12
yy/mm/dd	In the year 2525, in the month of July, mankind will be alive on the 28th day	2525-07-28
dd-mm-yy	I said on the 28th of July in the year 2525	2525-07-28
mmm.dd.yyyy	9/14/58	1958-09-14
yy/mm/dd	47/03/29	1947-03-29
mmm.dd.yyyy	oct 28 1975	1975-10-28
mmddyy	Nov 14th, 1985	1985-11-14

34.6.3. The timestamp Type

The timestamp type in C enables your programs to deal with data of the SQL type timestamp. See Section 8.5 for the equivalent type in the PostgreSQL server.

The following functions can be used to work with the timestamp type:

`PGTYPEStimestamp_from_asc`

> Parse a timestamp from its textual representation into a timestamp variable.
>
> `timestamp PGTYPEStimestamp_from_asc(char *str, char **endptr);`
> The function receives the string to parse (`str`) and a pointer to a C char* (`endptr`). At the moment ECPG always parses the complete string and so it currently does not support to store the address of the first invalid character in `*endptr`. You can safely set `endptr` to NULL.
>
> The function returns the parsed timestamp on success. On error, `PGTYPESInvalidTimestamp` is returned and `errno` is set to `PGTYPES_TS_BAD_TIMESTAMP`. See *PGTYPESInvalidTimestamp* for important notes on this value.
>
> In general, the input string can contain any combination of an allowed date specification, a whitespace character and an allowed time specification. Note that time zones are not supported by ECPG. It can parse them but does not apply any calculation as the PostgreSQL server does for example. Timezone specifiers are silently discarded.
>
> Table 34-5 contains a few examples for input strings.
>
> **Table 34-5. Valid Input Formats for `PGTYPEStimestamp_from_asc`**
>
> | Input | Result |
> |---|---|
> | 1999-01-08 04:05:06 | 1999-01-08 04:05:06 |
> | January 8 04:05:06 1999 PST | 1999-01-08 04:05:06 |
> | 1999-Jan-08 04:05:06.789-8 | 1999-01-08 04:05:06.789 (time zone specifier ignored) |
> | J2451187 04:05-08:00 | 1999-01-08 04:05:00 (time zone specifier ignored) |

`PGTYPEStimestamp_to_asc`

> Converts a date to a C char* string.
>
> `char *PGTYPEStimestamp_to_asc(timestamp tstamp);`
> The function receives the timestamp `tstamp` as its only argument and returns an allocated string that contains the textual representation of the timestamp.

`PGTYPEStimestamp_current`

> Retrieve the current timestamp.
>
> `void PGTYPEStimestamp_current(timestamp *ts);`
> The function retrieves the current timestamp and saves it into the timestamp variable that `ts` points to.

PGTYPEStimestamp_fmt_asc

Convert a timestamp variable to a C char* using a format mask.

`int PGTYPEStimestamp_fmt_asc(timestamp *ts, char *output, int str_len, char *fmts`

The function receives a pointer to the timestamp to convert as its first argument (`ts`), a pointer to the output buffer (`output`), the maximal length that has been allocated for the output buffer (`str_len`) and the format mask to use for the conversion (`fmtstr`).

Upon success, the function returns 0 and a negative value if an error occurred.

You can use the following format specifiers for the format mask. The format specifiers are the same ones that are used in the `strftime` function in libc. Any non-format specifier will be copied into the output buffer.

- `%A` - is replaced by national representation of the full weekday name.

- `%a` - is replaced by national representation of the abbreviated weekday name.

- `%B` - is replaced by national representation of the full month name.

- `%b` - is replaced by national representation of the abbreviated month name.

- `%C` - is replaced by (year / 100) as decimal number; single digits are preceded by a zero.

- `%c` - is replaced by national representation of time and date.

- `%D` - is equivalent to `%m/%d/%y`.

- `%d` - is replaced by the day of the month as a decimal number (01-31).

- `%E* %O*` - POSIX locale extensions. The sequences `%Ec %EC %Ex %EX %Ey %EY %Od %Oe %OH %OI %Om %OM %OS %Ou %OU %OV %Ow %OW %Oy` are supposed to provide alternative representations.

  Additionally `%OB` implemented to represent alternative months names (used standalone, without day mentioned).

- `%e` - is replaced by the day of month as a decimal number (1-31); single digits are preceded by a blank.

- `%F` - is equivalent to `%Y-%m-%d`.

- `%G` - is replaced by a year as a decimal number with century. This year is the one that contains the greater part of the week (Monday as the first day of the week).

- `%g` - is replaced by the same year as in `%G`, but as a decimal number without century (00-99).

- `%H` - is replaced by the hour (24-hour clock) as a decimal number (00-23).

- `%h` - the same as `%b`.

- `%I` - is replaced by the hour (12-hour clock) as a decimal number (01-12).

- `%j` - is replaced by the day of the year as a decimal number (001-366).

- `%k` - is replaced by the hour (24-hour clock) as a decimal number (0-23); single digits are preceded by a blank.

- `%l` - is replaced by the hour (12-hour clock) as a decimal number (1-12); single digits are preceded by a blank.

- `%M` - is replaced by the minute as a decimal number (00-59).

- `%m` - is replaced by the month as a decimal number (01-12).

- `%n` - is replaced by a newline.

- `%O*` - the same as `%E*`.

- `%p` - is replaced by national representation of either "ante meridiem" or "post meridiem" as appropriate.

- `%R` - is equivalent to `%H:%M`.

- `%r` - is equivalent to `%I:%M:%S %p`.

- `%S` - is replaced by the second as a decimal number (00-60).

- `%s` - is replaced by the number of seconds since the Epoch, UTC.

- `%T` - is equivalent to `%H:%M:%S`

- `%t` - is replaced by a tab.

- `%U` - is replaced by the week number of the year (Sunday as the first day of the week) as a decimal number (00-53).

- `%u` - is replaced by the weekday (Monday as the first day of the week) as a decimal number (1-7).

- `%V` - is replaced by the week number of the year (Monday as the first day of the week) as a decimal number (01-53). If the week containing January 1 has four or more days in the new year, then it is week 1; otherwise it is the last week of the previous year, and the next week is week 1.

- `%v` - is equivalent to `%e-%b-%Y`.

- `%W` - is replaced by the week number of the year (Monday as the first day of the week) as a decimal number (00-53).

- `%w` - is replaced by the weekday (Sunday as the first day of the week) as a decimal number (0-6).

- `%X` - is replaced by national representation of the time.

- `%x` - is replaced by national representation of the date.

- `%Y` - is replaced by the year with century as a decimal number.

- `%y` - is replaced by the year without century as a decimal number (00-99).

- `%Z` - is replaced by the time zone name.

- `%z` - is replaced by the time zone offset from UTC; a leading plus sign stands for east of UTC, a minus sign for west of UTC, hours and minutes follow with two digits each and no delimiter between them (common form for RFC 822 date headers).

- `%+` - is replaced by national representation of the date and time.

- `%-*` - GNU libc extension. Do not do any padding when performing numerical outputs.

- `$_*` - GNU libc extension. Explicitly specify space for padding.

- `%0*` - GNU libc extension. Explicitly specify zero for padding.

- `%%` - is replaced by `%`.

`PGTYPEStimestamp_sub`

Subtract one timestamp from another one and save the result in a variable of type interval.

```
int PGTYPEStimestamp_sub(timestamp *ts1, timestamp *ts2, interval *iv);
```

The function will subtract the timestamp variable that `ts2` points to from the timestamp variable that `ts1` points to and will store the result in the interval variable that `iv` points to.

Upon success, the function returns 0 and a negative value if an error occurred.

PGTYPEStimestamp_defmt_asc

Parse a timestamp value from its textual representation using a formatting mask.

```
int PGTYPEStimestamp_defmt_asc(char *str, char *fmt, timestamp *d);
```
The function receives the textual representation of a timestamp in the variable `str` as well as the formatting mask to use in the variable `fmt`. The result will be stored in the variable that `d` points to.

If the formatting mask `fmt` is NULL, the function will fall back to the default formatting mask which is `%Y-%m-%d %H:%M:%S`.

This is the reverse function to *PGTYPEStimestamp_fmt_asc*. See the documentation there in order to find out about the possible formatting mask entries.

PGTYPEStimestamp_add_interval

Add an interval variable to a timestamp variable.

```
int PGTYPEStimestamp_add_interval(timestamp *tin, interval *span, timestamp *tout
```
The function receives a pointer to a timestamp variable `tin` and a pointer to an interval variable `span`. It adds the interval to the timestamp and saves the resulting timestamp in the variable that `tout` points to.

Upon success, the function returns 0 and a negative value if an error occurred.

PGTYPEStimestamp_sub_interval

Subtract an interval variable from a timestamp variable.

```
int PGTYPEStimestamp_sub_interval(timestamp *tin, interval *span, timestamp *tout
```
The function subtracts the interval variable that `span` points to from the timestamp variable that `tin` points to and saves the result into the variable that `tout` points to.

Upon success, the function returns 0 and a negative value if an error occurred.

34.6.4. The interval Type

The interval type in C enables your programs to deal with data of the SQL type interval. See Section 8.5 for the equivalent type in the PostgreSQL server.

The following functions can be used to work with the interval type:

PGTYPESinterval_new

Return a pointer to a newly allocated interval variable.

```
interval *PGTYPESinterval_new(void);
```

PGTYPESinterval_free

Release the memory of a previously allocated interval variable.

```
void PGTYPESinterval_new(interval *intvl);
```

PGTYPESinterval_from_asc

Parse an interval from its textual representation.

`interval *PGTYPESinterval_from_asc(char *str, char **endptr);`
The function parses the input string `str` and returns a pointer to an allocated interval variable. At the moment ECPG always parses the complete string and so it currently does not support to store the address of the first invalid character in `*endptr`. You can safely set `endptr` to NULL.

PGTYPESinterval_to_asc

Convert a variable of type interval to its textual representation.

`char *PGTYPESinterval_to_asc(interval *span);`
The function converts the interval variable that `span` points to into a C char*. The output looks like this example: `@ 1 day 12 hours 59 mins 10 secs`.

PGTYPESinterval_copy

Copy a variable of type interval.

`int PGTYPESinterval_copy(interval *intvlsrc, interval *intvldest);`
The function copies the interval variable that `intvlsrc` points to into the variable that `intvldest` points to. Note that you need to allocate the memory for the destination variable before.

34.6.5. The decimal Type

The decimal type is similar to the numeric type. However it is limited to a maximum precision of 30 significant digits. In contrast to the numeric type which can be created on the heap only, the decimal type can be created either on the stack or on the heap (by means of the functions `PGTYPESdecimal_new` and `PGTYPESdecimal_free`). There are a lot of other functions that deal with the decimal type in the Informix compatibility mode described in Section 34.15.

The following functions can be used to work with the decimal type and are not only contained in the `libcompat` library.

PGTYPESdecimal_new

Request a pointer to a newly allocated decimal variable.

`decimal *PGTYPESdecimal_new(void);`

PGTYPESdecimal_free

Free a decimal type, release all of its memory.

`void PGTYPESdecimal_free(decimal *var);`

34.6.6. errno Values of pgtypeslib

PGTYPES_NUM_BAD_NUMERIC

> An argument should contain a numeric variable (or point to a numeric variable) but in fact its in-memory representation was invalid.

PGTYPES_NUM_OVERFLOW

> An overflow occurred. Since the numeric type can deal with almost arbitrary precision, converting a numeric variable into other types might cause overflow.

PGTYPES_NUM_UNDERFLOW

> An underflow occurred. Since the numeric type can deal with almost arbitrary precision, converting a numeric variable into other types might cause underflow.

PGTYPES_NUM_DIVIDE_ZERO

> A division by zero has been attempted.

PGTYPES_DATE_BAD_DATE

> An invalid date string was passed to the PGTYPESdate_from_asc function.

PGTYPES_DATE_ERR_EARGS

> Invalid arguments were passed to the PGTYPESdate_defmt_asc function.

PGTYPES_DATE_ERR_ENOSHORTDATE

> An invalid token in the input string was found by the PGTYPESdate_defmt_asc function.

PGTYPES_INTVL_BAD_INTERVAL

> An invalid interval string was passed to the PGTYPESinterval_from_asc function, or an invalid interval value was passed to the PGTYPESinterval_to_asc function.

PGTYPES_DATE_ERR_ENOTDMY

> There was a mismatch in the day/month/year assignment in the PGTYPESdate_defmt_asc function.

PGTYPES_DATE_BAD_DAY

> An invalid day of the month value was found by the PGTYPESdate_defmt_asc function.

PGTYPES_DATE_BAD_MONTH

> An invalid month value was found by the PGTYPESdate_defmt_asc function.

PGTYPES_TS_BAD_TIMESTAMP

> An invalid timestamp string pass passed to the PGTYPEStimestamp_from_asc function, or an invalid timestamp value was passed to the PGTYPEStimestamp_to_asc function.

PGTYPES_TS_ERR_EINFTIME

> An infinite timestamp value was encountered in a context that cannot handle it.

34.6.7. Special Constants of pgtypeslib

PGTYPESInvalidTimestamp

> A value of type timestamp representing an invalid time stamp. This is returned by the function PGTYPEStimestamp_from_asc on parse error. Note that due to the internal representation of the timestamp data type, PGTYPESInvalidTimestamp is also a valid timestamp at the same time. It is set to 1899-12-31 23:59:59. In order to detect errors, make sure that your application does not only test for PGTYPESInvalidTimestamp but also for errno != 0 after each call to PGTYPEStimestamp_from_asc.

34.7. Using Descriptor Areas

An SQL descriptor area is a more sophisticated method for processing the result of a SELECT, FETCH or a DESCRIBE statement. An SQL descriptor area groups the data of one row of data together with metadata items into one data structure. The metadata is particularly useful when executing dynamic SQL statements, where the nature of the result columns might not be known ahead of time. PostgreSQL provides two ways to use Descriptor Areas: the named SQL Descriptor Areas and the C-structure SQLDAs.

34.7.1. Named SQL Descriptor Areas

A named SQL descriptor area consists of a header, which contains information concerning the entire descriptor, and one or more item descriptor areas, which basically each describe one column in the result row.

Before you can use an SQL descriptor area, you need to allocate one:

EXEC SQL ALLOCATE DESCRIPTOR *identifier*;

The identifier serves as the "variable name" of the descriptor area. When you don't need the descriptor anymore, you should deallocate it:

EXEC SQL DEALLOCATE DESCRIPTOR *identifier*;

To use a descriptor area, specify it as the storage target in an INTO clause, instead of listing host variables:

EXEC SQL FETCH NEXT FROM mycursor INTO SQL DESCRIPTOR mydesc;

If the result set is empty, the Descriptor Area will still contain the metadata from the query, i.e. the field names.

For not yet executed prepared queries, the DESCRIBE statement can be used to get the metadata of the result set:

EXEC SQL BEGIN DECLARE SECTION;

```
char *sql_stmt = "SELECT * FROM table1";
EXEC SQL END DECLARE SECTION;

EXEC SQL PREPARE stmt1 FROM :sql_stmt;
EXEC SQL DESCRIBE stmt1 INTO SQL DESCRIPTOR mydesc;
```

Before PostgreSQL 9.0, the `SQL` keyword was optional, so using `DESCRIPTOR` and `SQL DESCRIPTOR` produced named SQL Descriptor Areas. Now it is mandatory, omitting the `SQL` keyword produces SQLDA Descriptor Areas, see Section 34.7.2.

In `DESCRIBE` and `FETCH` statements, the `INTO` and `USING` keywords can be used to similarly: they produce the result set and the metadata in a Descriptor Area.

Now how do you get the data out of the descriptor area? You can think of the descriptor area as a structure with named fields. To retrieve the value of a field from the header and store it into a host variable, use the following command:

```
EXEC SQL GET DESCRIPTOR name :hostvar = field;
```

Currently, there is only one header field defined: *COUNT*, which tells how many item descriptor areas exist (that is, how many columns are contained in the result). The host variable needs to be of an integer type. To get a field from the item descriptor area, use the following command:

```
EXEC SQL GET DESCRIPTOR name VALUE num :hostvar = field;
```

num can be a literal integer or a host variable containing an integer. Possible fields are:

CARDINALITY (integer)

    number of rows in the result set

DATA

    actual data item (therefore, the data type of this field depends on the query)

DATETIME_INTERVAL_CODE (integer)

    When TYPE is 9, DATETIME_INTERVAL_CODE will have a value of 1 for DATE, 2 for TIME, 3 for TIMESTAMP, 4 for TIME WITH TIME ZONE, or 5 for TIMESTAMP WITH TIME ZONE.

DATETIME_INTERVAL_PRECISION (integer)

    not implemented

INDICATOR (integer)

    the indicator (indicating a null value or a value truncation)

KEY_MEMBER (integer)

    not implemented

LENGTH (integer)

    length of the datum in characters

NAME (string)

   name of the column

NULLABLE (integer)

   not implemented

OCTET_LENGTH (integer)

   length of the character representation of the datum in bytes

PRECISION (integer)

   precision (for type numeric)

RETURNED_LENGTH (integer)

   length of the datum in characters

RETURNED_OCTET_LENGTH (integer)

   length of the character representation of the datum in bytes

SCALE (integer)

   scale (for type numeric)

TYPE (integer)

   numeric code of the data type of the column

In EXECUTE, DECLARE and OPEN statements, the effect of the INTO and USING keywords are different. A Descriptor Area can also be manually built to provide the input parameters for a query or a cursor and USING SQL DESCRIPTOR *name* is the way to pass the input parameters into a parameterized query. The statement to build a named SQL Descriptor Area is below:

```
EXEC SQL SET DESCRIPTOR name VALUE num field = :hostvar;
```

PostgreSQL supports retrieving more that one record in one FETCH statement and storing the data in host variables in this case assumes that the variable is an array. E.g.:

```
EXEC SQL BEGIN DECLARE SECTION;
int id[5];
EXEC SQL END DECLARE SECTION;

EXEC SQL FETCH 5 FROM mycursor INTO SQL DESCRIPTOR mydesc;

EXEC SQL GET DESCRIPTOR mydesc VALUE 1 :id = DATA;
```

34.7.2. SQLDA Descriptor Areas

An SQLDA Descriptor Area is a C language structure which can be also used to get the result set and the metadata of a query. One structure stores one record from the result set.

```
EXEC SQL include sqlda.h;
sqlda_t          *mysqlda;

EXEC SQL FETCH 3 FROM mycursor INTO DESCRIPTOR mysqlda;
```

Note that the SQL keyword is omitted. The paragraphs about the use cases of the INTO and USING keywords in Section 34.7.1 also apply here with an addition. In a DESCRIBE statement the DESCRIPTOR keyword can be completely omitted if the INTO keyword is used:

```
EXEC SQL DESCRIBE prepared_statement INTO mysqlda;
```

The general flow of a program that uses SQLDA is:

1. Prepare a query, and declare a cursor for it.

2. Declare an SQLDA for the result rows.

3. Declare an SQLDA for the input parameters, and initialize them (memory allocation, parameter settings).

4. Open a cursor with the input SQLDA.

5. Fetch rows from the cursor, and store them into an output SQLDA.

6. Read values from the output SQLDA into the host variables (with conversion if necessary).

7. Close the cursor.

8. Free the memory area allocated for the input SQLDA.

34.7.2.1. SQLDA Data Structure

SQLDA uses three data structure types: sqlda_t, sqlvar_t, and struct sqlname.

> **Tip:** PostgreSQL's SQLDA has a similar data structure to the one in IBM DB2 Universal Database, so some technical information on DB2's SQLDA could help understanding PostgreSQL's one better.

34.7.2.1.1. sqlda_t Structure

The structure type sqlda_t is the type of the actual SQLDA. It holds one record. And two or more sqlda_t structures can be connected in a linked list with the pointer in the desc_next field, thus representing an ordered collection of rows. So, when two or more rows are fetched, the application can read them by following the desc_next pointer in each sqlda_t node.

The definition of sqlda_t is:

```
struct sqlda_struct
```

```
{
    char           sqldaid[8];
    long           sqldabc;
    short          sqln;
    short          sqld;
    struct sqlda_struct *desc_next;
    struct sqlvar_struct sqlvar[1];
};

typedef struct sqlda_struct sqlda_t;
```

The meaning of the fields is:

sqldaid

It contains the literal string "SQLDA ".

sqldabc

It contains the size of the allocated space in bytes.

sqln

It contains the number of input parameters for a parameterized query in case it's passed into OPEN, DECLARE or EXECUTE statements using the USING keyword. In case it's used as output of SELECT, EXECUTE or FETCH statements, its value is the same as sqld statement

sqld

It contains the number of fields in a result set.

desc_next

If the query returns more than one record, multiple linked SQLDA structures are returned, and desc_next holds a pointer to the next entry in the list.

sqlvar

This is the array of the columns in the result set.

34.7.2.1.2. sqlvar_t Structure

The structure type sqlvar_t holds a column value and metadata such as type and length. The definition of the type is:

```
struct sqlvar_struct
{
    short          sqltype;
    short          sqllen;
    char           *sqldata;
    short          *sqlind;
    struct sqlname sqlname;
};

typedef struct sqlvar_struct sqlvar_t;
```

The meaning of the fields is:

`sqltype`

Contains the type identifier of the field. For values, see `enum ECPGttype` in `ecpgtype.h`.

`sqllen`

Contains the binary length of the field. e.g. 4 bytes for `ECPGt_int`.

`sqldata`

Points to the data. The format of the data is described in Section 34.4.4.

`sqlind`

Points to the null indicator. 0 means not null, -1 means null.

`sqlname`

The name of the field.

34.7.2.1.3. struct sqlname Structure

A `struct sqlname` structure holds a column name. It is used as a member of the `sqlvar_t` structure. The definition of the structure is:

```
#define NAMEDATALEN 64

struct sqlname
{
        short           length;
        char            data[NAMEDATALEN];
};
```

The meaning of the fields is:

`length`

Contains the length of the field name.

`data`

Contains the actual field name.

34.7.2.2. Retrieving a Result Set Using an SQLDA

The general steps to retrieve a query result set through an SQLDA are:

1. Declare an `sqlda_t` structure to receive the result set.

2. Execute FETCH/EXECUTE/DESCRIBE commands to process a query specifying the declared SQLDA.

3. Check the number of records in the result set by looking at sqln, a member of the sqlda_t structure.

4. Get the values of each column from sqlvar[0], sqlvar[1], etc., members of the sqlda_t structure.

5. Go to next row (sqlda_t structure) by following the desc_next pointer, a member of the sqlda_t structure.

6. Repeat above as you need.

Here is an example retrieving a result set through an SQLDA.

First, declare a sqlda_t structure to receive the result set.

```
sqlda_t *sqlda1;
```

Next, specify the SQLDA in a command. This is a FETCH command example.

```
EXEC SQL FETCH NEXT FROM cur1 INTO DESCRIPTOR sqlda1;
```

Run a loop following the linked list to retrieve the rows.

```
sqlda_t *cur_sqlda;

for (cur_sqlda = sqlda1;
     cur_sqlda != NULL;
     cur_sqlda = cur_sqlda->desc_next)
{
    ...
}
```

Inside the loop, run another loop to retrieve each column data (sqlvar_t structure) of the row.

```
for (i = 0; i < cur_sqlda->sqld; i++)
{
    sqlvar_t v = cur_sqlda->sqlvar[i];
    char *sqldata = v.sqldata;
    short sqllen  = v.sqllen;
    ...
}
```

To get a column value, check the sqltype value, a member of the sqlvar_t structure. Then, switch to an appropriate way, depending on the column type, to copy data from the sqlvar field to a host variable.

```
char var_buf[1024];

switch (v.sqltype)
{
```

```
    case ECPGt_char:
        memset(&var_buf, 0, sizeof(var_buf));
        memcpy(&var_buf, sqldata, (sizeof(var_buf) <= sqllen ? sizeof(var_buf) - 1 :
        break;

    case ECPGt_int: /* integer */
        memcpy(&intval, sqldata, sqllen);
        snprintf(var_buf, sizeof(var_buf), "%d", intval);
        break;

    ...
}
```

34.7.2.3. Passing Query Parameters Using an SQLDA

The general steps to use an SQLDA to pass input parameters to a prepared query are:

1.   Create a prepared query (prepared statement)

2.   Declare a sqlda_t structure as an input SQLDA.

3.   Allocate memory area (as sqlda_t structure) for the input SQLDA.

4.   Set (copy) input values in the allocated memory.

5.   Open a cursor with specifying the input SQLDA.

Here is an example.

First, create a prepared statement.

```
EXEC SQL BEGIN DECLARE SECTION;
char query[1024] = "SELECT d.oid, * FROM pg_database d, pg_stat_database s WHERE d.o
EXEC SQL END DECLARE SECTION;

EXEC SQL PREPARE stmt1 FROM :query;
```

Next, allocate memory for an SQLDA, and set the number of input parameters in `sqln`, a member variable of the `sqlda_t` structure. When two or more input parameters are required for the prepared query, the application has to allocate additional memory space which is calculated by (nr. of params - 1) * sizeof(sqlvar_t). The example shown here allocates memory space for two input parameters.

```
sqlda_t *sqlda2;

sqlda2 = (sqlda_t *) malloc(sizeof(sqlda_t) + sizeof(sqlvar_t));
memset(sqlda2, 0, sizeof(sqlda_t) + sizeof(sqlvar_t));

sqlda2->sqln = 2; /* number of input variables */
```

After memory allocation, store the parameter values into the `sqlvar[]` array. (This is same array used for retrieving column values when the SQLDA is receiving a result set.) In this example, the input parameters are `"postgres"`, having a string type, and `1`, having an integer type.

```
sqlda2->sqlvar[0].sqltype = ECPGt_char;
sqlda2->sqlvar[0].sqldata = "postgres";
sqlda2->sqlvar[0].sqllen  = 8;

int intval = 1;
sqlda2->sqlvar[1].sqltype = ECPGt_int;
sqlda2->sqlvar[1].sqldata = (char *) &intval;
sqlda2->sqlvar[1].sqllen  = sizeof(intval);
```

By opening a cursor and specifying the SQLDA that was set up beforehand, the input parameters are passed to the prepared statement.

```
EXEC SQL OPEN cur1 USING DESCRIPTOR sqlda2;
```

Finally, after using input SQLDAs, the allocated memory space must be freed explicitly, unlike SQLDAs used for receiving query results.

```
free(sqlda2);
```

34.7.2.4. A Sample Application Using SQLDA

Here is an example program, which describes how to fetch access statistics of the databases, specified by the input parameters, from the system catalogs.

This application joins two system tables, pg_database and pg_stat_database on the database OID, and also fetches and shows the database statistics which are retrieved by two input parameters (a database postgres, and OID 1).

First, declare an SQLDA for input and an SQLDA for output.

```
EXEC SQL include sqlda.h;

sqlda_t *sqlda1; /* an output descriptor */
sqlda_t *sqlda2; /* an input descriptor  */
```

Next, connect to the database, prepare a statement, and declare a cursor for the prepared statement.

```
int
main(void)
{
    EXEC SQL BEGIN DECLARE SECTION;
    char query[1024] = "SELECT d.oid,* FROM pg_database d, pg_stat_database s WHERE
```

```
EXEC SQL END DECLARE SECTION;

EXEC SQL CONNECT TO testdb AS con1 USER testuser;

EXEC SQL PREPARE stmt1 FROM :query;
EXEC SQL DECLARE cur1 CURSOR FOR stmt1;
```

Next, put some values in the input SQLDA for the input parameters. Allocate memory for the input SQLDA, and set the number of input parameters to `sqln`. Store type, value, and value length into `sqltype`, `sqldata`, and `sqllen` in the `sqlvar` structure.

```
/* Create SQLDA structure for input parameters. */
sqlda2 = (sqlda_t *) malloc(sizeof(sqlda_t) + sizeof(sqlvar_t));
memset(sqlda2, 0, sizeof(sqlda_t) + sizeof(sqlvar_t));
sqlda2->sqln = 2; /* number of input variables */

sqlda2->sqlvar[0].sqltype = ECPGt_char;
sqlda2->sqlvar[0].sqldata = "postgres";
sqlda2->sqlvar[0].sqllen  = 8;

intval = 1;
sqlda2->sqlvar[1].sqltype = ECPGt_int;
sqlda2->sqlvar[1].sqldata = (char *)&intval;
sqlda2->sqlvar[1].sqllen  = sizeof(intval);
```

After setting up the input SQLDA, open a cursor with the input SQLDA.

```
/* Open a cursor with input parameters. */
EXEC SQL OPEN cur1 USING DESCRIPTOR sqlda2;
```

Fetch rows into the output SQLDA from the opened cursor. (Generally, you have to call FETCH repeatedly in the loop, to fetch all rows in the result set.)

```
while (1)
{
    sqlda_t *cur_sqlda;

    /* Assign descriptor to the cursor */
    EXEC SQL FETCH NEXT FROM cur1 INTO DESCRIPTOR sqlda1;
```

Next, retrieve the fetched records from the SQLDA, by following the linked list of the `sqlda_t` structure.

```
for (cur_sqlda = sqlda1 ;
     cur_sqlda != NULL ;
     cur_sqlda = cur_sqlda->desc_next)
{
    ...
```

Read each columns in the first record. The number of columns is stored in `sqld`, the actual data of the first column is stored in `sqlvar[0]`, both members of the `sqlda_t` structure.

```
/* Print every column in a row. */
for (i = 0; i < sqlda1->sqld; i++)
{
    sqlvar_t v = sqlda1->sqlvar[i];
    char *sqldata = v.sqldata;
    short sqllen  = v.sqllen;

    strncpy(name_buf, v.sqlname.data, v.sqlname.length);
    name_buf[v.sqlname.length] = '\0';
```

Now, the column data is stored in the variable `v`. Copy every datum into host variables, looking at `v.sqltype` for the type of the column.

```
switch (v.sqltype) {
    int intval;
    double doubleval;
    unsigned long long int longlongval;

    case ECPGt_char:
        memset(&var_buf, 0, sizeof(var_buf));
        memcpy(&var_buf, sqldata, (sizeof(var_buf) <= sqllen ? sizeof(va
        break;

    case ECPGt_int: /* integer */
        memcpy(&intval, sqldata, sqllen);
        snprintf(var_buf, sizeof(var_buf), "%d", intval);
        break;

    ...

    default:
        ...
}

    printf("%s = %s (type: %d)\n", name_buf, var_buf, v.sqltype);
}
```

Close the cursor after processing all of records, and disconnect from the database.

```
EXEC SQL CLOSE cur1;
EXEC SQL COMMIT;

EXEC SQL DISCONNECT ALL;
```

The whole program is shown in Example 34-1.

Example 34-1. Example SQLDA Program

```
#include <stdlib.h>
#include <string.h>
#include <stdlib.h>
#include <stdio.h>
#include <unistd.h>

EXEC SQL include sqlda.h;

sqlda_t *sqlda1; /* descriptor for output */
sqlda_t *sqlda2; /* descriptor for input */

EXEC SQL WHENEVER NOT FOUND DO BREAK;
EXEC SQL WHENEVER SQLERROR STOP;

int
main(void)
{
    EXEC SQL BEGIN DECLARE SECTION;
    char query[1024] = "SELECT d.oid,* FROM pg_database d, pg_stat_database s WHERE

    int intval;
    unsigned long long int longlongval;
    EXEC SQL END DECLARE SECTION;

    EXEC SQL CONNECT TO uptimedb AS con1 USER uptime;

    EXEC SQL PREPARE stmt1 FROM :query;
    EXEC SQL DECLARE cur1 CURSOR FOR stmt1;

    /* Create a SQLDA structure for an input parameter */
    sqlda2 = (sqlda_t *)malloc(sizeof(sqlda_t) + sizeof(sqlvar_t));
    memset(sqlda2, 0, sizeof(sqlda_t) + sizeof(sqlvar_t));
    sqlda2->sqln = 2; /* a number of input variables */

    sqlda2->sqlvar[0].sqltype = ECPGt_char;
    sqlda2->sqlvar[0].sqldata = "postgres";
    sqlda2->sqlvar[0].sqllen  = 8;

    intval = 1;
    sqlda2->sqlvar[1].sqltype = ECPGt_int;
    sqlda2->sqlvar[1].sqldata = (char *) &intval;
    sqlda2->sqlvar[1].sqllen  = sizeof(intval);

    /* Open a cursor with input parameters. */
    EXEC SQL OPEN cur1 USING DESCRIPTOR sqlda2;

    while (1)
    {
        sqlda_t *cur_sqlda;
```

```
/* Assign descriptor to the cursor  */
EXEC SQL FETCH NEXT FROM cur1 INTO DESCRIPTOR sqlda1;

for (cur_sqlda = sqlda1 ;
     cur_sqlda != NULL ;
     cur_sqlda = cur_sqlda->desc_next)
{
    int i;
    char name_buf[1024];
    char var_buf[1024];

    /* Print every column in a row. */
    for (i=0 ; i<cur_sqlda->sqld ; i++)
    {
        sqlvar_t v = cur_sqlda->sqlvar[i];
        char *sqldata = v.sqldata;
        short sqllen  = v.sqllen;

        strncpy(name_buf, v.sqlname.data, v.sqlname.length);
        name_buf[v.sqlname.length] = '\0';

        switch (v.sqltype)
        {
            case ECPGt_char:
                memset(&var_buf, 0, sizeof(var_buf));
                memcpy(&var_buf, sqldata, (sizeof(var_buf)<=sqllen ? sizeof(
                break;

            case ECPGt_int: /* integer */
                memcpy(&intval, sqldata, sqllen);
                snprintf(var_buf, sizeof(var_buf), "%d", intval);
                break;

            case ECPGt_long_long: /* bigint */
                memcpy(&longlongval, sqldata, sqllen);
                snprintf(var_buf, sizeof(var_buf), "%lld", longlongval);
                break;

            default:
            {
                int i;
                memset(var_buf, 0, sizeof(var_buf));
                for (i = 0; i < sqllen; i++)
                {
                    char tmpbuf[16];
                    snprintf(tmpbuf, sizeof(tmpbuf), "%02x ", (unsigned char
                    strncat(var_buf, tmpbuf, sizeof(var_buf));
                }
            }
                break;
        }
```

```
                printf("%s = %s (type: %d)\n", name_buf, var_buf, v.sqltype);
            }

            printf("\n");
        }
    }

    EXEC SQL CLOSE cur1;
    EXEC SQL COMMIT;

    EXEC SQL DISCONNECT ALL;

    return 0;
}
```

The output of this example should look something like the following (some numbers will vary).

```
oid = 1 (type: 1)
datname = template1 (type: 1)
datdba = 10 (type: 1)
encoding = 0 (type: 5)
datistemplate = t (type: 1)
datallowconn = t (type: 1)
datconnlimit = -1 (type: 5)
datlastsysoid = 11510 (type: 1)
datfrozenxid = 379 (type: 1)
dattablespace = 1663 (type: 1)
datconfig =  (type: 1)
datacl = {=c/uptime,uptime=CTc/uptime} (type: 1)
datid = 1 (type: 1)
datname = template1 (type: 1)
numbackends = 0 (type: 5)
xact_commit = 113606 (type: 9)
xact_rollback = 0 (type: 9)
blks_read = 130 (type: 9)
blks_hit = 7341714 (type: 9)
tup_returned = 38262679 (type: 9)
tup_fetched = 1836281 (type: 9)
tup_inserted = 0 (type: 9)
tup_updated = 0 (type: 9)
tup_deleted = 0 (type: 9)

oid = 11511 (type: 1)
datname = postgres (type: 1)
datdba = 10 (type: 1)
encoding = 0 (type: 5)
datistemplate = f (type: 1)
datallowconn = t (type: 1)
datconnlimit = -1 (type: 5)
datlastsysoid = 11510 (type: 1)
datfrozenxid = 379 (type: 1)
dattablespace = 1663 (type: 1)
datconfig =  (type: 1)
datacl =  (type: 1)
```

```
datid = 11511 (type: 1)
datname = postgres (type: 1)
numbackends = 0 (type: 5)
xact_commit = 221069 (type: 9)
xact_rollback = 18 (type: 9)
blks_read = 1176 (type: 9)
blks_hit = 13943750 (type: 9)
tup_returned = 77410091 (type: 9)
tup_fetched = 3253694 (type: 9)
tup_inserted = 0 (type: 9)
tup_updated = 0 (type: 9)
tup_deleted = 0 (type: 9)
```

34.8. Error Handling

This section describes how you can handle exceptional conditions and warnings in an embedded SQL program. There are two nonexclusive facilities for this.

- Callbacks can be configured to handle warning and error conditions using the WHENEVER command.
- Detailed information about the error or warning can be obtained from the sqlca variable.

34.8.1. Setting Callbacks

One simple method to catch errors and warnings is to set a specific action to be executed whenever a particular condition occurs. In general:

```
EXEC SQL WHENEVER condition action;
```

condition can be one of the following:

SQLERROR

   The specified action is called whenever an error occurs during the execution of an SQL statement.

SQLWARNING

   The specified action is called whenever a warning occurs during the execution of an SQL statement.

NOT FOUND

   The specified action is called whenever an SQL statement retrieves or affects zero rows. (This condition is not an error, but you might be interested in handling it specially.)

action can be one of the following:

```
CONTINUE
```

This effectively means that the condition is ignored. This is the default.

```
GOTO label
GO TO label
```

Jump to the specified label (using a C `goto` statement).

```
SQLPRINT
```

Print a message to standard error. This is useful for simple programs or during prototyping. The details of the message cannot be configured.

```
STOP
```

Call `exit(1)`, which will terminate the program.

```
DO BREAK
```

Execute the C statement `break`. This should only be used in loops or `switch` statements.

```
CALL name (args)
DO name (args)
```

Call the specified C functions with the specified arguments.

The SQL standard only provides for the actions CONTINUE and GOTO (and GO TO).

Here is an example that you might want to use in a simple program. It prints a simple message when a warning occurs and aborts the program when an error happens:

```
EXEC SQL WHENEVER SQLWARNING SQLPRINT;
EXEC SQL WHENEVER SQLERROR STOP;
```

The statement EXEC SQL WHENEVER is a directive of the SQL preprocessor, not a C statement. The error or warning actions that it sets apply to all embedded SQL statements that appear below the point where the handler is set, unless a different action was set for the same condition between the first EXEC SQL WHENEVER and the SQL statement causing the condition, regardless of the flow of control in the C program. So neither of the two following C program excerpts will have the desired effect:

```
/*
 * WRONG
 */
int main(int argc, char *argv[])
{
    ...
    if (verbose) {
        EXEC SQL WHENEVER SQLWARNING SQLPRINT;
    }
    ...
    EXEC SQL SELECT ...;
    ...
}

/*
 * WRONG
```

```
 */
int main(int argc, char *argv[])
{
    ...
    set_error_handler();
    ...
    EXEC SQL SELECT ...;
    ...
}

static void set_error_handler(void)
{
    EXEC SQL WHENEVER SQLERROR STOP;
}
```

34.8.2. sqlca

For more powerful error handling, the embedded SQL interface provides a global variable with the name `sqlca` (SQL communication area) that has the following structure:

```
struct
{
    char sqlcaid[8];
    long sqlabc;
    long sqlcode;
    struct
    {
        int sqlerrml;
        char sqlerrmc[SQLERRMC_LEN];
    } sqlerrm;
    char sqlerrp[8];
    long sqlerrd[6];
    char sqlwarn[8];
    char sqlstate[5];
} sqlca;
```

(In a multithreaded program, every thread automatically gets its own copy of `sqlca`. This works similarly to the handling of the standard C global variable `errno`.)

`sqlca` covers both warnings and errors. If multiple warnings or errors occur during the execution of a statement, then `sqlca` will only contain information about the last one.

If no error occurred in the last SQL statement, `sqlca.sqlcode` will be 0 and `sqlca.sqlstate` will be `"00000"`. If a warning or error occurred, then `sqlca.sqlcode` will be negative and `sqlca.sqlstate` will be different from `"00000"`. A positive `sqlca.sqlcode` indicates a harmless condition, such as that the last query returned zero rows. `sqlcode` and `sqlstate` are two different error code schemes; details appear below.

If the last SQL statement was successful, then `sqlca.sqlerrd[1]` contains the OID of the processed row, if applicable, and `sqlca.sqlerrd[2]` contains the number of processed or returned rows, if applicable to the command.

In case of an error or warning, `sqlca.sqlerrm.sqlerrmc` will contain a string that describes the error. The field `sqlca.sqlerrm.sqlerrml` contains the length of the error message that is stored in `sqlca.sqlerrm.sqlerrmc` (the result of `strlen()`, not really interesting for a C programmer). Note that some messages are too long to fit in the fixed-size `sqlerrmc` array; they will be truncated.

In case of a warning, `sqlca.sqlwarn[2]` is set to `W`. (In all other cases, it is set to something different from `W`.) If `sqlca.sqlwarn[1]` is set to `W`, then a value was truncated when it was stored in a host variable. `sqlca.sqlwarn[0]` is set to `W` if any of the other elements are set to indicate a warning.

The fields `sqlcaid`, `sqlcabc`, `sqlerrp`, and the remaining elements of `sqlerrd` and `sqlwarn` currently contain no useful information.

The structure `sqlca` is not defined in the SQL standard, but is implemented in several other SQL database systems. The definitions are similar at the core, but if you want to write portable applications, then you should investigate the different implementations carefully.

Here is one example that combines the use of `WHENEVER` and `sqlca`, printing out the contents of `sqlca` when an error occurs. This is perhaps useful for debugging or prototyping applications, before installing a more "user-friendly" error handler.

```
EXEC SQL WHENEVER SQLERROR CALL print_sqlca();

void
print_sqlca()
{
    fprintf(stderr, "==== sqlca ====\n");
    fprintf(stderr, "sqlcode: %ld\n", sqlca.sqlcode);
    fprintf(stderr, "sqlerrm.sqlerrml: %d\n", sqlca.sqlerrm.sqlerrml);
    fprintf(stderr, "sqlerrm.sqlerrmc: %s\n", sqlca.sqlerrm.sqlerrmc);
    fprintf(stderr, "sqlerrd: %ld %ld %ld %ld %ld %ld\n", sqlca.sqlerrd[0],sqlca.sql
                                                           sqlca.sqlerrd[3],sqlca.sql
    fprintf(stderr, "sqlwarn: %d %d %d %d %d %d %d %d\n", sqlca.sqlwarn[0], sqlca.sq
                                                          sqlca.sqlwarn[3], sqlca.sq
                                                          sqlca.sqlwarn[6], sqlca.sq
    fprintf(stderr, "sqlstate: %5s\n", sqlca.sqlstate);
    fprintf(stderr, "==============\n");
}
```

The result could look as follows (here an error due to a misspelled table name):

```
==== sqlca ====
sqlcode: -400
sqlerrm.sqlerrml: 49
sqlerrm.sqlerrmc: relation "pg_databasep" does not exist on line 38
sqlerrd: 0 0 0 0 0 0
sqlwarn: 0 0 0 0 0 0 0 0
sqlstate: 42P01
==============
```

34.8.3. SQLSTATE VS. SQLCODE

The fields `sqlca.sqlstate` and `sqlca.sqlcode` are two different schemes that provide error codes. Both are derived from the SQL standard, but SQLCODE has been marked deprecated in the SQL-92 edition of the standard and has been dropped in later editions. Therefore, new applications are strongly encouraged to use SQLSTATE.

SQLSTATE is a five-character array. The five characters contain digits or upper-case letters that represent codes of various error and warning conditions. SQLSTATE has a hierarchical scheme: the first two characters indicate the general class of the condition, the last three characters indicate a subclass of the general condition. A successful state is indicated by the code 00000. The SQLSTATE codes are for the most part defined in the SQL standard. The PostgreSQL server natively supports SQLSTATE error codes; therefore a high degree of consistency can be achieved by using this error code scheme throughout all applications. For further information see Appendix A.

SQLCODE, the deprecated error code scheme, is a simple integer. A value of 0 indicates success, a positive value indicates success with additional information, a negative value indicates an error. The SQL standard only defines the positive value +100, which indicates that the last command returned or affected zero rows, and no specific negative values. Therefore, this scheme can only achieve poor portability and does not have a hierarchical code assignment. Historically, the embedded SQL processor for PostgreSQL has assigned some specific SQLCODE values for its use, which are listed below with their numeric value and their symbolic name. Remember that these are not portable to other SQL implementations. To simplify the porting of applications to the SQLSTATE scheme, the corresponding SQLSTATE is also listed. There is, however, no one-to-one or one-to-many mapping between the two schemes (indeed it is many-to-many), so you should consult the global SQLSTATE listing in Appendix A in each case.

These are the assigned SQLCODE values:

0 (ECPG_NO_ERROR)

> Indicates no error. (SQLSTATE 00000)

100 (ECPG_NOT_FOUND)

> This is a harmless condition indicating that the last command retrieved or processed zero rows, or that you are at the end of the cursor. (SQLSTATE 02000)
>
> When processing a cursor in a loop, you could use this code as a way to detect when to abort the loop, like this:

```
while (1)
{
    EXEC SQL FETCH ... ;
    if (sqlca.sqlcode == ECPG_NOT_FOUND)
        break;
}
```

> But WHENEVER NOT FOUND DO BREAK effectively does this internally, so there is usually no advantage in writing this out explicitly.

-12 (ECPG_OUT_OF_MEMORY)

> Indicates that your virtual memory is exhausted. The numeric value is defined as -ENOMEM. (SQLSTATE YE001)

-200 (`ECPG_UNSUPPORTED`)

Indicates the preprocessor has generated something that the library does not know about. Perhaps you are running incompatible versions of the preprocessor and the library. (SQLSTATE YE002)

-201 (`ECPG_TOO_MANY_ARGUMENTS`)

This means that the command specified more host variables than the command expected. (SQLSTATE 07001 or 07002)

-202 (`ECPG_TOO_FEW_ARGUMENTS`)

This means that the command specified fewer host variables than the command expected. (SQLSTATE 07001 or 07002)

-203 (`ECPG_TOO_MANY_MATCHES`)

This means a query has returned multiple rows but the statement was only prepared to store one result row (for example, because the specified variables are not arrays). (SQLSTATE 21000)

-204 (`ECPG_INT_FORMAT`)

The host variable is of type `int` and the datum in the database is of a different type and contains a value that cannot be interpreted as an `int`. The library uses `strtol()` for this conversion. (SQLSTATE 42804)

-205 (`ECPG_UINT_FORMAT`)

The host variable is of type `unsigned int` and the datum in the database is of a different type and contains a value that cannot be interpreted as an `unsigned int`. The library uses `strtoul()` for this conversion. (SQLSTATE 42804)

-206 (`ECPG_FLOAT_FORMAT`)

The host variable is of type `float` and the datum in the database is of another type and contains a value that cannot be interpreted as a `float`. The library uses `strtod()` for this conversion. (SQLSTATE 42804)

-207 (`ECPG_NUMERIC_FORMAT`)

The host variable is of type `numeric` and the datum in the database is of another type and contains a value that cannot be interpreted as a `numeric` value. (SQLSTATE 42804)

-208 (`ECPG_INTERVAL_FORMAT`)

The host variable is of type `interval` and the datum in the database is of another type and contains a value that cannot be interpreted as an `interval` value. (SQLSTATE 42804)

-209 (`ECPG_DATE_FORMAT`)

The host variable is of type `date` and the datum in the database is of another type and contains a value that cannot be interpreted as a `date` value. (SQLSTATE 42804)

-210 (`ECPG_TIMESTAMP_FORMAT`)

The host variable is of type `timestamp` and the datum in the database is of another type and contains a value that cannot be interpreted as a `timestamp` value. (SQLSTATE 42804)

-211 (`ECPG_CONVERT_BOOL`)

This means the host variable is of type `bool` and the datum in the database is neither 't' nor 'f'. (SQLSTATE 42804)

-212 (`ECPG_EMPTY`)

The statement sent to the PostgreSQL server was empty. (This cannot normally happen in an embedded SQL program, so it might point to an internal error.) (SQLSTATE YE002)

-213 (`ECPG_MISSING_INDICATOR`)

A null value was returned and no null indicator variable was supplied. (SQLSTATE 22002)

-214 (`ECPG_NO_ARRAY`)

An ordinary variable was used in a place that requires an array. (SQLSTATE 42804)

-215 (`ECPG_DATA_NOT_ARRAY`)

The database returned an ordinary variable in a place that requires array value. (SQLSTATE 42804)

-220 (`ECPG_NO_CONN`)

The program tried to access a connection that does not exist. (SQLSTATE 08003)

-221 (`ECPG_NOT_CONN`)

The program tried to access a connection that does exist but is not open. (This is an internal error.) (SQLSTATE YE002)

-230 (`ECPG_INVALID_STMT`)

The statement you are trying to use has not been prepared. (SQLSTATE 26000)

-239 (`ECPG_INFORMIX_DUPLICATE_KEY`)

Duplicate key error, violation of unique constraint (Informix compatibility mode). (SQLSTATE 23505)

-240 (`ECPG_UNKNOWN_DESCRIPTOR`)

The descriptor specified was not found. The statement you are trying to use has not been prepared. (SQLSTATE 33000)

-241 (`ECPG_INVALID_DESCRIPTOR_INDEX`)

The descriptor index specified was out of range. (SQLSTATE 07009)

-242 (`ECPG_UNKNOWN_DESCRIPTOR_ITEM`)

An invalid descriptor item was requested. (This is an internal error.) (SQLSTATE YE002)

-243 (`ECPG_VAR_NOT_NUMERIC`)

During the execution of a dynamic statement, the database returned a numeric value and the host variable was not numeric. (SQLSTATE 07006)

-244 (`ECPG_VAR_NOT_CHAR`)

During the execution of a dynamic statement, the database returned a non-numeric value and the host variable was numeric. (SQLSTATE 07006)

-284 (`ECPG_INFORMIX_SUBSELECT_NOT_ONE`)

A result of the subquery is not single row (Informix compatibility mode). (SQLSTATE 21000)

-400 (`ECPG_PGSQL`)

Some error caused by the PostgreSQL server. The message contains the error message from the PostgreSQL server.

-401 (`ECPG_TRANS`)

> The PostgreSQL server signaled that we cannot start, commit, or rollback the transaction. (SQL-STATE 08007)

-402 (`ECPG_CONNECT`)

> The connection attempt to the database did not succeed. (SQLSTATE 08001)

-403 (`ECPG_DUPLICATE_KEY`)

> Duplicate key error, violation of unique constraint. (SQLSTATE 23505)

-404 (`ECPG_SUBSELECT_NOT_ONE`)

> A result for the subquery is not single row. (SQLSTATE 21000)

-602 (`ECPG_WARNING_UNKNOWN_PORTAL`)

> An invalid cursor name was specified. (SQLSTATE 34000)

-603 (`ECPG_WARNING_IN_TRANSACTION`)

> Transaction is in progress. (SQLSTATE 25001)

-604 (`ECPG_WARNING_NO_TRANSACTION`)

> There is no active (in-progress) transaction. (SQLSTATE 25P01)

-605 (`ECPG_WARNING_PORTAL_EXISTS`)

> An existing cursor name was specified. (SQLSTATE 42P03)

34.9. Preprocessor Directives

Several preprocessor directives are available that modify how the `ecpg` preprocessor parses and processes a file.

34.9.1. Including Files

To include an external file into your embedded SQL program, use:

```
EXEC SQL INCLUDE filename;
EXEC SQL INCLUDE <filename>;
EXEC SQL INCLUDE "filename";
```

The embedded SQL preprocessor will look for a file named `filename.h`, preprocess it, and include it in the resulting C output. Thus, embedded SQL statements in the included file are handled correctly.

The `ecpg` preprocessor will search a file at several directories in following order:

- current directory
- /usr/local/include

- PostgreSQL include directory, defined at build time (e.g., `/usr/local/pgsql/include`)

- `/usr/include`

But when `EXEC SQL INCLUDE "filename"` is used, only the current directory is searched.

In each directory, the preprocessor will first look for the file name as given, and if not found will append `.h` to the file name and try again (unless the specified file name already has that suffix).

Note that `EXEC SQL INCLUDE` is *not* the same as:

```
#include <filename.h>
```

because this file would not be subject to SQL command preprocessing. Naturally, you can continue to use the C `#include` directive to include other header files.

> **Note:** The include file name is case-sensitive, even though the rest of the `EXEC SQL INCLUDE` command follows the normal SQL case-sensitivity rules.

34.9.2. The define and undef Directives

Similar to the directive `#define` that is known from C, embedded SQL has a similar concept:

```
EXEC SQL DEFINE name;
EXEC SQL DEFINE name value;
```

So you can define a name:

```
EXEC SQL DEFINE HAVE_FEATURE;
```

And you can also define constants:

```
EXEC SQL DEFINE MYNUMBER 12;
EXEC SQL DEFINE MYSTRING 'abc';
```

Use `undef` to remove a previous definition:

```
EXEC SQL UNDEF MYNUMBER;
```

Of course you can continue to use the C versions `#define` and `#undef` in your embedded SQL program. The difference is where your defined values get evaluated. If you use `EXEC SQL DEFINE` then the `ecpg` preprocessor evaluates the defines and substitutes the values. For example if you write:

```
EXEC SQL DEFINE MYNUMBER 12;
...
EXEC SQL UPDATE Tbl SET col = MYNUMBER;
```

then `ecpg` will already do the substitution and your C compiler will never see any name or identifier `MYNUMBER`. Note that you cannot use `#define` for a constant that you are going to use in an embedded SQL query because in this case the embedded SQL precompiler is not able to see this declaration.

34.9.3. ifdef, ifndef, else, elif, and endif Directives

You can use the following directives to compile code sections conditionally:

```
EXEC SQL ifdef name;
```

Checks a *name* and processes subsequent lines if *name* has been created with EXEC SQL define *name*.

```
EXEC SQL ifndef name;
```

Checks a *name* and processes subsequent lines if *name* has *not* been created with EXEC SQL define *name*.

```
EXEC SQL else;
```

Starts processing an alternative section to a section introduced by either EXEC SQL ifdef *name* or EXEC SQL ifndef *name*.

```
EXEC SQL elif name;
```

Checks *name* and starts an alternative section if *name* has been created with EXEC SQL define *name*.

```
EXEC SQL endif;
```

Ends an alternative section.

Example:

```
EXEC SQL ifndef TZVAR;
EXEC SQL SET TIMEZONE TO 'GMT';
EXEC SQL elif TZNAME;
EXEC SQL SET TIMEZONE TO TZNAME;
EXEC SQL else;
EXEC SQL SET TIMEZONE TO TZVAR;
EXEC SQL endif;
```

34.10. Processing Embedded SQL Programs

Now that you have an idea how to form embedded SQL C programs, you probably want to know how to compile them. Before compiling you run the file through the embedded SQL C preprocessor, which converts the SQL statements you used to special function calls. After compiling, you must link with a special library that contains the needed functions. These functions fetch information from the arguments, perform the SQL command using the libpq interface, and put the result in the arguments specified for output.

The preprocessor program is called ecpg and is included in a normal PostgreSQL installation. Embedded SQL programs are typically named with an extension .pgc. If you have a program file called prog1.pgc, you can preprocess it by simply calling:

```
ecpg prog1.pgc
```

This will create a file called `prog1.c`. If your input files do not follow the suggested naming pattern, you can specify the output file explicitly using the `-o` option.

The preprocessed file can be compiled normally, for example:

```
cc -c prog1.c
```

The generated C source files include header files from the PostgreSQL installation, so if you installed PostgreSQL in a location that is not searched by default, you have to add an option such as `-I/usr/local/pgsql/include` to the compilation command line.

To link an embedded SQL program, you need to include the `libecpg` library, like so:

```
cc -o myprog prog1.o prog2.o ... -lecpg
```

Again, you might have to add an option like `-L/usr/local/pgsql/lib` to that command line.

You can use `pg_config` or `pkg-config` with package name `libecpg` to get the paths for your installation.

If you manage the build process of a larger project using make, it might be convenient to include the following implicit rule to your makefiles:

```
ECPG = ecpg

%.c: %.pgc
        $(ECPG) $<
```

The complete syntax of the `ecpg` command is detailed in ecpg.

The ecpg library is thread-safe by default. However, you might need to use some threading command-line options to compile your client code.

34.11. Library Functions

The `libecpg` library primarily contains "hidden" functions that are used to implement the functionality expressed by the embedded SQL commands. But there are some functions that can usefully be called directly. Note that this makes your code unportable.

- `ECPGdebug(int on, FILE *stream)` turns on debug logging if called with the first argument non-zero. Debug logging is done on `stream`. The log contains all SQL statements with all the input variables inserted, and the results from the PostgreSQL server. This can be very useful when searching for errors in your SQL statements.

    Note: On Windows, if the ecpg libraries and an application are compiled with different flags, this function call will crash the application because the internal representation of the `FILE` pointers differ. Specifically, multithreaded/single-threaded, release/debug, and static/dynamic flags should be the same for the library and all applications using that library.

- `ECPGget_PGconn(const char *connection_name)` returns the library database connection handle identified by the given name. If `connection_name` is set to `NULL`, the current connection handle is returned. If no connection handle can be identified, the function returns `NULL`. The returned connection handle can be used to call any other functions from libpq, if necessary.

  > **Note:** It is a bad idea to manipulate database connection handles made from ecpg directly with libpq routines.

- `ECPGtransactionStatus(const char *connection_name)` returns the current transaction status of the given connection identified by `connection_name`. See Section 32.2 and libpq's `PQtransactionStatus()` for details about the returned status codes.

- `ECPGstatus(int lineno, const char* connection_name)` returns true if you are connected to a database and false if not. `connection_name` can be `NULL` if a single connection is being used.

34.12. Large Objects

Large objects are not directly supported by ECPG, but ECPG application can manipulate large objects through the libpq large object functions, obtaining the necessary `PGconn` object by calling the `ECPGget_PGconn()` function. (However, use of the `ECPGget_PGconn()` function and touching `PGconn` objects directly should be done very carefully and ideally not mixed with other ECPG database access calls.)

For more details about the `ECPGget_PGconn()`, see Section 34.11. For information about the large object function interface, see Chapter 33.

Large object functions have to be called in a transaction block, so when autocommit is off, `BEGIN` commands have to be issued explicitly.

Example 34-2 shows an example program that illustrates how to create, write, and read a large object in an ECPG application.

Example 34-2. ECPG Program Accessing Large Objects

```
#include <stdio.h>
#include <stdlib.h>
#include <libpq-fe.h>
#include <libpq/libpq-fs.h>

EXEC SQL WHENEVER SQLERROR STOP;

int
main(void)
{
```

```
PGconn      *conn;
Oid         loid;
int         fd;
char        buf[256];
int         buflen = 256;
char        buf2[256];
int         rc;

memset(buf, 1, buflen);

EXEC SQL CONNECT TO testdb AS con1;

conn = ECPGget_PGconn("con1");
printf("conn = %p\n", conn);

/* create */
loid = lo_create(conn, 0);
if (loid < 0)
    printf("lo_create() failed: %s", PQerrorMessage(conn));

printf("loid = %d\n", loid);

/* write test */
fd = lo_open(conn, loid, INV_READ|INV_WRITE);
if (fd < 0)
    printf("lo_open() failed: %s", PQerrorMessage(conn));

printf("fd = %d\n", fd);

rc = lo_write(conn, fd, buf, buflen);
if (rc < 0)
    printf("lo_write() failed\n");

rc = lo_close(conn, fd);
if (rc < 0)
    printf("lo_close() failed: %s", PQerrorMessage(conn));

/* read test */
fd = lo_open(conn, loid, INV_READ);
if (fd < 0)
    printf("lo_open() failed: %s", PQerrorMessage(conn));

printf("fd = %d\n", fd);

rc = lo_read(conn, fd, buf2, buflen);
if (rc < 0)
    printf("lo_read() failed\n");

rc = lo_close(conn, fd);
if (rc < 0)
    printf("lo_close() failed: %s", PQerrorMessage(conn));

/* check */
```

```
rc = memcmp(buf, buf2, buflen);
printf("memcmp() = %d\n", rc);

/* cleanup */
rc = lo_unlink(conn, loid);
if (rc < 0)
    printf("lo_unlink() failed: %s", PQerrorMessage(conn));

EXEC SQL COMMIT;
EXEC SQL DISCONNECT ALL;
return 0;
}
```

34.13. C++ Applications

ECPG has some limited support for C++ applications. This section describes some caveats.

The ecpg preprocessor takes an input file written in C (or something like C) and embedded SQL commands, converts the embedded SQL commands into C language chunks, and finally generates a .c file. The header file declarations of the library functions used by the C language chunks that ecpg generates are wrapped in extern "C" { ... } blocks when used under C++, so they should work seamlessly in C++.

In general, however, the ecpg preprocessor only understands C; it does not handle the special syntax and reserved words of the C++ language. So, some embedded SQL code written in C++ application code that uses complicated features specific to C++ might fail to be preprocessed correctly or might not work as expected.

A safe way to use the embedded SQL code in a C++ application is hiding the ECPG calls in a C module, which the C++ application code calls into to access the database, and linking that together with the rest of the C++ code. See Section 34.13.2 about that.

34.13.1. Scope for Host Variables

The ecpg preprocessor understands the scope of variables in C. In the C language, this is rather simple because the scopes of variables is based on their code blocks. In C++, however, the class member variables are referenced in a different code block from the declared position, so the ecpg preprocessor will not understand the scope of the class member variables.

For example, in the following case, the ecpg preprocessor cannot find any declaration for the variable dbname in the test method, so an error will occur.

```
class TestCpp
{
    EXEC SQL BEGIN DECLARE SECTION;
    char dbname[1024];
    EXEC SQL END DECLARE SECTION;

  public:
    TestCpp();
```

```
    void test();
    ~TestCpp();
};

TestCpp::TestCpp()
{
    EXEC SQL CONNECT TO testdb1;
}

void Test::test()
{
    EXEC SQL SELECT current_database() INTO :dbname;
    printf("current_database = %s\n", dbname);
}

TestCpp::~TestCpp()
{
    EXEC SQL DISCONNECT ALL;
}
```

This code will result in an error like this:

ecpg test_cpp.pgc
```
test_cpp.pgc:28: ERROR: variable "dbname" is not declared
```

To avoid this scope issue, the `test` method could be modified to use a local variable as intermediate storage. But this approach is only a poor workaround, because it uglifies the code and reduces performance.

```
void TestCpp::test()
{
    EXEC SQL BEGIN DECLARE SECTION;
    char tmp[1024];
    EXEC SQL END DECLARE SECTION;

    EXEC SQL SELECT current_database() INTO :tmp;
    strlcpy(dbname, tmp, sizeof(tmp));

    printf("current_database = %s\n", dbname);
}
```

34.13.2. C++ Application Development with External C Module

If you understand these technical limitations of the `ecpg` preprocessor in C++, you might come to the conclusion that linking C objects and C++ objects at the link stage to enable C++ applications to use ECPG features could be better than writing some embedded SQL commands in C++ code directly. This section describes a way to separate some embedded SQL commands from C++ application code with a simple example. In this example, the application is implemented in C++, while C and ECPG is used to connect to the PostgreSQL server.

Three kinds of files have to be created: a C file (`*.pgc`), a header file, and a C++ file:

`test_mod.pgc`

> A sub-routine module to execute SQL commands embedded in C. It is going to be converted into
> `test_mod.c` by the preprocessor.
>
> ```c
> #include "test_mod.h"
> #include <stdio.h>
>
> void
> db_connect()
> {
>     EXEC SQL CONNECT TO testdb1;
> }
>
> void
> db_test()
> {
>     EXEC SQL BEGIN DECLARE SECTION;
>     char dbname[1024];
>     EXEC SQL END DECLARE SECTION;
>
>     EXEC SQL SELECT current_database() INTO :dbname;
>     printf("current_database = %s\n", dbname);
> }
>
> void
> db_disconnect()
> {
>     EXEC SQL DISCONNECT ALL;
> }
> ```

`test_mod.h`

> A header file with declarations of the functions in the C module (`test_mod.pgc`). It is included by
> `test_cpp.cpp`. This file has to have an `extern "C"` block around the declarations, because it will
> be linked from the C++ module.
>
> ```c
> #ifdef __cplusplus
> extern "C" {
> #endif
>
> void db_connect();
> void db_test();
> void db_disconnect();
>
> #ifdef __cplusplus
> }
> #endif
> ```

`test_cpp.cpp`

The main code for the application, including the `main` routine, and in this example a C++ class.

```
#include "test_mod.h"

class TestCpp
{
  public:
    TestCpp();
    void test();
    ~TestCpp();
};

TestCpp::TestCpp()
{
    db_connect();
}

void
TestCpp::test()
{
    db_test();
}

TestCpp::~TestCpp()
{
    db_disconnect();
}

int
main(void)
{
    TestCpp *t = new TestCpp();

    t->test();
    return 0;
}
```

To build the application, proceed as follows. Convert `test_mod.pgc` into `test_mod.c` by running `ecpg`, and generate `test_mod.o` by compiling `test_mod.c` with the C compiler:

```
ecpg -o test_mod.c test_mod.pgc
cc -c test_mod.c -o test_mod.o
```

Next, generate `test_cpp.o` by compiling `test_cpp.cpp` with the C++ compiler:

```
c++ -c test_cpp.cpp -o test_cpp.o
```

Finally, link these object files, `test_cpp.o` and `test_mod.o`, into one executable, using the C++ compiler driver:

```
c++ test_cpp.o test_mod.o -lecpg -o test_cpp
```

34.14. Embedded SQL Commands

This section describes all SQL commands that are specific to embedded SQL. Also refer to the SQL commands listed in Reference I, *SQL Commands*, which can also be used in embedded SQL, unless stated otherwise.

ALLOCATE DESCRIPTOR

Name

ALLOCATE DESCRIPTOR — allocate an SQL descriptor area

Synopsis

```
ALLOCATE DESCRIPTOR name
```

Description

ALLOCATE DESCRIPTOR allocates a new named SQL descriptor area, which can be used to exchange data between the PostgreSQL server and the host program.

Descriptor areas should be freed after use using the DEALLOCATE DESCRIPTOR command.

Parameters

name

A name of SQL descriptor, case sensitive. This can be an SQL identifier or a host variable.

Examples

```
EXEC SQL ALLOCATE DESCRIPTOR mydesc;
```

Compatibility

`ALLOCATE DESCRIPTOR` is specified in the SQL standard.

See Also

DEALLOCATE DESCRIPTOR, GET DESCRIPTOR, SET DESCRIPTOR

CONNECT

Name

CONNECT — establish a database connection

Synopsis

```
CONNECT TO connection_target [ AS connection_name ] [ USER connection_user ]
CONNECT TO DEFAULT
CONNECT connection_user
DATABASE connection_target
```

Description

The CONNECT command establishes a connection between the client and the PostgreSQL server.

Parameters

connection_target

    connection_target specifies the target server of the connection on one of several forms.

    [database_name] [@host] [:port]

        Connect over TCP/IP

    unix:postgresql://host [:port] / [database_name] [?connection_option]

        Connect over Unix-domain sockets

    tcp:postgresql://host [:port] / [database_name] [?connection_option]

        Connect over TCP/IP

    SQL string constant

        containing a value in one of the above forms

    host variable

        host variable of type char[] or VARCHAR[] containing a value in one of the above forms

connection_object

    An optional identifier for the connection, so that it can be referred to in other commands. This can be an SQL identifier or a host variable.

connection_user

> The user name for the database connection.

> This parameter can also specify user name and password, using one the forms *user_name*/*password*, *user_name* IDENTIFIED BY *password*, or *user_name* USING *password*.

> User name and password can be SQL identifiers, string constants, or host variables.

DEFAULT

> Use all default connection parameters, as defined by libpq.

Examples

Here a several variants for specifying connection parameters:

```
EXEC SQL CONNECT TO "connectdb" AS main;
EXEC SQL CONNECT TO "connectdb" AS second;
EXEC SQL CONNECT TO "unix:postgresql://200.46.204.71/connectdb" AS main USER connect
EXEC SQL CONNECT TO "unix:postgresql://localhost/connectdb" AS main USER connectuser
EXEC SQL CONNECT TO 'connectdb' AS main;
EXEC SQL CONNECT TO 'unix:postgresql://localhost/connectdb' AS main USER :user;
EXEC SQL CONNECT TO :db AS :id;
EXEC SQL CONNECT TO :db USER connectuser USING :pw;
EXEC SQL CONNECT TO @localhost AS main USER connectdb;
EXEC SQL CONNECT TO REGRESSDB1 as main;
EXEC SQL CONNECT TO AS main USER connectdb;
EXEC SQL CONNECT TO connectdb AS :id;
EXEC SQL CONNECT TO connectdb AS main USER connectuser/connectdb;
EXEC SQL CONNECT TO connectdb AS main;
EXEC SQL CONNECT TO connectdb@localhost AS main;
EXEC SQL CONNECT TO tcp:postgresql://localhost/ USER connectdb;
EXEC SQL CONNECT TO tcp:postgresql://localhost/connectdb USER connectuser IDENTIFIED
EXEC SQL CONNECT TO tcp:postgresql://localhost:20/connectdb USER connectuser IDENTIF
EXEC SQL CONNECT TO unix:postgresql://localhost/ AS main USER connectdb;
EXEC SQL CONNECT TO unix:postgresql://localhost/connectdb AS main USER connectuser;
EXEC SQL CONNECT TO unix:postgresql://localhost/connectdb USER connectuser IDENTIFIE
EXEC SQL CONNECT TO unix:postgresql://localhost/connectdb USER connectuser USING "co
EXEC SQL CONNECT TO unix:postgresql://localhost/connectdb?connect_timeout=14 USER co
```

Here is an example program that illustrates the use of host variables to specify connection parameters:

```
int
main(void)
{
EXEC SQL BEGIN DECLARE SECTION;
    char *dbname     = "testdb";    /* database name */
    char *user       = "testuser";  /* connection user name */
    char *connection = "tcp:postgresql://localhost:5432/testdb";
                                    /* connection string */
    char ver[256];                  /* buffer to store the version string */
```

```
EXEC SQL END DECLARE SECTION;

    ECPGdebug(1, stderr);

    EXEC SQL CONNECT TO :dbname USER :user;
    EXEC SQL SELECT version() INTO :ver;
    EXEC SQL DISCONNECT;

    printf("version: %s\n", ver);

    EXEC SQL CONNECT TO :connection USER :user;
    EXEC SQL SELECT version() INTO :ver;
    EXEC SQL DISCONNECT;

    printf("version: %s\n", ver);

    return 0;
}
```

Compatibility

CONNECT is specified in the SQL standard, but the format of the connection parameters is implementation-specific.

See Also

DISCONNECT, SET CONNECTION

DEALLOCATE DESCRIPTOR

Name

DEALLOCATE DESCRIPTOR — deallocate an SQL descriptor area

Synopsis

```
DEALLOCATE DESCRIPTOR name
```

Description

DEALLOCATE DESCRIPTOR deallocates a named SQL descriptor area.

Parameters

name

> The name of the descriptor which is going to be deallocated. It is case sensitive. This can be an SQL identifier or a host variable.

Examples

```
EXEC SQL DEALLOCATE DESCRIPTOR mydesc;
```

Compatibility

DEALLOCATE DESCRIPTOR is specified in the SQL standard.

See Also

ALLOCATE DESCRIPTOR, GET DESCRIPTOR, SET DESCRIPTOR

DECLARE

Name

DECLARE — define a cursor

Synopsis

```
DECLARE cursor_name [ BINARY ] [ INSENSITIVE ] [ [ NO ] SCROLL ] CURSOR [ { WITH | WI'
DECLARE cursor_name [ BINARY ] [ INSENSITIVE ] [ [ NO ] SCROLL ] CURSOR [ { WITH | WI'
```

Description

DECLARE declares a cursor for iterating over the result set of a prepared statement. This command has slightly different semantics from the direct SQL command DECLARE: Whereas the latter executes a query and prepares the result set for retrieval, this embedded SQL command merely declares a name as a "loop variable" for iterating over the result set of a query; the actual execution happens when the cursor is opened with the OPEN command.

Parameters

cursor_name

A cursor name, case sensitive. This can be an SQL identifier or a host variable.

prepared_name

The name of a prepared query, either as an SQL identifier or a host variable.

query

A SELECT or VALUES command which will provide the rows to be returned by the cursor.

For the meaning of the cursor options, see DECLARE.

Examples

Examples declaring a cursor for a query:

```
EXEC SQL DECLARE C CURSOR FOR SELECT * FROM My_Table;
EXEC SQL DECLARE C CURSOR FOR SELECT Item1 FROM T;
EXEC SQL DECLARE cur1 CURSOR FOR SELECT version();
```

An example declaring a cursor for a prepared statement:

```
EXEC SQL PREPARE stmt1 AS SELECT version();
```

```
EXEC SQL DECLARE cur1 CURSOR FOR stmt1;
```

Compatibility

DECLARE is specified in the SQL standard.

See Also

OPEN, CLOSE, DECLARE

DESCRIBE

Name

DESCRIBE — obtain information about a prepared statement or result set

Synopsis

```
DESCRIBE [ OUTPUT ] prepared_name USING [ SQL ] DESCRIPTOR descriptor_name
DESCRIBE [ OUTPUT ] prepared_name INTO [ SQL ] DESCRIPTOR descriptor_name
DESCRIBE [ OUTPUT ] prepared_name INTO sqlda_name
```

Description

DESCRIBE retrieves metadata information about the result columns contained in a prepared statement, without actually fetching a row.

Parameters

prepared_name

The name of a prepared statement. This can be an SQL identifier or a host variable.

descriptor_name

A descriptor name. It is case sensitive. It can be an SQL identifier or a host variable.

sqlda_name

The name of an SQLDA variable.

Examples

```
EXEC SQL ALLOCATE DESCRIPTOR mydesc;
EXEC SQL PREPARE stmt1 FROM :sql_stmt;
EXEC SQL DESCRIBE stmt1 INTO SQL DESCRIPTOR mydesc;
EXEC SQL GET DESCRIPTOR mydesc VALUE 1 :charvar = NAME;
EXEC SQL DEALLOCATE DESCRIPTOR mydesc;
```

Compatibility

DESCRIBE is specified in the SQL standard.

See Also

ALLOCATE DESCRIPTOR, GET DESCRIPTOR

DISCONNECT

Name

DISCONNECT — terminate a database connection

Synopsis

```
DISCONNECT connection_name
DISCONNECT [ CURRENT ]
DISCONNECT DEFAULT
DISCONNECT ALL
```

Description

DISCONNECT closes a connection (or all connections) to the database.

Parameters

connection_name

A database connection name established by the CONNECT command.

CURRENT

Close the "current" connection, which is either the most recently opened connection, or the connection set by the SET CONNECTION command. This is also the default if no argument is given to the DISCONNECT command.

DEFAULT

Close the default connection.

ALL

Close all open connections.

Examples

```
int
main(void)
{
    EXEC SQL CONNECT TO testdb AS DEFAULT USER testuser;
    EXEC SQL CONNECT TO testdb AS con1 USER testuser;
    EXEC SQL CONNECT TO testdb AS con2 USER testuser;
    EXEC SQL CONNECT TO testdb AS con3 USER testuser;

    EXEC SQL DISCONNECT CURRENT;  /* close con3         */
```

```
EXEC SQL DISCONNECT DEFAULT;    /* close DEFAULT       */
EXEC SQL DISCONNECT ALL;        /* close con2 and con1 */

return 0;
}
```

Compatibility

DISCONNECT is specified in the SQL standard.

See Also

CONNECT, SET CONNECTION

EXECUTE IMMEDIATE

Name

EXECUTE IMMEDIATE — dynamically prepare and execute a statement

Synopsis

```
EXECUTE IMMEDIATE string
```

Description

EXECUTE IMMEDIATE immediately prepares and executes a dynamically specified SQL statement, without retrieving result rows.

Parameters

string

A literal C string or a host variable containing the SQL statement to be executed.

Examples

Here is an example that executes an INSERT statement using EXECUTE IMMEDIATE and a host variable named command:

```
sprintf(command, "INSERT INTO test (name, amount, letter) VALUES ('db: "r1"', 1, 'f'
EXEC SQL EXECUTE IMMEDIATE :command;
```

Compatibility

EXECUTE IMMEDIATE is specified in the SQL standard.

GET DESCRIPTOR

Name

GET DESCRIPTOR — get information from an SQL descriptor area

Synopsis

```
GET DESCRIPTOR descriptor_name :cvariable = descriptor_header_item [, ... ]
GET DESCRIPTOR descriptor_name VALUE column_number :cvariable = descriptor_item [, ... ]
```

Description

GET DESCRIPTOR retrieves information about a query result set from an SQL descriptor area and stores it into host variables. A descriptor area is typically populated using FETCH or SELECT before using this command to transfer the information into host language variables.

This command has two forms: The first form retrieves descriptor "header" items, which apply to the result set in its entirety. One example is the row count. The second form, which requires the column number as additional parameter, retrieves information about a particular column. Examples are the column name and the actual column value.

Parameters

descriptor_name

> A descriptor name.

descriptor_header_item

> A token identifying which header information item to retrieve. Only COUNT, to get the number of columns in the result set, is currently supported.

column_number

> The number of the column about which information is to be retrieved. The count starts at 1.

descriptor_item

> A token identifying which item of information about a column to retrieve. See Section 34.7.1 for a list of supported items.

cvariable

> A host variable that will receive the data retrieved from the descriptor area.

Examples

An example to retrieve the number of columns in a result set:

```
EXEC SQL GET DESCRIPTOR d :d_count = COUNT;
```

An example to retrieve a data length in the first column:

```
EXEC SQL GET DESCRIPTOR d VALUE 1 :d_returned_octet_length = RETURNED_OCTET_LENGTH;
```

An example to retrieve the data body of the second column as a string:

```
EXEC SQL GET DESCRIPTOR d VALUE 2 :d_data = DATA;
```

Here is an example for a whole procedure of executing `SELECT current_database();` and showing the number of columns, the column data length, and the column data:

```
int
main(void)
{
EXEC SQL BEGIN DECLARE SECTION;
    int   d_count;
    char d_data[1024];
    int   d_returned_octet_length;
EXEC SQL END DECLARE SECTION;

    EXEC SQL CONNECT TO testdb AS con1 USER testuser;
    EXEC SQL ALLOCATE DESCRIPTOR d;

    /* Declare, open a cursor, and assign a descriptor to the cursor  */
    EXEC SQL DECLARE cur CURSOR FOR SELECT current_database();
    EXEC SQL OPEN cur;
    EXEC SQL FETCH NEXT FROM cur INTO SQL DESCRIPTOR d;

    /* Get a number of total columns */
    EXEC SQL GET DESCRIPTOR d :d_count = COUNT;
    printf("d_count              = %d\n", d_count);

    /* Get length of a returned column */
    EXEC SQL GET DESCRIPTOR d VALUE 1 :d_returned_octet_length = RETURNED_OCTET_LENG'
    printf("d_returned_octet_length = %d\n", d_returned_octet_length);

    /* Fetch the returned column as a string */
    EXEC SQL GET DESCRIPTOR d VALUE 1 :d_data = DATA;
    printf("d_data               = %s\n", d_data);

    /* Closing */
    EXEC SQL CLOSE cur;
    EXEC SQL COMMIT;
```

```
    EXEC SQL DEALLOCATE DESCRIPTOR d;
    EXEC SQL DISCONNECT ALL;

    return 0;
}
```

When the example is executed, the result will look like this:

```
d_count               = 1
d_returned_octet_length = 6
d_data                = testdb
```

Compatibility

GET DESCRIPTOR is specified in the SQL standard.

See Also

ALLOCATE DESCRIPTOR, SET DESCRIPTOR

OPEN

Name

OPEN — open a dynamic cursor

Synopsis

```
OPEN cursor_name
OPEN cursor_name USING value [, ... ]
OPEN cursor_name USING SQL DESCRIPTOR descriptor_name
```

Description

OPEN opens a cursor and optionally binds actual values to the placeholders in the cursor's declaration. The cursor must previously have been declared with the DECLARE command. The execution of OPEN causes the query to start executing on the server.

Parameters

cursor_name

> The name of the cursor to be opened. This can be an SQL identifier or a host variable.

value

> A value to be bound to a placeholder in the cursor. This can be an SQL constant, a host variable, or a host variable with indicator.

descriptor_name

> The name of a descriptor containing values to be bound to the placeholders in the cursor. This can be an SQL identifier or a host variable.

Examples

```
EXEC SQL OPEN a;
EXEC SQL OPEN d USING 1, 'test';
EXEC SQL OPEN c1 USING SQL DESCRIPTOR mydesc;
EXEC SQL OPEN :curname1;
```

Compatibility

OPEN is specified in the SQL standard.

See Also

DECLARE, CLOSE

PREPARE

Name

PREPARE — prepare a statement for execution

Synopsis

```
PREPARE name FROM string
```

Description

PREPARE prepares a statement dynamically specified as a string for execution. This is different from the direct SQL statement PREPARE, which can also be used in embedded programs. The EXECUTE command is used to execute either kind of prepared statement.

Parameters

prepared_name

An identifier for the prepared query.

string

A literal C string or a host variable containing a preparable statement, one of the SELECT, INSERT, UPDATE, or DELETE.

Examples

```
char *stmt = "SELECT * FROM test1 WHERE a = ? AND b = ?";

EXEC SQL ALLOCATE DESCRIPTOR outdesc;
EXEC SQL PREPARE foo FROM :stmt;

EXEC SQL EXECUTE foo USING SQL DESCRIPTOR indesc INTO SQL DESCRIPTOR outdesc;
```

Compatibility

PREPARE is specified in the SQL standard.

See Also

EXECUTE

SET AUTOCOMMIT

Name

`SET AUTOCOMMIT` — set the autocommit behavior of the current session

Synopsis

```
SET AUTOCOMMIT { = | TO } { ON | OFF }
```

Description

`SET AUTOCOMMIT` sets the autocommit behavior of the current database session. By default, embedded SQL programs are *not* in autocommit mode, so `COMMIT` needs to be issued explicitly when desired. This command can change the session to autocommit mode, where each individual statement is committed implicitly.

Compatibility

`SET AUTOCOMMIT` is an extension of PostgreSQL ECPG.

SET CONNECTION

Name

SET CONNECTION — select a database connection

Synopsis

```
SET CONNECTION [ TO | = ] connection_name
```

Description

SET CONNECTION sets the "current" database connection, which is the one that all commands use unless overridden.

Parameters

connection_name

A database connection name established by the CONNECT command.

DEFAULT

Set the connection to the default connection.

Examples

```
EXEC SQL SET CONNECTION TO con2;
EXEC SQL SET CONNECTION = con1;
```

Compatibility

SET CONNECTION is specified in the SQL standard.

See Also

CONNECT, DISCONNECT

SET DESCRIPTOR

Name

SET DESCRIPTOR — set information in an SQL descriptor area

Synopsis

```
SET DESCRIPTOR descriptor_name descriptor_header_item = value [, ... ]
SET DESCRIPTOR descriptor_name VALUE number descriptor_item = value [, ...]
```

Description

SET DESCRIPTOR populates an SQL descriptor area with values. The descriptor area is then typically used to bind parameters in a prepared query execution.

This command has two forms: The first form applies to the descriptor "header", which is independent of a particular datum. The second form assigns values to particular datums, identified by number.

Parameters

descriptor_name

A descriptor name.

descriptor_header_item

A token identifying which header information item to set. Only COUNT, to set the number of descriptor items, is currently supported.

number

The number of the descriptor item to set. The count starts at 1.

descriptor_item

A token identifying which item of information to set in the descriptor. See Section 34.7.1 for a list of supported items.

value

A value to store into the descriptor item. This can be an SQL constant or a host variable.

Examples

```
EXEC SQL SET DESCRIPTOR indesc COUNT = 1;
EXEC SQL SET DESCRIPTOR indesc VALUE 1 DATA = 2;
EXEC SQL SET DESCRIPTOR indesc VALUE 1 DATA = :val1;
EXEC SQL SET DESCRIPTOR indesc VALUE 2 INDICATOR = :val1, DATA = 'some string';
```

```
EXEC SQL SET DESCRIPTOR indesc VALUE 2 INDICATOR = :val2null, DATA = :val2;
```

Compatibility

SET DESCRIPTOR is specified in the SQL standard.

See Also

ALLOCATE DESCRIPTOR, GET DESCRIPTOR

TYPE

Name

TYPE — define a new data type

Synopsis

```
TYPE type_name IS ctype
```

Description

The TYPE command defines a new C type. It is equivalent to putting a typedef into a declare section.

This command is only recognized when ecpg is run with the -c option.

Parameters

type_name

The name for the new type. It must be a valid C type name.

ctype

A C type specification.

Examples

```
EXEC SQL TYPE customer IS
    struct
    {
        varchar name[50];
        int     phone;
    };

EXEC SQL TYPE cust_ind IS
    struct ind
    {
        short   name_ind;
        short   phone_ind;
    };

EXEC SQL TYPE c IS char reference;
EXEC SQL TYPE ind IS union { int integer; short smallint; };
EXEC SQL TYPE intarray IS int[AMOUNT];
EXEC SQL TYPE str IS varchar[BUFFERSIZ];
EXEC SQL TYPE string IS char[11];
```

Here is an example program that uses EXEC SQL TYPE:

```
EXEC SQL WHENEVER SQLERROR SQLPRINT;

EXEC SQL TYPE tt IS
    struct
    {
        varchar v[256];
        int     i;
    };

EXEC SQL TYPE tt_ind IS
    struct ind {
        short   v_ind;
        short   i_ind;
    };

int
main(void)
{
EXEC SQL BEGIN DECLARE SECTION;
    tt t;
    tt_ind t_ind;
EXEC SQL END DECLARE SECTION;

    EXEC SQL CONNECT TO testdb AS con1;

    EXEC SQL SELECT current_database(), 256 INTO :t:t_ind LIMIT 1;

    printf("t.v = %s\n", t.v.arr);
    printf("t.i = %d\n", t.i);

    printf("t_ind.v_ind = %d\n", t_ind.v_ind);
    printf("t_ind.i_ind = %d\n", t_ind.i_ind);

    EXEC SQL DISCONNECT con1;

    return 0;
}
```

The output from this program looks like this:

```
t.v = testdb
t.i = 256
t_ind.v_ind = 0
t_ind.i_ind = 0
```

Compatibility

The TYPE command is a PostgreSQL extension.

VAR

Name

VAR — define a variable

Synopsis

```
VAR varname IS ctype
```

Description

The VAR command assigns a new C data type to a host variable. The host variable must be previously declared in a declare section.

Parameters

varname

A C variable name.

ctype

A C type specification.

Examples

```
Exec sql begin declare section;
short a;
exec sql end declare section;
EXEC SQL VAR a IS int;
```

Compatibility

The VAR command is a PostgreSQL extension.

WHENEVER

Name

WHENEVER — specify the action to be taken when an SQL statement causes a specific class condition to be raised

Synopsis

```
WHENEVER { NOT FOUND | SQLERROR | SQLWARNING } action
```

Description

Define a behavior which is called on the special cases (Rows not found, SQL warnings or errors) in the result of SQL execution.

Parameters

See Section 34.8.1 for a description of the parameters.

Examples

```
EXEC SQL WHENEVER NOT FOUND CONTINUE;
EXEC SQL WHENEVER NOT FOUND DO BREAK;
EXEC SQL WHENEVER SQLWARNING SQLPRINT;
EXEC SQL WHENEVER SQLWARNING DO warn();
EXEC SQL WHENEVER SQLERROR sqlprint;
EXEC SQL WHENEVER SQLERROR CALL print2();
EXEC SQL WHENEVER SQLERROR DO handle_error("select");
EXEC SQL WHENEVER SQLERROR DO sqlnotice(NULL, NONO);
EXEC SQL WHENEVER SQLERROR DO sqlprint();
EXEC SQL WHENEVER SQLERROR GOTO error_label;
EXEC SQL WHENEVER SQLERROR STOP;
```

A typical application is the use of WHENEVER NOT FOUND BREAK to handle looping through result sets:

```
int
main(void)
{
    EXEC SQL CONNECT TO testdb AS con1;
    EXEC SQL ALLOCATE DESCRIPTOR d;
    EXEC SQL DECLARE cur CURSOR FOR SELECT current_database(), 'hoge', 256;
    EXEC SQL OPEN cur;

    /* when end of result set reached, break out of while loop */
```

```
EXEC SQL WHENEVER NOT FOUND DO BREAK;

while (1)
{
    EXEC SQL FETCH NEXT FROM cur INTO SQL DESCRIPTOR d;
    ...
}

EXEC SQL CLOSE cur;
EXEC SQL COMMIT;

EXEC SQL DEALLOCATE DESCRIPTOR d;
EXEC SQL DISCONNECT ALL;

return 0;
}
```

Compatibility

WHENEVER is specified in the SQL standard, but most of the actions are PostgreSQL extensions.

34.15. Informix Compatibility Mode

`ecpg` can be run in a so-called *Informix compatibility mode*. If this mode is active, it tries to behave as if it were the Informix precompiler for Informix E/SQL. Generally spoken this will allow you to use the dollar sign instead of the `EXEC SQL` primitive to introduce embedded SQL commands:

```
$int j = 3;
$CONNECT TO :dbname;
$CREATE TABLE test(i INT PRIMARY KEY, j INT);
$INSERT INTO test(i, j) VALUES (7, :j);
$COMMIT;
```

> **Note:** There must not be any white space between the `$` and a following preprocessor directive, that is, `include`, `define`, `ifdef`, etc. Otherwise, the preprocessor will parse the token as a host variable.

There are two compatibility modes: `INFORMIX`, `INFORMIX_SE`

When linking programs that use this compatibility mode, remember to link against `libcompat` that is shipped with ECPG.

Besides the previously explained syntactic sugar, the Informix compatibility mode ports some functions for input, output and transformation of data as well as embedded SQL statements known from E/SQL to ECPG.

Informix compatibility mode is closely connected to the pgtypeslib library of ECPG. pgtypeslib maps SQL data types to data types within the C host program and most of the additional functions of the Informix compatibility mode allow you to operate on those C host program types. Note however that the extent of the compatibility is limited. It does not try to copy Informix behavior; it allows you to do more or less the same operations and gives you functions that have the same name and the same basic behavior but it is no drop-in replacement if you are using Informix at the moment. Moreover, some of the data types are different. For example, PostgreSQL's datetime and interval types do not know about ranges like for example `YEAR TO MINUTE` so you won't find support in ECPG for that either.

34.15.1. Additional Types

The Informix-special "string" pseudo-type for storing right-trimmed character string data is now supported in Informix-mode without using `typedef`. In fact, in Informix-mode, ECPG refuses to process source files that contain `typedef sometype string;`

```
EXEC SQL BEGIN DECLARE SECTION;
string userid; /* this variable will contain trimmed data */
EXEC SQL END DECLARE SECTION;

EXEC SQL FETCH MYCUR INTO :userid;
```

34.15.2. Additional/Missing Embedded SQL Statements

CLOSE DATABASE

This statement closes the current connection. In fact, this is a synonym for ECPG's DISCONNECT CURRENT:

```
$CLOSE DATABASE;                    /* close the current connection */
EXEC SQL CLOSE DATABASE;
```

FREE cursor_name

Due to the differences how ECPG works compared to Informix's ESQL/C (i.e. which steps are purely grammar transformations and which steps rely on the underlying run-time library) there is no FREE cursor_name statement in ECPG. This is because in ECPG, DECLARE CURSOR doesn't translate to a function call into the run-time library that uses to the cursor name. This means that there's no run-time bookkeeping of SQL cursors in the ECPG run-time library, only in the PostgreSQL server.

FREE statement_name

FREE statement_name is a synonym for DEALLOCATE PREPARE statement_name.

34.15.3. Informix-compatible SQLDA Descriptor Areas

Informix-compatible mode supports a different structure than the one described in Section 34.7.2. See below:

```
struct sqlvar_compat
{
    short    sqltype;
    int      sqllen;
    char     *sqldata;
    short    *sqlind;
    char     *sqlname;
    char     *sqlformat;
    short    sqlitype;
    short    sqlilen;
    char     *sqlidata;
    int      sqlxid;
    char     *sqltypename;
    short    sqltypelen;
    short    sqlownerlen;
    short    sqlsourcetype;
    char     *sqlownername;
    int      sqlsourceid;
    char     *sqlilongdata;
    int      sqlflags;
    void     *sqlreserved;
};

struct sqlda_compat
```

```
{
    short   sqld;
    struct sqlvar_compat *sqlvar;
    char    desc_name[19];
    short   desc_occ;
    struct sqlda_compat *desc_next;
    void    *reserved;
};

typedef struct sqlvar_compat      sqlvar_t;
typedef struct sqlda_compat       sqlda_t;
```

The global properties are:

sqld

> The number of fields in the SQLDA descriptor.

sqlvar

> Pointer to the per-field properties.

desc_name

> Unused, filled with zero-bytes.

desc_occ

> Size of the allocated structure.

desc_next

> Pointer to the next SQLDA structure if the result set contains more than one record.

reserved

> Unused pointer, contains NULL. Kept for Informix-compatibility.

The per-field properties are below, they are stored in the sqlvar array:

sqltype

> Type of the field. Constants are in sqltypes.h

sqllen

> Length of the field data.

sqldata

> Pointer to the field data. The pointer is of char * type, the data pointed by it is in a binary format.
> Example:

```
int intval;

switch (sqldata->sqlvar[i].sqltype)
{
    case SQLINTEGER:
        intval = *(int *)sqldata->sqlvar[i].sqldata;
        break;
```

```
    ...
}
```

sqlind

> Pointer to the NULL indicator. If returned by DESCRIBE or FETCH then it's always a valid pointer. If used as input for EXECUTE ... USING sqlda; then NULL-pointer value means that the value for this field is non-NULL. Otherwise a valid pointer and sqlitype has to be properly set. Example:

```
if (*(int2 *)sqldata->sqlvar[i].sqlind != 0)
    printf("value is NULL\n");
```

sqlname

> Name of the field. 0-terminated string.

sqlformat

> Reserved in Informix, value of PQfformat() for the field.

sqlitype

> Type of the NULL indicator data. It's always SQLSMINT when returning data from the server. When the SQLDA is used for a parameterized query, the data is treated according to the set type.

sqlilen

> Length of the NULL indicator data.

sqlxid

> Extended type of the field, result of PQftype().

sqltypename
sqltypelen
sqlownerlen
sqlsourcetype
sqlownername
sqlsourceid
sqlflags
sqlreserved

> Unused.

sqlilongdata

> It equals to sqldata if sqllen is larger than 32kB.

Example:

```
EXEC SQL INCLUDE sqlda.h;

    sqlda_t        *sqlda; /* This doesn't need to be under embedded DECLARE SECTION

    EXEC SQL BEGIN DECLARE SECTION;
    char *prep_stmt = "select * from table1";
    int i;
    EXEC SQL END DECLARE SECTION;

    ...
```

```
EXEC SQL PREPARE mystmt FROM :prep_stmt;

EXEC SQL DESCRIBE mystmt INTO sqlda;

printf("# of fields: %d\n", sqlda->sqld);
for (i = 0; i < sqlda->sqld; i++)
  printf("field %d: \"%s\"\n", sqlda->sqlvar[i]->sqlname);

EXEC SQL DECLARE mycursor CURSOR FOR mystmt;
EXEC SQL OPEN mycursor;
EXEC SQL WHENEVER NOT FOUND GOTO out;

while (1)
{
  EXEC SQL FETCH mycursor USING sqlda;
}

EXEC SQL CLOSE mycursor;

free(sqlda); /* The main structure is all to be free(),
             * sqlda and sqlda->sqlvar is in one allocated area */
```

For more information, see the `sqlda.h` header and the `src/interfaces/ecpg/test/compat_informix/sql` regression test.

34.15.4. Additional Functions

decadd

Add two decimal type values.

`int decadd(decimal *arg1, decimal *arg2, decimal *sum);`
The function receives a pointer to the first operand of type decimal (`arg1`), a pointer to the second operand of type decimal (`arg2`) and a pointer to a value of type decimal that will contain the sum (`sum`). On success, the function returns 0. `ECPG_INFORMIX_NUM_OVERFLOW` is returned in case of overflow and `ECPG_INFORMIX_NUM_UNDERFLOW` in case of underflow. -1 is returned for other failures and `errno` is set to the respective `errno` number of the pgtypeslib.

deccmp

Compare two variables of type decimal.

`int deccmp(decimal *arg1, decimal *arg2);`
The function receives a pointer to the first decimal value (`arg1`), a pointer to the second decimal value (`arg2`) and returns an integer value that indicates which is the bigger value.

- 1, if the value that `arg1` points to is bigger than the value that `var2` points to

- -1, if the value that `arg1` points to is smaller than the value that `arg2` points to

- 0, if the value that `arg1` points to and the value that `arg2` points to are equal deccopy

> Copy a decimal value.
>
> `void deccopy(decimal *src, decimal *target);`
> The function receives a pointer to the decimal value that should be copied as the first argument (`src`) and a pointer to the target structure of type decimal (`target`) as the second argument.

deccvasc

> Convert a value from its ASCII representation into a decimal type.
>
> `int deccvasc(char *cp, int len, decimal *np);`
> The function receives a pointer to string that contains the string representation of the number to be converted (`cp`) as well as its length `len`. `np` is a pointer to the decimal value that saves the result of the operation.
>
> Valid formats are for example: `-2`, `.794`, `+3.44`, `592.49E07` or `-32.84e-4`.
>
> The function returns 0 on success. If overflow or underflow occurred, `ECPG_INFORMIX_NUM_OVERFLOW` or `ECPG_INFORMIX_NUM_UNDERFLOW` is returned. If the ASCII representation could not be parsed, `ECPG_INFORMIX_BAD_NUMERIC` is returned or `ECPG_INFORMIX_BAD_EXPONENT` if this problem occurred while parsing the exponent.

deccvdbl

> Convert a value of type double to a value of type decimal.
>
> `int deccvdbl(double dbl, decimal *np);`
> The function receives the variable of type double that should be converted as its first argument (`dbl`). As the second argument (`np`), the function receives a pointer to the decimal variable that should hold the result of the operation.
>
> The function returns 0 on success and a negative value if the conversion failed.

deccvint

> Convert a value of type int to a value of type decimal.
>
> `int deccvint(int in, decimal *np);`
> The function receives the variable of type int that should be converted as its first argument (`in`). As the second argument (`np`), the function receives a pointer to the decimal variable that should hold the result of the operation.
>
> The function returns 0 on success and a negative value if the conversion failed.

deccvlong

> Convert a value of type long to a value of type decimal.
>
> `int deccvlong(long lng, decimal *np);`
> The function receives the variable of type long that should be converted as its first argument (`lng`). As the second argument (`np`), the function receives a pointer to the decimal variable that should hold the result of the operation.
>
> The function returns 0 on success and a negative value if the conversion failed.

decdiv

> Divide two variables of type decimal.
>
> `int decdiv(decimal *n1, decimal *n2, decimal *result);`

The function receives pointers to the variables that are the first (n1) and the second (n2) operands and calculates n1/n2. result is a pointer to the variable that should hold the result of the operation.

On success, 0 is returned and a negative value if the division fails. If overflow or underflow occurred, the function returns `ECPG_INFORMIX_NUM_OVERFLOW` or `ECPG_INFORMIX_NUM_UNDERFLOW` respectively. If an attempt to divide by zero is observed, the function returns `ECPG_INFORMIX_DIVIDE_ZERO`.

`decmul`

Multiply two decimal values.

`int decmul(decimal *n1, decimal *n2, decimal *result);`

The function receives pointers to the variables that are the first (n1) and the second (n2) operands and calculates n1*n2. result is a pointer to the variable that should hold the result of the operation.

On success, 0 is returned and a negative value if the multiplication fails. If overflow or underflow occurred, the function returns `ECPG_INFORMIX_NUM_OVERFLOW` or `ECPG_INFORMIX_NUM_UNDERFLOW` respectively.

`decsub`

Subtract one decimal value from another.

`int decsub(decimal *n1, decimal *n2, decimal *result);`

The function receives pointers to the variables that are the first (n1) and the second (n2) operands and calculates n1-n2. result is a pointer to the variable that should hold the result of the operation.

On success, 0 is returned and a negative value if the subtraction fails. If overflow or underflow occurred, the function returns `ECPG_INFORMIX_NUM_OVERFLOW` or `ECPG_INFORMIX_NUM_UNDERFLOW` respectively.

`dectoasc`

Convert a variable of type decimal to its ASCII representation in a C char* string.

`int dectoasc(decimal *np, char *cp, int len, int right)`

The function receives a pointer to a variable of type decimal (np) that it converts to its textual representation. cp is the buffer that should hold the result of the operation. The parameter `right` specifies, how many digits right of the decimal point should be included in the output. The result will be rounded to this number of decimal digits. Setting `right` to -1 indicates that all available decimal digits should be included in the output. If the length of the output buffer, which is indicated by `len` is not sufficient to hold the textual representation including the trailing zero byte, only a single `*` character is stored in the result and -1 is returned.

The function returns either -1 if the buffer `cp` was too small or `ECPG_INFORMIX_OUT_OF_MEMORY` if memory was exhausted.

`dectodbl`

Convert a variable of type decimal to a double.

`int dectodbl(decimal *np, double *dblp);`

The function receives a pointer to the decimal value to convert (np) and a pointer to the double variable that should hold the result of the operation (dblp).

On success, 0 is returned and a negative value if the conversion failed.

dectoint

> Convert a variable to type decimal to an integer.
>
> `int dectoint(decimal *np, int *ip);`
> The function receives a pointer to the decimal value to convert (`np`) and a pointer to the integer variable that should hold the result of the operation (`ip`).
>
> On success, 0 is returned and a negative value if the conversion failed. If an overflow occurred, `ECPG_INFORMIX_NUM_OVERFLOW` is returned.
>
> Note that the ECPG implementation differs from the Informix implementation. Informix limits an integer to the range from -32767 to 32767, while the limits in the ECPG implementation depend on the architecture (`-INT_MAX .. INT_MAX`).

dectolong

> Convert a variable to type decimal to a long integer.
>
> `int dectolong(decimal *np, long *lngp);`
> The function receives a pointer to the decimal value to convert (`np`) and a pointer to the long variable that should hold the result of the operation (`lngp`).
>
> On success, 0 is returned and a negative value if the conversion failed. If an overflow occurred, `ECPG_INFORMIX_NUM_OVERFLOW` is returned.
>
> Note that the ECPG implementation differs from the Informix implementation. Informix limits a long integer to the range from -2,147,483,647 to 2,147,483,647, while the limits in the ECPG implementation depend on the architecture (`-LONG_MAX .. LONG_MAX`).

rdatestr

> Converts a date to a C char* string.
>
> `int rdatestr(date d, char *str);`
> The function receives two arguments, the first one is the date to convert (`d`) and the second one is a pointer to the target string. The output format is always `yyyy-mm-dd`, so you need to allocate at least 11 bytes (including the zero-byte terminator) for the string.
>
> The function returns 0 on success and a negative value in case of error.
>
> Note that ECPG's implementation differs from the Informix implementation. In Informix the format can be influenced by setting environment variables. In ECPG however, you cannot change the output format.

rstrdate

> Parse the textual representation of a date.
>
> `int rstrdate(char *str, date *d);`
> The function receives the textual representation of the date to convert (`str`) and a pointer to a variable of type date (`d`). This function does not allow you to specify a format mask. It uses the default format mask of Informix which is `mm/dd/yyyy`. Internally, this function is implemented by means of `rdefmtdate`. Therefore, `rstrdate` is not faster and if you have the choice you should opt for `rdefmtdate` which allows you to specify the format mask explicitly.
>
> The function returns the same values as `rdefmtdate`.

`rtoday`

Get the current date.

```
void rtoday(date *d);
```
The function receives a pointer to a date variable (d) that it sets to the current date.

Internally this function uses the *PGTYPESdate_today* function.

`rjulmdy`

Extract the values for the day, the month and the year from a variable of type date.

```
int rjulmdy(date d, short mdy[3]);
```
The function receives the date d and a pointer to an array of 3 short integer values mdy. The variable name indicates the sequential order: mdy[0] will be set to contain the number of the month, mdy[1] will be set to the value of the day and mdy[2] will contain the year.

The function always returns 0 at the moment.

Internally the function uses the *PGTYPESdate_julmdy* function.

`rdefmtdate`

Use a format mask to convert a character string to a value of type date.

```
int rdefmtdate(date *d, char *fmt, char *str);
```
The function receives a pointer to the date value that should hold the result of the operation (d), the format mask to use for parsing the date (fmt) and the C char* string containing the textual representation of the date (str). The textual representation is expected to match the format mask. However you do not need to have a 1:1 mapping of the string to the format mask. The function only analyzes the sequential order and looks for the literals yy or yyyy that indicate the position of the year, mm to indicate the position of the month and dd to indicate the position of the day.

The function returns the following values:

- 0 - The function terminated successfully.

- ECPG_INFORMIX_ENOSHORTDATE - The date does not contain delimiters between day, month and year. In this case the input string must be exactly 6 or 8 bytes long but isn't.

- ECPG_INFORMIX_ENOTDMY - The format string did not correctly indicate the sequential order of year, month and day.

- ECPG_INFORMIX_BAD_DAY - The input string does not contain a valid day.

- ECPG_INFORMIX_BAD_MONTH - The input string does not contain a valid month.

- ECPG_INFORMIX_BAD_YEAR - The input string does not contain a valid year.

Internally this function is implemented to use the *PGTYPESdate_defmt_asc* function. See the reference there for a table of example input.

`rfmtdate`

Convert a variable of type date to its textual representation using a format mask.

```
int rfmtdate(date d, char *fmt, char *str);
```
The function receives the date to convert (d), the format mask (fmt) and the string that will hold the textual representation of the date (str).

On success, 0 is returned and a negative value if an error occurred.

Internally this function uses the *PGTYPESdate_fmt_asc* function, see the reference there for examples.

rmdyjul

Create a date value from an array of 3 short integers that specify the day, the month and the year of the date.

```
int rmdyjul(short mdy[3], date *d);
```
The function receives the array of the 3 short integers (mdy) and a pointer to a variable of type date that should hold the result of the operation.

Currently the function returns always 0.

Internally the function is implemented to use the function *PGTYPESdate_mdyjul*.

rdayofweek

Return a number representing the day of the week for a date value.

```
int rdayofweek(date d);
```
The function receives the date variable d as its only argument and returns an integer that indicates the day of the week for this date.

- 0 - Sunday

- 1 - Monday

- 2 - Tuesday

- 3 - Wednesday

- 4 - Thursday

- 5 - Friday

- 6 - Saturday

Internally the function is implemented to use the function *PGTYPESdate_dayofweek*.

dtcurrent

Retrieve the current timestamp.

```
void dtcurrent(timestamp *ts);
```
The function retrieves the current timestamp and saves it into the timestamp variable that ts points to.

dtcvasc

Parses a timestamp from its textual representation into a timestamp variable.

```
int dtcvasc(char *str, timestamp *ts);
```
The function receives the string to parse (str) and a pointer to the timestamp variable that should hold the result of the operation (ts).

The function returns 0 on success and a negative value in case of error.

Internally this function uses the *PGTYPEStimestamp_from_asc* function. See the reference there for a table with example inputs.

dtcvfmtasc

> Parses a timestamp from its textual representation using a format mask into a timestamp variable.
>
> dtcvfmtasc(char *inbuf, char *fmtstr, timestamp *dtvalue)
> The function receives the string to parse (inbuf), the format mask to use (fmtstr) and a pointer to the timestamp variable that should hold the result of the operation (dtvalue).
>
> This function is implemented by means of the *PGTYPEStimestamp_defmt_asc* function. See the documentation there for a list of format specifiers that can be used.
>
> The function returns 0 on success and a negative value in case of error.

dtsub

> Subtract one timestamp from another and return a variable of type interval.
>
> int dtsub(timestamp *ts1, timestamp *ts2, interval *iv);
> The function will subtract the timestamp variable that ts2 points to from the timestamp variable that ts1 points to and will store the result in the interval variable that iv points to.
>
> Upon success, the function returns 0 and a negative value if an error occurred.

dttoasc

> Convert a timestamp variable to a C char* string.
>
> int dttoasc(timestamp *ts, char *output);
> The function receives a pointer to the timestamp variable to convert (ts) and the string that should hold the result of the operation (output). It converts ts to its textual representation according to the SQL standard, which is be YYYY-MM-DD HH:MM:SS.
>
> Upon success, the function returns 0 and a negative value if an error occurred.

dttofmtasc

> Convert a timestamp variable to a C char* using a format mask.
>
> int dttofmtasc(timestamp *ts, char *output, int str_len, char *fmtstr);
> The function receives a pointer to the timestamp to convert as its first argument (ts), a pointer to the output buffer (output), the maximal length that has been allocated for the output buffer (str_len) and the format mask to use for the conversion (fmtstr).
>
> Upon success, the function returns 0 and a negative value if an error occurred.
>
> Internally, this function uses the *PGTYPEStimestamp_fmt_asc* function. See the reference there for information on what format mask specifiers can be used.

intoasc

> Convert an interval variable to a C char* string.
>
> int intoasc(interval *i, char *str);
> The function receives a pointer to the interval variable to convert (i) and the string that should hold the result of the operation (str). It converts i to its textual representation according to the SQL standard, which is be YYYY-MM-DD HH:MM:SS.
>
> Upon success, the function returns 0 and a negative value if an error occurred.

`rfmtlong`

Convert a long integer value to its textual representation using a format mask.

`int rfmtlong(long lng_val, char *fmt, char *outbuf);`

The function receives the long value `lng_val`, the format mask `fmt` and a pointer to the output buffer `outbuf`. It converts the long value according to the format mask to its textual representation.

The format mask can be composed of the following format specifying characters:

- `*` (asterisk) - if this position would be blank otherwise, fill it with an asterisk.

- `&` (ampersand) - if this position would be blank otherwise, fill it with a zero.

- `#` - turn leading zeroes into blanks.

- `<` - left-justify the number in the string.

- `,` (comma) - group numbers of four or more digits into groups of three digits separated by a comma.

- `.` (period) - this character separates the whole-number part of the number from the fractional part.

- `–` (minus) - the minus sign appears if the number is a negative value.

- `+` (plus) - the plus sign appears if the number is a positive value.

- `(` - this replaces the minus sign in front of the negative number. The minus sign will not appear.

- `)` - this character replaces the minus and is printed behind the negative value.

- `$` - the currency symbol.

`rupshift`

Convert a string to upper case.

`void rupshift(char *str);`

The function receives a pointer to the string and transforms every lower case character to upper case.

`byleng`

Return the number of characters in a string without counting trailing blanks.

`int byleng(char *str, int len);`

The function expects a fixed-length string as its first argument (`str`) and its length as its second argument (`len`). It returns the number of significant characters, that is the length of the string without trailing blanks.

`ldchar`

Copy a fixed-length string into a null-terminated string.

`void ldchar(char *src, int len, char *dest);`

The function receives the fixed-length string to copy (`src`), its length (`len`) and a pointer to the destination memory (`dest`). Note that you need to reserve at least `len+1` bytes for the string that `dest` points to. The function copies at most `len` bytes to the new location (less if the source string has trailing blanks) and adds the null-terminator.

rgetmsg

```
int rgetmsg(int msgnum, char *s, int maxsize);
```
This function exists but is not implemented at the moment!

rtypalign

```
int rtypalign(int offset, int type);
```
This function exists but is not implemented at the moment!

rtypmsize

```
int rtypmsize(int type, int len);
```
This function exists but is not implemented at the moment!

rtypwidth

```
int rtypwidth(int sqltype, int sqllen);
```
This function exists but is not implemented at the moment!

rsetnull

Set a variable to NULL.

```
int rsetnull(int t, char *ptr);
```
The function receives an integer that indicates the type of the variable and a pointer to the variable itself that is cast to a C char* pointer.

The following types exist:

- CCHARTYPE - For a variable of type char or char*
- CSHORTTYPE - For a variable of type short int
- CINTTYPE - For a variable of type int
- CBOOLTYPE - For a variable of type boolean
- CFLOATTYPE - For a variable of type float
- CLONGTYPE - For a variable of type long
- CDOUBLETYPE - For a variable of type double
- CDECIMALTYPE - For a variable of type decimal
- CDATETYPE - For a variable of type date
- CDTIMETYPE - For a variable of type timestamp

Here is an example of a call to this function:

```
$char c[] = "abc       ";
$short s = 17;
$int i = -74874;

rsetnull(CCHARTYPE, (char *) c);
rsetnull(CSHORTTYPE, (char *) &s);
rsetnull(CINTTYPE, (char *) &i);
```

```
risnull
```

Test if a variable is NULL.

```
int risnull(int t, char *ptr);
```
The function receives the type of the variable to test (`t`) as well a pointer to this variable (`ptr`). Note that the latter needs to be cast to a char*. See the function *rsetnull* for a list of possible variable types.

Here is an example of how to use this function:

```
$char c[] = "abc       ";
$short s = 17;
$int i = -74874;

risnull(CCHARTYPE, (char *) c);
risnull(CSHORTTYPE, (char *) &s);
risnull(CINTTYPE, (char *) &i);
```

34.15.5. Additional Constants

Note that all constants here describe errors and all of them are defined to represent negative values. In the descriptions of the different constants you can also find the value that the constants represent in the current implementation. However you should not rely on this number. You can however rely on the fact all of them are defined to represent negative values.

```
ECPG_INFORMIX_NUM_OVERFLOW
```

Functions return this value if an overflow occurred in a calculation. Internally it is defined as -1200 (the Informix definition).

```
ECPG_INFORMIX_NUM_UNDERFLOW
```

Functions return this value if an underflow occurred in a calculation. Internally it is defined as -1201 (the Informix definition).

```
ECPG_INFORMIX_DIVIDE_ZERO
```

Functions return this value if an attempt to divide by zero is observed. Internally it is defined as -1202 (the Informix definition).

```
ECPG_INFORMIX_BAD_YEAR
```

Functions return this value if a bad value for a year was found while parsing a date. Internally it is defined as -1204 (the Informix definition).

```
ECPG_INFORMIX_BAD_MONTH
```

Functions return this value if a bad value for a month was found while parsing a date. Internally it is defined as -1205 (the Informix definition).

```
ECPG_INFORMIX_BAD_DAY
```

Functions return this value if a bad value for a day was found while parsing a date. Internally it is defined as -1206 (the Informix definition).

ECPG_INFORMIX_ENOSHORTDATE

Functions return this value if a parsing routine needs a short date representation but did not get the date string in the right length. Internally it is defined as -1209 (the Informix definition).

ECPG_INFORMIX_DATE_CONVERT

Functions return this value if an error occurred during date formatting. Internally it is defined as -1210 (the Informix definition).

ECPG_INFORMIX_OUT_OF_MEMORY

Functions return this value if memory was exhausted during their operation. Internally it is defined as -1211 (the Informix definition).

ECPG_INFORMIX_ENOTDMY

Functions return this value if a parsing routine was supposed to get a format mask (like mmddyy) but not all fields were listed correctly. Internally it is defined as -1212 (the Informix definition).

ECPG_INFORMIX_BAD_NUMERIC

Functions return this value either if a parsing routine cannot parse the textual representation for a numeric value because it contains errors or if a routine cannot complete a calculation involving numeric variables because at least one of the numeric variables is invalid. Internally it is defined as -1213 (the Informix definition).

ECPG_INFORMIX_BAD_EXPONENT

Functions return this value if a parsing routine cannot parse an exponent. Internally it is defined as -1216 (the Informix definition).

ECPG_INFORMIX_BAD_DATE

Functions return this value if a parsing routine cannot parse a date. Internally it is defined as -1218 (the Informix definition).

ECPG_INFORMIX_EXTRA_CHARS

Functions return this value if a parsing routine is passed extra characters it cannot parse. Internally it is defined as -1264 (the Informix definition).

34.16. Internals

This section explains how ECPG works internally. This information can occasionally be useful to help users understand how to use ECPG.

The first four lines written by ecpg to the output are fixed lines. Two are comments and two are include lines necessary to interface to the library. Then the preprocessor reads through the file and writes output. Normally it just echoes everything to the output.

When it sees an EXEC SQL statement, it intervenes and changes it. The command starts with EXEC SQL and ends with ; . Everything in between is treated as an SQL statement and parsed for variable substitution.

Variable substitution occurs when a symbol starts with a colon (:). The variable with that name is looked up among the variables that were previously declared within a EXEC SQL DECLARE section.

The most important function in the library is ECPGdo, which takes care of executing most commands. It takes a variable number of arguments. This can easily add up to 50 or so arguments, and we hope this will not be a problem on any platform.

The arguments are:

A line number

This is the line number of the original line; used in error messages only.

A string

This is the SQL command that is to be issued. It is modified by the input variables, i.e., the variables that where not known at compile time but are to be entered in the command. Where the variables should go the string contains ?.

Input variables

Every input variable causes ten arguments to be created. (See below.)

ECPGt_EOIT

An enum telling that there are no more input variables.

Output variables

Every output variable causes ten arguments to be created. (See below.) These variables are filled by the function.

ECPGt_EORT

An enum telling that there are no more variables.

For every variable that is part of the SQL command, the function gets ten arguments:

1. The type as a special symbol.

2. A pointer to the value or a pointer to the pointer.

3. The size of the variable if it is a char or varchar.

4. The number of elements in the array (for array fetches).

5. The offset to the next element in the array (for array fetches).

6. The type of the indicator variable as a special symbol.

7. A pointer to the indicator variable.

8. 0

9. The number of elements in the indicator array (for array fetches).

10. The offset to the next element in the indicator array (for array fetches).

Note that not all SQL commands are treated in this way. For instance, an open cursor statement like:

```
EXEC SQL OPEN cursor;
```

is not copied to the output. Instead, the cursor's DECLARE command is used at the position of the OPEN command because it indeed opens the cursor.

Here is a complete example describing the output of the preprocessor of a file foo.pgc (details might change with each particular version of the preprocessor):

```
EXEC SQL BEGIN DECLARE SECTION;
int index;
int result;
EXEC SQL END DECLARE SECTION;
...
EXEC SQL SELECT res INTO :result FROM mytable WHERE index = :index;
```

is translated into:

```
/* Processed by ecpg (2.6.0) */
/* These two include files are added by the preprocessor */
#include <ecpgtype.h>;
#include <ecpglib.h>;

/* exec sql begin declare section */

#line 1 "foo.pgc"

 int index;
 int result;
/* exec sql end declare section */
...
ECPGdo(__LINE__, NULL, "SELECT res FROM mytable WHERE index = ?      ",
        ECPGt_int,&(index),1L,1L,sizeof(int),
        ECPGt_NO_INDICATOR, NULL , 0L, 0L, 0L, ECPGt_EOIT,
        ECPGt_int,&(result),1L,1L,sizeof(int),
        ECPGt_NO_INDICATOR, NULL , 0L, 0L, 0L, ECPGt_EORT);
#line 147 "foo.pgc"
```

(The indentation here is added for readability and not something the preprocessor does.)

Chapter 35. The Information Schema

The information schema consists of a set of views that contain information about the objects defined in the current database. The information schema is defined in the SQL standard and can therefore be expected to be portable and remain stable — unlike the system catalogs, which are specific to PostgreSQL and are modeled after implementation concerns. The information schema views do not, however, contain information about PostgreSQL-specific features; to inquire about those you need to query the system catalogs or other PostgreSQL-specific views.

> **Note:** When querying the database for constraint information, it is possible for a standard-compliant query that expects to return one row to return several. This is because the SQL standard requires constraint names to be unique within a schema, but PostgreSQL does not enforce this restriction. PostgreSQL automatically-generated constraint names avoid duplicates in the same schema, but users can specify such duplicate names.
>
> This problem can appear when querying information schema views such as `check_constraint_routine_usage`, `check_constraints`, `domain_constraints`, and `referential_constraints`. Some other views have similar issues but contain the table name to help distinguish duplicate rows, e.g., `constraint_column_usage`, `constraint_table_usage`, `table_constraints`.

35.1. The Schema

The information schema itself is a schema named `information_schema`. This schema automatically exists in all databases. The owner of this schema is the initial database user in the cluster, and that user naturally has all the privileges on this schema, including the ability to drop it (but the space savings achieved by that are minuscule).

By default, the information schema is not in the schema search path, so you need to access all objects in it through qualified names. Since the names of some of the objects in the information schema are generic names that might occur in user applications, you should be careful if you want to put the information schema in the path.

35.2. Data Types

The columns of the information schema views use special data types that are defined in the information schema. These are defined as simple domains over ordinary built-in types. You should not use these types for work outside the information schema, but your applications must be prepared for them if they select from the information schema.

These types are:

`cardinal_number`

A nonnegative integer.

`character_data`

> A character string (without specific maximum length).

`sql_identifier`

> A character string. This type is used for SQL identifiers, the type `character_data` is used for any other kind of text data.

`time_stamp`

> A domain over the type `timestamp with time zone`

`yes_or_no`

> A character string domain that contains either `YES` or `NO`. This is used to represent Boolean (true/false) data in the information schema. (The information schema was invented before the type `boolean` was added to the SQL standard, so this convention is necessary to keep the information schema backward compatible.)

Every column in the information schema has one of these five types.

35.3. `information_schema_catalog_name`

`information_schema_catalog_name` is a table that always contains one row and one column containing the name of the current database (current catalog, in SQL terminology).

Table 35-1. `information_schema_catalog_name` Columns

Name	Data Type	Description
`catalog_name`	`sql_identifier`	Name of the database that contains this information schema

35.4. `administrable_role_authorizations`

The view `administrable_role_authorizations` identifies all roles that the current user has the admin option for.

Table 35-2. `administrable_role_authorizations` Columns

Name	Data Type	Description
`grantee`	`sql_identifier`	Name of the role to which this role membership was granted (can be the current user, or a different role in case of nested role memberships)
`role_name`	`sql_identifier`	Name of a role

Name	Data Type	Description
is_grantable	yes_or_no	Always YES

35.5. `applicable_roles`

The view `applicable_roles` identifies all roles whose privileges the current user can use. This means there is some chain of role grants from the current user to the role in question. The current user itself is also an applicable role. The set of applicable roles is generally used for permission checking.

Table 35-3. `applicable_roles` Columns

Name	Data Type	Description
grantee	sql_identifier	Name of the role to which this role membership was granted (can be the current user, or a different role in case of nested role memberships)
role_name	sql_identifier	Name of a role
is_grantable	yes_or_no	YES if the grantee has the admin option on the role, NO if not

35.6. `attributes`

The view `attributes` contains information about the attributes of composite data types defined in the database. (Note that the view does not give information about table columns, which are sometimes called attributes in PostgreSQL contexts.) Only those attributes are shown that the current user has access to (by way of being the owner of or having some privilege on the type).

Table 35-4. `attributes` Columns

Name	Data Type	Description
udt_catalog	sql_identifier	Name of the database containing the data type (always the current database)
udt_schema	sql_identifier	Name of the schema containing the data type
udt_name	sql_identifier	Name of the data type
attribute_name	sql_identifier	Name of the attribute
ordinal_position	cardinal_number	Ordinal position of the attribute within the data type (count starts at 1)

Name	Data Type	Description
attribute_default	character_data	Default expression of the attribute
is_nullable	yes_or_no	YES if the attribute is possibly nullable, NO if it is known not nullable.
data_type	character_data	Data type of the attribute, if it is a built-in type, or ARRAY if it is some array (in that case, see the view element_types), else USER-DEFINED (in that case, the type is identified in attribute_udt_name and associated columns).
character_maximum_length	cardinal_number	If data_type identifies a character or bit string type, the declared maximum length; null for all other data types or if no maximum length was declared.
character_octet_length	cardinal_number	If data_type identifies a character type, the maximum possible length in octets (bytes) of a datum; null for all other data types. The maximum octet length depends on the declared character maximum length (see above) and the server encoding.
character_set_catalog	sql_identifier	Applies to a feature not available in PostgreSQL
character_set_schema	sql_identifier	Applies to a feature not available in PostgreSQL
character_set_name	sql_identifier	Applies to a feature not available in PostgreSQL
collation_catalog	sql_identifier	Name of the database containing the collation of the attribute (always the current database), null if default or the data type of the attribute is not collatable
collation_schema	sql_identifier	Name of the schema containing the collation of the attribute, null if default or the data type of the attribute is not collatable

Name	Data Type	Description
collation_name	sql_identifier	Name of the collation of the attribute, null if default or the data type of the attribute is not collatable
numeric_precision	cardinal_number	If data_type identifies a numeric type, this column contains the (declared or implicit) precision of the type for this attribute. The precision indicates the number of significant digits. It can be expressed in decimal (base 10) or binary (base 2) terms, as specified in the column numeric_precision_radix. For all other data types, this column is null.
numeric_precision_radix	cardinal_number	If data_type identifies a numeric type, this column indicates in which base the values in the columns numeric_precision and numeric_scale are expressed. The value is either 2 or 10. For all other data types, this column is null.
numeric_scale	cardinal_number	If data_type identifies an exact numeric type, this column contains the (declared or implicit) scale of the type for this attribute. The scale indicates the number of significant digits to the right of the decimal point. It can be expressed in decimal (base 10) or binary (base 2) terms, as specified in the column numeric_precision_radix. For all other data types, this column is null.

Name	Data Type	Description
datetime_precision	cardinal_number	If data_type identifies a date, time, timestamp, or interval type, this column contains the (declared or implicit) fractional seconds precision of the type for this attribute, that is, the number of decimal digits maintained following the decimal point in the seconds value. For all other data types, this column is null.
interval_type	character_data	If data_type identifies an interval type, this column contains the specification which fields the intervals include for this attribute, e.g., YEAR TO MONTH, DAY TO SECOND, etc. If no field restrictions were specified (that is, the interval accepts all fields), and for all other data types, this field is null.
interval_precision	cardinal_number	Applies to a feature not available in PostgreSQL (see datetime_precision for the fractional seconds precision of interval type attributes)
attribute_udt_catalog	sql_identifier	Name of the database that the attribute data type is defined in (always the current database)
attribute_udt_schema	sql_identifier	Name of the schema that the attribute data type is defined in
attribute_udt_name	sql_identifier	Name of the attribute data type
scope_catalog	sql_identifier	Applies to a feature not available in PostgreSQL
scope_schema	sql_identifier	Applies to a feature not available in PostgreSQL
scope_name	sql_identifier	Applies to a feature not available in PostgreSQL
maximum_cardinality	cardinal_number	Always null, because arrays always have unlimited maximum cardinality in PostgreSQL

Name	Data Type	Description
dtd_identifier	sql_identifier	An identifier of the data type descriptor of the column, unique among the data type descriptors pertaining to the table. This is mainly useful for joining with other instances of such identifiers. (The specific format of the identifier is not defined and not guaranteed to remain the same in future versions.)
is_derived_reference_attribute	yes_or_no	Applies to a feature not available in PostgreSQL

See also under Section 35.16, a similarly structured view, for further information on some of the columns.

35.7. `character_sets`

The view `character_sets` identifies the character sets available in the current database. Since PostgreSQL does not support multiple character sets within one database, this view only shows one, which is the database encoding.

Take note of how the following terms are used in the SQL standard:

character repertoire

An abstract collection of characters, for example UNICODE, UCS, or LATIN1. Not exposed as an SQL object, but visible in this view.

character encoding form

An encoding of some character repertoire. Most older character repertoires only use one encoding form, and so there are no separate names for them (e.g., LATIN1 is an encoding form applicable to the LATIN1 repertoire). But for example Unicode has the encoding forms UTF8, UTF16, etc. (not all supported by PostgreSQL). Encoding forms are not exposed as an SQL object, but are visible in this view.

character set

A named SQL object that identifies a character repertoire, a character encoding, and a default collation. A predefined character set would typically have the same name as an encoding form, but users could define other names. For example, the character set UTF8 would typically identify the character repertoire UCS, encoding form UTF8, and some default collation.

You can think of an "encoding" in PostgreSQL either as a character set or a character encoding form. They will have the same name, and there can only be one in one database.

Table 35-5. `character_sets` Columns

Name	Data Type	Description

Name	Data Type	Description
character_set_catalog	sql_identifier	Character sets are currently not implemented as schema objects, so this column is null.
character_set_schema	sql_identifier	Character sets are currently not implemented as schema objects, so this column is null.
character_set_name	sql_identifier	Name of the character set, currently implemented as showing the name of the database encoding
character_repertoire	sql_identifier	Character repertoire, showing UCS if the encoding is UTF8, else just the encoding name
form_of_use	sql_identifier	Character encoding form, same as the database encoding
default_collate_catalog	sql_identifier	Name of the database containing the default collation (always the current database, if any collation is identified)
default_collate_schema	sql_identifier	Name of the schema containing the default collation
default_collate_name	sql_identifier	Name of the default collation. The default collation is identified as the collation that matches the COLLATE and CTYPE settings of the current database. If there is no such collation, then this column and the associated schema and catalog columns are null.

35.8. check_constraint_routine_usage

The view check_constraint_routine_usage identifies routines (functions and procedures) that are used by a check constraint. Only those routines are shown that are owned by a currently enabled role.

Table 35-6. check_constraint_routine_usage Columns

Name	Data Type	Description
constraint_catalog	sql_identifier	Name of the database containing the constraint (always the current database)

Name	Data Type	Description
constraint_schema	sql_identifier	Name of the schema containing the constraint
constraint_name	sql_identifier	Name of the constraint
specific_catalog	sql_identifier	Name of the database containing the function (always the current database)
specific_schema	sql_identifier	Name of the schema containing the function
specific_name	sql_identifier	The "specific name" of the function. See Section 35.40 for more information.

35.9. check_constraints

The view check_constraints contains all check constraints, either defined on a table or on a domain, that are owned by a currently enabled role. (The owner of the table or domain is the owner of the constraint.)

Table 35-7. check_constraints Columns

Name	Data Type	Description
constraint_catalog	sql_identifier	Name of the database containing the constraint (always the current database)
constraint_schema	sql_identifier	Name of the schema containing the constraint
constraint_name	sql_identifier	Name of the constraint
check_clause	character_data	The check expression of the check constraint

35.10. collations

The view collations contains the collations available in the current database.

Table 35-8. collations Columns

Name	Data Type	Description
collation_catalog	sql_identifier	Name of the database containing the collation (always the current database)

Name	Data Type	Description
collation_schema	sql_identifier	Name of the schema containing the collation
collation_name	sql_identifier	Name of the default collation
pad_attribute	character_data	Always NO PAD (The alternative PAD SPACE is not supported by PostgreSQL.)

35.11. collation_character_set_applicability

The view collation_character_set_applicability identifies which character set the available collations are applicable to. In PostgreSQL, there is only one character set per database (see explanation in Section 35.7), so this view does not provide much useful information.

Table 35-9. collation_character_set_applicability Columns

Name	Data Type	Description
collation_catalog	sql_identifier	Name of the database containing the collation (always the current database)
collation_schema	sql_identifier	Name of the schema containing the collation
collation_name	sql_identifier	Name of the default collation
character_set_catalog	sql_identifier	Character sets are currently not implemented as schema objects, so this column is null
character_set_schema	sql_identifier	Character sets are currently not implemented as schema objects, so this column is null
character_set_name	sql_identifier	Name of the character set

35.12. column_domain_usage

The view column_domain_usage identifies all columns (of a table or a view) that make use of some domain defined in the current database and owned by a currently enabled role.

Table 35-10. column_domain_usage Columns

Name	Data Type	Description

Name	Data Type	Description
domain_catalog	sql_identifier	Name of the database containing the domain (always the current database)
domain_schema	sql_identifier	Name of the schema containing the domain
domain_name	sql_identifier	Name of the domain
table_catalog	sql_identifier	Name of the database containing the table (always the current database)
table_schema	sql_identifier	Name of the schema containing the table
table_name	sql_identifier	Name of the table
column_name	sql_identifier	Name of the column

35.13. `column_options`

The view `column_options` contains all the options defined for foreign table columns in the current database. Only those foreign table columns are shown that the current user has access to (by way of being the owner or having some privilege).

Table 35-11. `column_options` Columns

Name	Data Type	Description
table_catalog	sql_identifier	Name of the database that contains the foreign table (always the current database)
table_schema	sql_identifier	Name of the schema that contains the foreign table
table_name	sql_identifier	Name of the foreign table
column_name	sql_identifier	Name of the column
option_name	sql_identifier	Name of an option
option_value	character_data	Value of the option

35.14. `column_privileges`

The view `column_privileges` identifies all privileges granted on columns to a currently enabled role or by a currently enabled role. There is one row for each combination of column, grantor, and grantee.

If a privilege has been granted on an entire table, it will show up in this view as a grant for each column, but only for the privilege types where column granularity is possible: SELECT, INSERT, UPDATE, REFERENCES.

Table 35-12. `column_privileges` **Columns**

Name	Data Type	Description
grantor	sql_identifier	Name of the role that granted the privilege
grantee	sql_identifier	Name of the role that the privilege was granted to
table_catalog	sql_identifier	Name of the database that contains the table that contains the column (always the current database)
table_schema	sql_identifier	Name of the schema that contains the table that contains the column
table_name	sql_identifier	Name of the table that contains the column
column_name	sql_identifier	Name of the column
privilege_type	character_data	Type of the privilege: SELECT, INSERT, UPDATE, or REFERENCES
is_grantable	yes_or_no	YES if the privilege is grantable, NO if not

35.15. `column_udt_usage`

The view `column_udt_usage` identifies all columns that use data types owned by a currently enabled role. Note that in PostgreSQL, built-in data types behave like user-defined types, so they are included here as well. See also Section 35.16 for details.

Table 35-13. `column_udt_usage` **Columns**

Name	Data Type	Description
udt_catalog	sql_identifier	Name of the database that the column data type (the underlying type of the domain, if applicable) is defined in (always the current database)
udt_schema	sql_identifier	Name of the schema that the column data type (the underlying type of the domain, if applicable) is defined in

Name	Data Type	Description
udt_name	sql_identifier	Name of the column data type (the underlying type of the domain, if applicable)
table_catalog	sql_identifier	Name of the database containing the table (always the current database)
table_schema	sql_identifier	Name of the schema containing the table
table_name	sql_identifier	Name of the table
column_name	sql_identifier	Name of the column

35.16. `columns`

The view `columns` contains information about all table columns (or view columns) in the database. System columns (`oid`, etc.) are not included. Only those columns are shown that the current user has access to (by way of being the owner or having some privilege).

Table 35-14. `columns` Columns

Name	Data Type	Description
table_catalog	sql_identifier	Name of the database containing the table (always the current database)
table_schema	sql_identifier	Name of the schema containing the table
table_name	sql_identifier	Name of the table
column_name	sql_identifier	Name of the column
ordinal_position	cardinal_number	Ordinal position of the column within the table (count starts at 1)
column_default	character_data	Default expression of the column
is_nullable	yes_or_no	YES if the column is possibly nullable, NO if it is known not nullable. A not-null constraint is one way a column can be known not nullable, but there can be others.

Name	Data Type	Description
data_type	character_data	Data type of the column, if it is a built-in type, or ARRAY if it is some array (in that case, see the view element_types), else USER-DEFINED (in that case, the type is identified in udt_name and associated columns). If the column is based on a domain, this column refers to the type underlying the domain (and the domain is identified in domain_name and associated columns).
character_maximum_length	cardinal_number	If data_type identifies a character or bit string type, the declared maximum length; null for all other data types or if no maximum length was declared.
character_octet_length	cardinal_number	If data_type identifies a character type, the maximum possible length in octets (bytes) of a datum; null for all other data types. The maximum octet length depends on the declared character maximum length (see above) and the server encoding.
numeric_precision	cardinal_number	If data_type identifies a numeric type, this column contains the (declared or implicit) precision of the type for this column. The precision indicates the number of significant digits. It can be expressed in decimal (base 10) or binary (base 2) terms, as specified in the column numeric_precision_radix. For all other data types, this column is null.

Name	Data Type	Description
numeric_precision_radix	cardinal_number	If data_type identifies a numeric type, this column indicates in which base the values in the columns numeric_precision and numeric_scale are expressed. The value is either 2 or 10. For all other data types, this column is null.
numeric_scale	cardinal_number	If data_type identifies an exact numeric type, this column contains the (declared or implicit) scale of the type for this column. The scale indicates the number of significant digits to the right of the decimal point. It can be expressed in decimal (base 10) or binary (base 2) terms, as specified in the column numeric_precision_radix. For all other data types, this column is null.
datetime_precision	cardinal_number	If data_type identifies a date, time, timestamp, or interval type, this column contains the (declared or implicit) fractional seconds precision of the type for this column, that is, the number of decimal digits maintained following the decimal point in the seconds value. For all other data types, this column is null.
interval_type	character_data	If data_type identifies an interval type, this column contains the specification which fields the intervals include for this column, e.g., YEAR TO MONTH, DAY TO SECOND, etc. If no field restrictions were specified (that is, the interval accepts all fields), and for all other data types, this field is null.

Name	Data Type	Description
interval_precision	cardinal_number	Applies to a feature not available in PostgreSQL (see datetime_precision for the fractional seconds precision of interval type columns)
character_set_catalog	sql_identifier	Applies to a feature not available in PostgreSQL
character_set_schema	sql_identifier	Applies to a feature not available in PostgreSQL
character_set_name	sql_identifier	Applies to a feature not available in PostgreSQL
collation_catalog	sql_identifier	Name of the database containing the collation of the column (always the current database), null if default or the data type of the column is not collatable
collation_schema	sql_identifier	Name of the schema containing the collation of the column, null if default or the data type of the column is not collatable
collation_name	sql_identifier	Name of the collation of the column, null if default or the data type of the column is not collatable
domain_catalog	sql_identifier	If the column has a domain type, the name of the database that the domain is defined in (always the current database), else null.
domain_schema	sql_identifier	If the column has a domain type, the name of the schema that the domain is defined in, else null.
domain_name	sql_identifier	If the column has a domain type, the name of the domain, else null.
udt_catalog	sql_identifier	Name of the database that the column data type (the underlying type of the domain, if applicable) is defined in (always the current database)
udt_schema	sql_identifier	Name of the schema that the column data type (the underlying type of the domain, if applicable) is defined in

Name	Data Type	Description
udt_name	sql_identifier	Name of the column data type (the underlying type of the domain, if applicable)
scope_catalog	sql_identifier	Applies to a feature not available in PostgreSQL
scope_schema	sql_identifier	Applies to a feature not available in PostgreSQL
scope_name	sql_identifier	Applies to a feature not available in PostgreSQL
maximum_cardinality	cardinal_number	Always null, because arrays always have unlimited maximum cardinality in PostgreSQL
dtd_identifier	sql_identifier	An identifier of the data type descriptor of the column, unique among the data type descriptors pertaining to the table. This is mainly useful for joining with other instances of such identifiers. (The specific format of the identifier is not defined and not guaranteed to remain the same in future versions.)
is_self_referencing	yes_or_no	Applies to a feature not available in PostgreSQL
is_identity	yes_or_no	Applies to a feature not available in PostgreSQL
identity_generation	character_data	Applies to a feature not available in PostgreSQL
identity_start	character_data	Applies to a feature not available in PostgreSQL
identity_increment	character_data	Applies to a feature not available in PostgreSQL
identity_maximum	character_data	Applies to a feature not available in PostgreSQL
identity_minimum	character_data	Applies to a feature not available in PostgreSQL
identity_cycle	yes_or_no	Applies to a feature not available in PostgreSQL
is_generated	character_data	Applies to a feature not available in PostgreSQL
generation_expression	character_data	Applies to a feature not available in PostgreSQL

Name	Data Type	Description
is_updatable	yes_or_no	YES if the column is updatable, NO if not (Columns in base tables are always updatable, columns in views not necessarily)

Since data types can be defined in a variety of ways in SQL, and PostgreSQL contains additional ways to define data types, their representation in the information schema can be somewhat difficult. The column data_type is supposed to identify the underlying built-in type of the column. In PostgreSQL, this means that the type is defined in the system catalog schema pg_catalog. This column might be useful if the application can handle the well-known built-in types specially (for example, format the numeric types differently or use the data in the precision columns). The columns udt_name, udt_schema, and udt_catalog always identify the underlying data type of the column, even if the column is based on a domain. (Since PostgreSQL treats built-in types like user-defined types, built-in types appear here as well. This is an extension of the SQL standard.) These columns should be used if an application wants to process data differently according to the type, because in that case it wouldn't matter if the column is really based on a domain. If the column is based on a domain, the identity of the domain is stored in the columns domain_name, domain_schema, and domain_catalog. If you want to pair up columns with their associated data types and treat domains as separate types, you could write coalesce(domain_name, udt_name), etc.

35.17. `constraint_column_usage`

The view constraint_column_usage identifies all columns in the current database that are used by some constraint. Only those columns are shown that are contained in a table owned by a currently enabled role. For a check constraint, this view identifies the columns that are used in the check expression. For a foreign key constraint, this view identifies the columns that the foreign key references. For a unique or primary key constraint, this view identifies the constrained columns.

Table 35-15. `constraint_column_usage` Columns

Name	Data Type	Description
table_catalog	sql_identifier	Name of the database that contains the table that contains the column that is used by some constraint (always the current database)
table_schema	sql_identifier	Name of the schema that contains the table that contains the column that is used by some constraint
table_name	sql_identifier	Name of the table that contains the column that is used by some constraint

Name	Data Type	Description
column_name	sql_identifier	Name of the column that is used by some constraint
constraint_catalog	sql_identifier	Name of the database that contains the constraint (always the current database)
constraint_schema	sql_identifier	Name of the schema that contains the constraint
constraint_name	sql_identifier	Name of the constraint

35.18. `constraint_table_usage`

The view `constraint_table_usage` identifies all tables in the current database that are used by some constraint and are owned by a currently enabled role. (This is different from the view `table_constraints`, which identifies all table constraints along with the table they are defined on.) For a foreign key constraint, this view identifies the table that the foreign key references. For a unique or primary key constraint, this view simply identifies the table the constraint belongs to. Check constraints and not-null constraints are not included in this view.

Table 35-16. `constraint_table_usage` Columns

Name	Data Type	Description
table_catalog	sql_identifier	Name of the database that contains the table that is used by some constraint (always the current database)
table_schema	sql_identifier	Name of the schema that contains the table that is used by some constraint
table_name	sql_identifier	Name of the table that is used by some constraint
constraint_catalog	sql_identifier	Name of the database that contains the constraint (always the current database)
constraint_schema	sql_identifier	Name of the schema that contains the constraint
constraint_name	sql_identifier	Name of the constraint

35.19. `data_type_privileges`

The view `data_type_privileges` identifies all data type descriptors that the current user has access to, by way of being the owner of the described object or having some privilege for it. A data type descriptor is generated whenever a data type is used in the definition of a table column, a domain, or a function (as parameter or return type) and stores some information about how the data type is used in that instance (for example, the declared maximum length, if applicable). Each data type descriptor is assigned an arbitrary identifier that is unique among the data type descriptor identifiers assigned for one object (table, domain, function). This view is probably not useful for applications, but it is used to define some other views in the information schema.

Table 35-17. `data_type_privileges` Columns

Name	Data Type	Description
object_catalog	sql_identifier	Name of the database that contains the described object (always the current database)
object_schema	sql_identifier	Name of the schema that contains the described object
object_name	sql_identifier	Name of the described object
object_type	character_data	The type of the described object: one of TABLE (the data type descriptor pertains to a column of that table), DOMAIN (the data type descriptors pertains to that domain), ROUTINE (the data type descriptor pertains to a parameter or the return data type of that function).
dtd_identifier	sql_identifier	The identifier of the data type descriptor, which is unique among the data type descriptors for that same object.

35.20. `domain_constraints`

The view `domain_constraints` contains all constraints belonging to domains defined in the current database. Only those domains are shown that the current user has access to (by way of being the owner or having some privilege).

Table 35-18. `domain_constraints` Columns

Name	Data Type	Description
constraint_catalog	sql_identifier	Name of the database that contains the constraint (always the current database)
constraint_schema	sql_identifier	Name of the schema that contains the constraint

Name	Data Type	Description
constraint_name	sql_identifier	Name of the constraint
domain_catalog	sql_identifier	Name of the database that contains the domain (always the current database)
domain_schema	sql_identifier	Name of the schema that contains the domain
domain_name	sql_identifier	Name of the domain
is_deferrable	yes_or_no	YES if the constraint is deferrable, NO if not
initially_deferred	yes_or_no	YES if the constraint is deferrable and initially deferred, NO if not

35.21. `domain_udt_usage`

The view `domain_udt_usage` identifies all domains that are based on data types owned by a currently enabled role. Note that in PostgreSQL, built-in data types behave like user-defined types, so they are included here as well.

Table 35-19. `domain_udt_usage` Columns

Name	Data Type	Description
udt_catalog	sql_identifier	Name of the database that the domain data type is defined in (always the current database)
udt_schema	sql_identifier	Name of the schema that the domain data type is defined in
udt_name	sql_identifier	Name of the domain data type
domain_catalog	sql_identifier	Name of the database that contains the domain (always the current database)
domain_schema	sql_identifier	Name of the schema that contains the domain
domain_name	sql_identifier	Name of the domain

35.22. `domains`

The view `domains` contains all domains defined in the current database. Only those domains are shown that the current user has access to (by way of being the owner or having some privilege).

Table 35-20. `domains` Columns

Name	Data Type	Description
domain_catalog	sql_identifier	Name of the database that contains the domain (always the current database)
domain_schema	sql_identifier	Name of the schema that contains the domain
domain_name	sql_identifier	Name of the domain
data_type	character_data	Data type of the domain, if it is a built-in type, or ARRAY if it is some array (in that case, see the view element_types), else USER-DEFINED (in that case, the type is identified in udt_name and associated columns).
character_maximum_length	cardinal_number	If the domain has a character or bit string type, the declared maximum length; null for all other data types or if no maximum length was declared.
character_octet_length	cardinal_number	If the domain has a character type, the maximum possible length in octets (bytes) of a datum; null for all other data types. The maximum octet length depends on the declared character maximum length (see above) and the server encoding.
character_set_catalog	sql_identifier	Applies to a feature not available in PostgreSQL
character_set_schema	sql_identifier	Applies to a feature not available in PostgreSQL
character_set_name	sql_identifier	Applies to a feature not available in PostgreSQL
collation_catalog	sql_identifier	Name of the database containing the collation of the domain (always the current database), null if default or the data type of the domain is not collatable
collation_schema	sql_identifier	Name of the schema containing the collation of the domain, null if default or the data type of the domain is not collatable

Name	Data Type	Description
collation_name	sql_identifier	Name of the collation of the domain, null if default or the data type of the domain is not collatable
numeric_precision	cardinal_number	If the domain has a numeric type, this column contains the (declared or implicit) precision of the type for this domain. The precision indicates the number of significant digits. It can be expressed in decimal (base 10) or binary (base 2) terms, as specified in the column numeric_precision_radix. For all other data types, this column is null.
numeric_precision_radix	cardinal_number	If the domain has a numeric type, this column indicates in which base the values in the columns numeric_precision and numeric_scale are expressed. The value is either 2 or 10. For all other data types, this column is null.
numeric_scale	cardinal_number	If the domain has an exact numeric type, this column contains the (declared or implicit) scale of the type for this domain. The scale indicates the number of significant digits to the right of the decimal point. It can be expressed in decimal (base 10) or binary (base 2) terms, as specified in the column numeric_precision_radix. For all other data types, this column is null.

Name	Data Type	Description
datetime_precision	cardinal_number	If data_type identifies a date, time, timestamp, or interval type, this column contains the (declared or implicit) fractional seconds precision of the type for this domain, that is, the number of decimal digits maintained following the decimal point in the seconds value. For all other data types, this column is null.
interval_type	character_data	If data_type identifies an interval type, this column contains the specification which fields the intervals include for this domain, e.g., YEAR TO MONTH, DAY TO SECOND, etc. If no field restrictions were specified (that is, the interval accepts all fields), and for all other data types, this field is null.
interval_precision	cardinal_number	Applies to a feature not available in PostgreSQL (see datetime_precision for the fractional seconds precision of interval type domains)
domain_default	character_data	Default expression of the domain
udt_catalog	sql_identifier	Name of the database that the domain data type is defined in (always the current database)
udt_schema	sql_identifier	Name of the schema that the domain data type is defined in
udt_name	sql_identifier	Name of the domain data type
scope_catalog	sql_identifier	Applies to a feature not available in PostgreSQL
scope_schema	sql_identifier	Applies to a feature not available in PostgreSQL
scope_name	sql_identifier	Applies to a feature not available in PostgreSQL
maximum_cardinality	cardinal_number	Always null, because arrays always have unlimited maximum cardinality in PostgreSQL

Name	Data Type	Description
dtd_identifier	sql_identifier	An identifier of the data type descriptor of the domain, unique among the data type descriptors pertaining to the domain (which is trivial, because a domain only contains one data type descriptor). This is mainly useful for joining with other instances of such identifiers. (The specific format of the identifier is not defined and not guaranteed to remain the same in future versions.)

35.23. `element_types`

The view `element_types` contains the data type descriptors of the elements of arrays. When a table column, composite-type attribute, domain, function parameter, or function return value is defined to be of an array type, the respective information schema view only contains ARRAY in the column `data_type`. To obtain information on the element type of the array, you can join the respective view with this view. For example, to show the columns of a table with data types and array element types, if applicable, you could do:

```
SELECT c.column_name, c.data_type, e.data_type AS element_type
FROM information_schema.columns c LEFT JOIN information_schema.element_types e
    ON ((c.table_catalog, c.table_schema, c.table_name, 'TABLE', c.dtd_identifier)
       = (e.object_catalog, e.object_schema, e.object_name, e.object_type, e.collect
WHERE c.table_schema = '...' AND c.table_name = '...'
ORDER BY c.ordinal_position;
```

This view only includes objects that the current user has access to, by way of being the owner or having some privilege.

Table 35-21. `element_types` Columns

Name	Data Type	Description
object_catalog	sql_identifier	Name of the database that contains the object that uses the array being described (always the current database)
object_schema	sql_identifier	Name of the schema that contains the object that uses the array being described
object_name	sql_identifier	Name of the object that uses the array being described

Name	Data Type	Description
object_type	character_data	The type of the object that uses the array being described: one of TABLE (the array is used by a column of that table), USER-DEFINED TYPE (the array is used by an attribute of that composite type), DOMAIN (the array is used by that domain), ROUTINE (the array is used by a parameter or the return data type of that function).
collection_type_identifier	sql_identifier	The identifier of the data type descriptor of the array being described. Use this to join with the dtd_identifier columns of other information schema views.
data_type	character_data	Data type of the array elements, if it is a built-in type, else USER-DEFINED (in that case, the type is identified in udt_name and associated columns).
character_maximum_length	cardinal_number	Always null, since this information is not applied to array element data types in PostgreSQL
character_octet_length	cardinal_number	Always null, since this information is not applied to array element data types in PostgreSQL
character_set_catalog	sql_identifier	Applies to a feature not available in PostgreSQL
character_set_schema	sql_identifier	Applies to a feature not available in PostgreSQL
character_set_name	sql_identifier	Applies to a feature not available in PostgreSQL
collation_catalog	sql_identifier	Name of the database containing the collation of the element type (always the current database), null if default or the data type of the element is not collatable

Name	Data Type	Description
collation_schema	sql_identifier	Name of the schema containing the collation of the element type, null if default or the data type of the element is not collatable
collation_name	sql_identifier	Name of the collation of the element type, null if default or the data type of the element is not collatable
numeric_precision	cardinal_number	Always null, since this information is not applied to array element data types in PostgreSQL
numeric_precision_radix	cardinal_number	Always null, since this information is not applied to array element data types in PostgreSQL
numeric_scale	cardinal_number	Always null, since this information is not applied to array element data types in PostgreSQL
datetime_precision	cardinal_number	Always null, since this information is not applied to array element data types in PostgreSQL
interval_type	character_data	Always null, since this information is not applied to array element data types in PostgreSQL
interval_precision	cardinal_number	Always null, since this information is not applied to array element data types in PostgreSQL
domain_default	character_data	Not yet implemented
udt_catalog	sql_identifier	Name of the database that the data type of the elements is defined in (always the current database)
udt_schema	sql_identifier	Name of the schema that the data type of the elements is defined in
udt_name	sql_identifier	Name of the data type of the elements
scope_catalog	sql_identifier	Applies to a feature not available in PostgreSQL

Name	Data Type	Description
scope_schema	sql_identifier	Applies to a feature not available in PostgreSQL
scope_name	sql_identifier	Applies to a feature not available in PostgreSQL
maximum_cardinality	cardinal_number	Always null, because arrays always have unlimited maximum cardinality in PostgreSQL
dtd_identifier	sql_identifier	An identifier of the data type descriptor of the element. This is currently not useful.

35.24. `enabled_roles`

The view `enabled_roles` identifies the currently "enabled roles". The enabled roles are recursively defined as the current user together with all roles that have been granted to the enabled roles with automatic inheritance. In other words, these are all roles that the current user has direct or indirect, automatically inheriting membership in.

For permission checking, the set of "applicable roles" is applied, which can be broader than the set of enabled roles. So generally, it is better to use the view `applicable_roles` instead of this one; see also there.

Table 35-22. `enabled_roles` Columns

Name	Data Type	Description
role_name	sql_identifier	Name of a role

35.25. `foreign_data_wrapper_options`

The view `foreign_data_wrapper_options` contains all the options defined for foreign-data wrappers in the current database. Only those foreign-data wrappers are shown that the current user has access to (by way of being the owner or having some privilege).

Table 35-23. `foreign_data_wrapper_options` Columns

Name	Data Type	Description
foreign_data_wrapper_catalog	sql_identifier	Name of the database that the foreign-data wrapper is defined in (always the current database)
foreign_data_wrapper_name	sql_identifier	Name of the foreign-data wrapper

Name	Data Type	Description
option_name	sql_identifier	Name of an option
option_value	character_data	Value of the option

35.26. `foreign_data_wrappers`

The view `foreign_data_wrappers` contains all foreign-data wrappers defined in the current database. Only those foreign-data wrappers are shown that the current user has access to (by way of being the owner or having some privilege).

Table 35-24. `foreign_data_wrappers` Columns

Name	Data Type	Description
foreign_data_wrapper_catalog	sql_identifier	Name of the database that contains the foreign-data wrapper (always the current database)
foreign_data_wrapper_name	sql_identifier	Name of the foreign-data wrapper
authorization_identifier	sql_identifier	Name of the owner of the foreign server
library_name	character_data	File name of the library that implementing this foreign-data wrapper
foreign_data_wrapper_language	character_data	Language used to implement this foreign-data wrapper

35.27. `foreign_server_options`

The view `foreign_server_options` contains all the options defined for foreign servers in the current database. Only those foreign servers are shown that the current user has access to (by way of being the owner or having some privilege).

Table 35-25. `foreign_server_options` Columns

Name	Data Type	Description
foreign_server_catalog	sql_identifier	Name of the database that the foreign server is defined in (always the current database)
foreign_server_name	sql_identifier	Name of the foreign server
option_name	sql_identifier	Name of an option

Name	Data Type	Description
option_value	character_data	Value of the option

35.28. `foreign_servers`

The view `foreign_servers` contains all foreign servers defined in the current database. Only those foreign servers are shown that the current user has access to (by way of being the owner or having some privilege).

Table 35-26. `foreign_servers` Columns

Name	Data Type	Description
foreign_server_catalog	sql_identifier	Name of the database that the foreign server is defined in (always the current database)
foreign_server_name	sql_identifier	Name of the foreign server
foreign_data_wrapper_catalog	sql_identifier	Name of the database that contains the foreign-data wrapper used by the foreign server (always the current database)
foreign_data_wrapper_name	sql_identifier	Name of the foreign-data wrapper used by the foreign server
foreign_server_type	character_data	Foreign server type information, if specified upon creation
foreign_server_version	character_data	Foreign server version information, if specified upon creation
authorization_identifier	sql_identifier	Name of the owner of the foreign server

35.29. `foreign_table_options`

The view `foreign_table_options` contains all the options defined for foreign tables in the current database. Only those foreign tables are shown that the current user has access to (by way of being the owner or having some privilege).

Table 35-27. `foreign_table_options` Columns

Name	Data Type	Description

Name	Data Type	Description
foreign_table_catalog	sql_identifier	Name of the database that contains the foreign table (always the current database)
foreign_table_schema	sql_identifier	Name of the schema that contains the foreign table
foreign_table_name	sql_identifier	Name of the foreign table
option_name	sql_identifier	Name of an option
option_value	character_data	Value of the option

35.30. `foreign_tables`

The view `foreign_tables` contains all foreign tables defined in the current database. Only those foreign tables are shown that the current user has access to (by way of being the owner or having some privilege).

Table 35-28. `foreign_tables` Columns

Name	Data Type	Description
foreign_table_catalog	sql_identifier	Name of the database that the foreign table is defined in (always the current database)
foreign_table_schema	sql_identifier	Name of the schema that contains the foreign table
foreign_table_name	sql_identifier	Name of the foreign table
foreign_server_catalog	sql_identifier	Name of the database that the foreign server is defined in (always the current database)
foreign_server_name	sql_identifier	Name of the foreign server

35.31. `key_column_usage`

The view `key_column_usage` identifies all columns in the current database that are restricted by some unique, primary key, or foreign key constraint. Check constraints are not included in this view. Only those columns are shown that the current user has access to, by way of being the owner or having some privilege.

Table 35-29. `key_column_usage` Columns

Name	Data Type	Description
constraint_catalog	sql_identifier	Name of the database that contains the constraint (always the current database)

Name	Data Type	Description
constraint_schema	sql_identifier	Name of the schema that contains the constraint
constraint_name	sql_identifier	Name of the constraint
table_catalog	sql_identifier	Name of the database that contains the table that contains the column that is restricted by this constraint (always the current database)
table_schema	sql_identifier	Name of the schema that contains the table that contains the column that is restricted by this constraint
table_name	sql_identifier	Name of the table that contains the column that is restricted by this constraint
column_name	sql_identifier	Name of the column that is restricted by this constraint
ordinal_position	cardinal_number	Ordinal position of the column within the constraint key (count starts at 1)
position_in_unique_constraint	cardinal_number	For a foreign-key constraint, ordinal position of the referenced column within its unique constraint (count starts at 1); otherwise null

35.32. parameters

The view parameters contains information about the parameters (arguments) of all functions in the current database. Only those functions are shown that the current user has access to (by way of being the owner or having some privilege).

Table 35-30. parameters Columns

Name	Data Type	Description
specific_catalog	sql_identifier	Name of the database containing the function (always the current database)
specific_schema	sql_identifier	Name of the schema containing the function

Name	Data Type	Description
specific_name	sql_identifier	The "specific name" of the function. See Section 35.40 for more information.
ordinal_position	cardinal_number	Ordinal position of the parameter in the argument list of the function (count starts at 1)
parameter_mode	character_data	IN for input parameter, OUT for output parameter, and INOUT for input/output parameter.
is_result	yes_or_no	Applies to a feature not available in PostgreSQL
as_locator	yes_or_no	Applies to a feature not available in PostgreSQL
parameter_name	sql_identifier	Name of the parameter, or null if the parameter has no name
data_type	character_data	Data type of the parameter, if it is a built-in type, or ARRAY if it is some array (in that case, see the view element_types), else USER-DEFINED (in that case, the type is identified in udt_name and associated columns).
character_maximum_length	cardinal_number	Always null, since this information is not applied to parameter data types in PostgreSQL
character_octet_length	cardinal_number	Always null, since this information is not applied to parameter data types in PostgreSQL
character_set_catalog	sql_identifier	Applies to a feature not available in PostgreSQL
character_set_schema	sql_identifier	Applies to a feature not available in PostgreSQL
character_set_name	sql_identifier	Applies to a feature not available in PostgreSQL
collation_catalog	sql_identifier	Always null, since this information is not applied to parameter data types in PostgreSQL

Name	Data Type	Description
collation_schema	sql_identifier	Always null, since this information is not applied to parameter data types in PostgreSQL
collation_name	sql_identifier	Always null, since this information is not applied to parameter data types in PostgreSQL
numeric_precision	cardinal_number	Always null, since this information is not applied to parameter data types in PostgreSQL
numeric_precision_radix	cardinal_number	Always null, since this information is not applied to parameter data types in PostgreSQL
numeric_scale	cardinal_number	Always null, since this information is not applied to parameter data types in PostgreSQL
datetime_precision	cardinal_number	Always null, since this information is not applied to parameter data types in PostgreSQL
interval_type	character_data	Always null, since this information is not applied to parameter data types in PostgreSQL
interval_precision	cardinal_number	Always null, since this information is not applied to parameter data types in PostgreSQL
udt_catalog	sql_identifier	Name of the database that the data type of the parameter is defined in (always the current database)
udt_schema	sql_identifier	Name of the schema that the data type of the parameter is defined in
udt_name	sql_identifier	Name of the data type of the parameter
scope_catalog	sql_identifier	Applies to a feature not available in PostgreSQL

Name	Data Type	Description
scope_schema	sql_identifier	Applies to a feature not available in PostgreSQL
scope_name	sql_identifier	Applies to a feature not available in PostgreSQL
maximum_cardinality	cardinal_number	Always null, because arrays always have unlimited maximum cardinality in PostgreSQL
dtd_identifier	sql_identifier	An identifier of the data type descriptor of the parameter, unique among the data type descriptors pertaining to the function. This is mainly useful for joining with other instances of such identifiers. (The specific format of the identifier is not defined and not guaranteed to remain the same in future versions.)
parameter_default	character_data	The default expression of the parameter, or null if none or if the function is not owned by a currently enabled role.

35.33. referential_constraints

The view referential_constraints contains all referential (foreign key) constraints in the current database. Only those constraints are shown for which the current user has write access to the referencing table (by way of being the owner or having some privilege other than SELECT).

Table 35-31. referential_constraints Columns

Name	Data Type	Description
constraint_catalog	sql_identifier	Name of the database containing the constraint (always the current database)
constraint_schema	sql_identifier	Name of the schema containing the constraint
constraint_name	sql_identifier	Name of the constraint
unique_constraint_catalog	sql_identifier	Name of the database that contains the unique or primary key constraint that the foreign key constraint references (always the current database)

Name	Data Type	Description
unique_constraint_schema	sql_identifier	Name of the schema that contains the unique or primary key constraint that the foreign key constraint references
unique_constraint_name	sql_identifier	Name of the unique or primary key constraint that the foreign key constraint references
match_option	character_data	Match option of the foreign key constraint: FULL, PARTIAL, or NONE.
update_rule	character_data	Update rule of the foreign key constraint: CASCADE, SET NULL, SET DEFAULT, RESTRICT, or NO ACTION.
delete_rule	character_data	Delete rule of the foreign key constraint: CASCADE, SET NULL, SET DEFAULT, RESTRICT, or NO ACTION.

35.34. `role_column_grants`

The view `role_column_grants` identifies all privileges granted on columns where the grantor or grantee is a currently enabled role. Further information can be found under `column_privileges`. The only effective difference between this view and `column_privileges` is that this view omits columns that have been made accessible to the current user by way of a grant to PUBLIC.

Table 35-32. `role_column_grants` Columns

Name	Data Type	Description
grantor	sql_identifier	Name of the role that granted the privilege
grantee	sql_identifier	Name of the role that the privilege was granted to
table_catalog	sql_identifier	Name of the database that contains the table that contains the column (always the current database)
table_schema	sql_identifier	Name of the schema that contains the table that contains the column
table_name	sql_identifier	Name of the table that contains the column

Name	Data Type	Description
column_name	sql_identifier	Name of the column
privilege_type	character_data	Type of the privilege: SELECT, INSERT, UPDATE, or REFERENCES
is_grantable	yes_or_no	YES if the privilege is grantable, NO if not

35.35. `role_routine_grants`

The view `role_routine_grants` identifies all privileges granted on functions where the grantor or grantee is a currently enabled role. Further information can be found under `routine_privileges`. The only effective difference between this view and `routine_privileges` is that this view omits functions that have been made accessible to the current user by way of a grant to PUBLIC.

Table 35-33. `role_routine_grants` Columns

Name	Data Type	Description
grantor	sql_identifier	Name of the role that granted the privilege
grantee	sql_identifier	Name of the role that the privilege was granted to
specific_catalog	sql_identifier	Name of the database containing the function (always the current database)
specific_schema	sql_identifier	Name of the schema containing the function
specific_name	sql_identifier	The "specific name" of the function. See Section 35.40 for more information.
routine_catalog	sql_identifier	Name of the database containing the function (always the current database)
routine_schema	sql_identifier	Name of the schema containing the function
routine_name	sql_identifier	Name of the function (might be duplicated in case of overloading)
privilege_type	character_data	Always EXECUTE (the only privilege type for functions)
is_grantable	yes_or_no	YES if the privilege is grantable, NO if not

35.36. `role_table_grants`

The view `role_table_grants` identifies all privileges granted on tables or views where the grantor or grantee is a currently enabled role. Further information can be found under `table_privileges`. The only effective difference between this view and `table_privileges` is that this view omits tables that have been made accessible to the current user by way of a grant to `PUBLIC`.

Table 35-34. `role_table_grants` Columns

Name	Data Type	Description
grantor	sql_identifier	Name of the role that granted the privilege
grantee	sql_identifier	Name of the role that the privilege was granted to
table_catalog	sql_identifier	Name of the database that contains the table (always the current database)
table_schema	sql_identifier	Name of the schema that contains the table
table_name	sql_identifier	Name of the table
privilege_type	character_data	Type of the privilege: SELECT, INSERT, UPDATE, DELETE, TRUNCATE, REFERENCES, or TRIGGER
is_grantable	yes_or_no	YES if the privilege is grantable, NO if not
with_hierarchy	yes_or_no	In the SQL standard, WITH HIERARCHY OPTION is a separate (sub-)privilege allowing certain operations on table inheritance hierarchies. In PostgreSQL, this is included in the SELECT privilege, so this column shows YES if the privilege is SELECT, else NO.

35.37. `role_udt_grants`

The view `role_udt_grants` is intended to identify USAGE privileges granted on user-defined types where the grantor or grantee is a currently enabled role. Further information can be found under `udt_privileges`. The only effective difference between this view and `udt_privileges` is that this view omits objects that have been made accessible to the current user by way of a grant to `PUBLIC`. Since data types do not have real privileges in PostgreSQL, but only an implicit grant to `PUBLIC`, this view is empty.

Table 35-35. `role_udt_grants` Columns

Name	Data Type	Description
grantor	sql_identifier	The name of the role that granted the privilege
grantee	sql_identifier	The name of the role that the privilege was granted to
udt_catalog	sql_identifier	Name of the database containing the type (always the current database)
udt_schema	sql_identifier	Name of the schema containing the type
udt_name	sql_identifier	Name of the type
privilege_type	character_data	Always TYPE USAGE
is_grantable	yes_or_no	YES if the privilege is grantable, NO if not

35.38. `role_usage_grants`

The view `role_usage_grants` identifies USAGE privileges granted on various kinds of objects where the grantor or grantee is a currently enabled role. Further information can be found under `usage_privileges`. The only effective difference between this view and `usage_privileges` is that this view omits objects that have been made accessible to the current user by way of a grant to PUBLIC.

Table 35-36. `role_usage_grants` Columns

Name	Data Type	Description
grantor	sql_identifier	The name of the role that granted the privilege
grantee	sql_identifier	The name of the role that the privilege was granted to
object_catalog	sql_identifier	Name of the database containing the object (always the current database)
object_schema	sql_identifier	Name of the schema containing the object, if applicable, else an empty string
object_name	sql_identifier	Name of the object
object_type	character_data	COLLATION or DOMAIN or FOREIGN DATA WRAPPER or FOREIGN SERVER or SEQUENCE
privilege_type	character_data	Always USAGE

Name	Data Type	Description
is_grantable	yes_or_no	YES if the privilege is grantable, NO if not

35.39. `routine_privileges`

The view `routine_privileges` identifies all privileges granted on functions to a currently enabled role or by a currently enabled role. There is one row for each combination of function, grantor, and grantee.

Table 35-37. `routine_privileges` Columns

Name	Data Type	Description
grantor	sql_identifier	Name of the role that granted the privilege
grantee	sql_identifier	Name of the role that the privilege was granted to
specific_catalog	sql_identifier	Name of the database containing the function (always the current database)
specific_schema	sql_identifier	Name of the schema containing the function
specific_name	sql_identifier	The "specific name" of the function. See Section 35.40 for more information.
routine_catalog	sql_identifier	Name of the database containing the function (always the current database)
routine_schema	sql_identifier	Name of the schema containing the function
routine_name	sql_identifier	Name of the function (might be duplicated in case of overloading)
privilege_type	character_data	Always EXECUTE (the only privilege type for functions)
is_grantable	yes_or_no	YES if the privilege is grantable, NO if not

35.40. `routines`

The view `routines` contains all functions in the current database. Only those functions are shown that the current user has access to (by way of being the owner or having some privilege).

Table 35-38. routines Columns

Name	Data Type	Description
specific_catalog	sql_identifier	Name of the database containing the function (always the current database)
specific_schema	sql_identifier	Name of the schema containing the function
specific_name	sql_identifier	The "specific name" of the function. This is a name that uniquely identifies the function in the schema, even if the real name of the function is overloaded. The format of the specific name is not defined, it should only be used to compare it to other instances of specific routine names.
routine_catalog	sql_identifier	Name of the database containing the function (always the current database)
routine_schema	sql_identifier	Name of the schema containing the function
routine_name	sql_identifier	Name of the function (might be duplicated in case of overloading)
routine_type	character_data	Always FUNCTION (In the future there might be other types of routines.)
module_catalog	sql_identifier	Applies to a feature not available in PostgreSQL
module_schema	sql_identifier	Applies to a feature not available in PostgreSQL
module_name	sql_identifier	Applies to a feature not available in PostgreSQL
udt_catalog	sql_identifier	Applies to a feature not available in PostgreSQL
udt_schema	sql_identifier	Applies to a feature not available in PostgreSQL
udt_name	sql_identifier	Applies to a feature not available in PostgreSQL

Name	Data Type	Description
data_type	character_data	Return data type of the function, if it is a built-in type, or ARRAY if it is some array (in that case, see the view element_types), else USER-DEFINED (in that case, the type is identified in type_udt_name and associated columns).
character_maximum_length	cardinal_number	Always null, since this information is not applied to return data types in PostgreSQL
character_octet_length	cardinal_number	Always null, since this information is not applied to return data types in PostgreSQL
character_set_catalog	sql_identifier	Applies to a feature not available in PostgreSQL
character_set_schema	sql_identifier	Applies to a feature not available in PostgreSQL
character_set_name	sql_identifier	Applies to a feature not available in PostgreSQL
collation_catalog	sql_identifier	Always null, since this information is not applied to return data types in PostgreSQL
collation_schema	sql_identifier	Always null, since this information is not applied to return data types in PostgreSQL
collation_name	sql_identifier	Always null, since this information is not applied to return data types in PostgreSQL
numeric_precision	cardinal_number	Always null, since this information is not applied to return data types in PostgreSQL
numeric_precision_radix	cardinal_number	Always null, since this information is not applied to return data types in PostgreSQL
numeric_scale	cardinal_number	Always null, since this information is not applied to return data types in PostgreSQL
datetime_precision	cardinal_number	Always null, since this information is not applied to return data types in PostgreSQL

Name	Data Type	Description
interval_type	character_data	Always null, since this information is not applied to return data types in PostgreSQL
interval_precision	cardinal_number	Always null, since this information is not applied to return data types in PostgreSQL
type_udt_catalog	sql_identifier	Name of the database that the return data type of the function is defined in (always the current database)
type_udt_schema	sql_identifier	Name of the schema that the return data type of the function is defined in
type_udt_name	sql_identifier	Name of the return data type of the function
scope_catalog	sql_identifier	Applies to a feature not available in PostgreSQL
scope_schema	sql_identifier	Applies to a feature not available in PostgreSQL
scope_name	sql_identifier	Applies to a feature not available in PostgreSQL
maximum_cardinality	cardinal_number	Always null, because arrays always have unlimited maximum cardinality in PostgreSQL
dtd_identifier	sql_identifier	An identifier of the data type descriptor of the return data type of this function, unique among the data type descriptors pertaining to the function. This is mainly useful for joining with other instances of such identifiers. (The specific format of the identifier is not defined and not guaranteed to remain the same in future versions.)
routine_body	character_data	If the function is an SQL function, then SQL, else EXTERNAL.

Name	Data Type	Description
routine_definition	character_data	The source text of the function (null if the function is not owned by a currently enabled role). (According to the SQL standard, this column is only applicable if routine_body is SQL, but in PostgreSQL it will contain whatever source text was specified when the function was created.)
external_name	character_data	If this function is a C function, then the external name (link symbol) of the function; else null. (This works out to be the same value that is shown in routine_definition.)
external_language	character_data	The language the function is written in
parameter_style	character_data	Always GENERAL (The SQL standard defines other parameter styles, which are not available in PostgreSQL.)
is_deterministic	yes_or_no	If the function is declared immutable (called deterministic in the SQL standard), then YES, else NO. (You cannot query the other volatility levels available in PostgreSQL through the information schema.)
sql_data_access	character_data	Always MODIFIES, meaning that the function possibly modifies SQL data. This information is not useful for PostgreSQL.
is_null_call	yes_or_no	If the function automatically returns null if any of its arguments are null, then YES, else NO.
sql_path	character_data	Applies to a feature not available in PostgreSQL

Name	Data Type	Description
schema_level_routine	yes_or_no	Always YES (The opposite would be a method of a user-defined type, which is a feature not available in PostgreSQL.)
max_dynamic_result_sets	cardinal_number	Applies to a feature not available in PostgreSQL
is_user_defined_cast	yes_or_no	Applies to a feature not available in PostgreSQL
is_implicitly_invocable	yes_or_no	Applies to a feature not available in PostgreSQL
security_type	character_data	If the function runs with the privileges of the current user, then INVOKER, if the function runs with the privileges of the user who defined it, then DEFINER.
to_sql_specific_catalog	sql_identifier	Applies to a feature not available in PostgreSQL
to_sql_specific_schema	sql_identifier	Applies to a feature not available in PostgreSQL
to_sql_specific_name	sql_identifier	Applies to a feature not available in PostgreSQL
as_locator	yes_or_no	Applies to a feature not available in PostgreSQL
created	time_stamp	Applies to a feature not available in PostgreSQL
last_altered	time_stamp	Applies to a feature not available in PostgreSQL
new_savepoint_level	yes_or_no	Applies to a feature not available in PostgreSQL
is_udt_dependent	yes_or_no	Currently always NO. The alternative YES applies to a feature not available in PostgreSQL.
result_cast_from_data_type	character_data	Applies to a feature not available in PostgreSQL
result_cast_as_locator	yes_or_no	Applies to a feature not available in PostgreSQL
result_cast_char_max_length	cardinal_number	Applies to a feature not available in PostgreSQL
result_cast_char_octet_length	character_data	Applies to a feature not available in PostgreSQL

Name	Data Type	Description
result_cast_char_set_catalog	sql_identifier	Applies to a feature not available in PostgreSQL
result_cast_char_set_schema	sql_identifier	Applies to a feature not available in PostgreSQL
result_cast_char_set_name	sql_identifier	Applies to a feature not available in PostgreSQL
result_cast_collation_catalog	sql_identifier	Applies to a feature not available in PostgreSQL
result_cast_collation_schema	sql_identifier	Applies to a feature not available in PostgreSQL
result_cast_collation_name	sql_identifier	Applies to a feature not available in PostgreSQL
result_cast_numeric_precision	cardinal_number	Applies to a feature not available in PostgreSQL
result_cast_numeric_precision_radix	cardinal_number	Applies to a feature not available in PostgreSQL
result_cast_numeric_scale	cardinal_number	Applies to a feature not available in PostgreSQL
result_cast_datetime_precision	character_data	Applies to a feature not available in PostgreSQL
result_cast_interval_type	character_data	Applies to a feature not available in PostgreSQL
result_cast_interval_precision	cardinal_number	Applies to a feature not available in PostgreSQL
result_cast_type_udt_catalog	sql_identifier	Applies to a feature not available in PostgreSQL
result_cast_type_udt_schema	sql_identifier	Applies to a feature not available in PostgreSQL
result_cast_type_udt_name	sql_identifier	Applies to a feature not available in PostgreSQL
result_cast_scope_catalog	sql_identifier	Applies to a feature not available in PostgreSQL
result_cast_scope_schema	sql_identifier	Applies to a feature not available in PostgreSQL
result_cast_scope_name	sql_identifier	Applies to a feature not available in PostgreSQL
result_cast_maximum_cardinality	cardinal_number	Applies to a feature not available in PostgreSQL
result_cast_dtd_identifier	sql_identifier	Applies to a feature not available in PostgreSQL

35.41. `schemata`

The view `schemata` contains all schemas in the current database that the current user has access to (by way of being the owner or having some privilege).

Table 35-39. `schemata` Columns

Name	Data Type	Description
catalog_name	sql_identifier	Name of the database that the schema is contained in (always the current database)
schema_name	sql_identifier	Name of the schema
schema_owner	sql_identifier	Name of the owner of the schema
default_character_set_catalog	sql_identifier	Applies to a feature not available in PostgreSQL
default_character_set_schema	sql_identifier	Applies to a feature not available in PostgreSQL
default_character_set_name	sql_identifier	Applies to a feature not available in PostgreSQL
sql_path	character_data	Applies to a feature not available in PostgreSQL

35.42. `sequences`

The view `sequences` contains all sequences defined in the current database. Only those sequences are shown that the current user has access to (by way of being the owner or having some privilege).

Table 35-40. `sequences` Columns

Name	Data Type	Description
sequence_catalog	sql_identifier	Name of the database that contains the sequence (always the current database)
sequence_schema	sql_identifier	Name of the schema that contains the sequence
sequence_name	sql_identifier	Name of the sequence
data_type	character_data	The data type of the sequence. In PostgreSQL, this is currently always `bigint`.

Name	Data Type	Description
numeric_precision	cardinal_number	This column contains the (declared or implicit) precision of the sequence data type (see above). The precision indicates the number of significant digits. It can be expressed in decimal (base 10) or binary (base 2) terms, as specified in the column numeric_precision_radix.
numeric_precision_radix	cardinal_number	This column indicates in which base the values in the columns numeric_precision and numeric_scale are expressed. The value is either 2 or 10.
numeric_scale	cardinal_number	This column contains the (declared or implicit) scale of the sequence data type (see above). The scale indicates the number of significant digits to the right of the decimal point. It can be expressed in decimal (base 10) or binary (base 2) terms, as specified in the column numeric_precision_radix.
start_value	character_data	The start value of the sequence
minimum_value	character_data	The minimum value of the sequence
maximum_value	character_data	The maximum value of the sequence
increment	character_data	The increment of the sequence
cycle_option	yes_or_no	YES if the sequence cycles, else NO

Note that in accordance with the SQL standard, the start, minimum, maximum, and increment values are returned as character strings.

35.43. sql_features

The table sql_features contains information about which formal features defined in the SQL standard are supported by PostgreSQL. This is the same information that is presented in Appendix D. There you can also find some additional background information.

Table 35-41. sql_features Columns

Name	Data Type	Description
feature_id	character_data	Identifier string of the feature
feature_name	character_data	Descriptive name of the feature
sub_feature_id	character_data	Identifier string of the subfeature, or a zero-length string if not a subfeature
sub_feature_name	character_data	Descriptive name of the subfeature, or a zero-length string if not a subfeature
is_supported	yes_or_no	YES if the feature is fully supported by the current version of PostgreSQL, NO if not
is_verified_by	character_data	Always null, since the PostgreSQL development group does not perform formal testing of feature conformance
comments	character_data	Possibly a comment about the supported status of the feature

35.44. `sql_implementation_info`

The table `sql_implementation_info` contains information about various aspects that are left implementation-defined by the SQL standard. This information is primarily intended for use in the context of the ODBC interface; users of other interfaces will probably find this information to be of little use. For this reason, the individual implementation information items are not described here; you will find them in the description of the ODBC interface.

Table 35-42. `sql_implementation_info` Columns

Name	Data Type	Description
implementation_info_id	character_data	Identifier string of the implementation information item
implementation_info_name	character_data	Descriptive name of the implementation information item
integer_value	cardinal_number	Value of the implementation information item, or null if the value is contained in the column character_value

Name	Data Type	Description
character_value	character_data	Value of the implementation information item, or null if the value is contained in the column integer_value
comments	character_data	Possibly a comment pertaining to the implementation information item

35.45. sql_languages

The table sql_languages contains one row for each SQL language binding that is supported by PostgreSQL. PostgreSQL supports direct SQL and embedded SQL in C; that is all you will learn from this table.

This table was removed from the SQL standard in SQL:2008, so there are no entries referring to standards later than SQL:2003.

Table 35-43. sql_languages Columns

Name	Data Type	Description
sql_language_source	character_data	The name of the source of the language definition; always ISO 9075, that is, the SQL standard
sql_language_year	character_data	The year the standard referenced in sql_language_source was approved.
sql_language_conformance	character_data	The standard conformance level for the language binding. For ISO 9075:2003 this is always CORE.
sql_language_integrity	character_data	Always null (This value is relevant to an earlier version of the SQL standard.)
sql_language_implementation	character_data	Always null
sql_language_binding_style	character_data	The language binding style, either DIRECT or EMBEDDED
sql_language_programming_language	character_data	The programming language, if the binding style is EMBEDDED, else null. PostgreSQL only supports the language C.

35.46. `sql_packages`

The table `sql_packages` contains information about which feature packages defined in the SQL standard are supported by PostgreSQL. Refer to Appendix D for background information on feature packages.

Table 35-44. `sql_packages` Columns

Name	Data Type	Description
`feature_id`	`character_data`	Identifier string of the package
`feature_name`	`character_data`	Descriptive name of the package
`is_supported`	`yes_or_no`	YES if the package is fully supported by the current version of PostgreSQL, NO if not
`is_verified_by`	`character_data`	Always null, since the PostgreSQL development group does not perform formal testing of feature conformance
`comments`	`character_data`	Possibly a comment about the supported status of the package

35.47. `sql_parts`

The table `sql_parts` contains information about which of the several parts of the SQL standard are supported by PostgreSQL.

Table 35-45. `sql_parts` Columns

Name	Data Type	Description
`feature_id`	`character_data`	An identifier string containing the number of the part
`feature_name`	`character_data`	Descriptive name of the part
`is_supported`	`yes_or_no`	YES if the part is fully supported by the current version of PostgreSQL, NO if not
`is_verified_by`	`character_data`	Always null, since the PostgreSQL development group does not perform formal testing of feature conformance
`comments`	`character_data`	Possibly a comment about the supported status of the part

35.48. `sql_sizing`

The table `sql_sizing` contains information about various size limits and maximum values in PostgreSQL. This information is primarily intended for use in the context of the ODBC interface; users of other interfaces will probably find this information to be of little use. For this reason, the individual sizing items are not described here; you will find them in the description of the ODBC interface.

Table 35-46. `sql_sizing` Columns

Name	Data Type	Description
sizing_id	cardinal_number	Identifier of the sizing item
sizing_name	character_data	Descriptive name of the sizing item
supported_value	cardinal_number	Value of the sizing item, or 0 if the size is unlimited or cannot be determined, or null if the features for which the sizing item is applicable are not supported
comments	character_data	Possibly a comment pertaining to the sizing item

35.49. `sql_sizing_profiles`

The table `sql_sizing_profiles` contains information about the `sql_sizing` values that are required by various profiles of the SQL standard. PostgreSQL does not track any SQL profiles, so this table is empty.

Table 35-47. `sql_sizing_profiles` Columns

Name	Data Type	Description
sizing_id	cardinal_number	Identifier of the sizing item
sizing_name	character_data	Descriptive name of the sizing item
profile_id	character_data	Identifier string of a profile
required_value	cardinal_number	The value required by the SQL profile for the sizing item, or 0 if the profile places no limit on the sizing item, or null if the profile does not require any of the features for which the sizing item is applicable
comments	character_data	Possibly a comment pertaining to the sizing item within the profile

35.50. `table_constraints`

The view `table_constraints` contains all constraints belonging to tables that the current user owns or has some privilege other than `SELECT` on.

Table 35-48. `table_constraints` Columns

Name	Data Type	Description
constraint_catalog	sql_identifier	Name of the database that contains the constraint (always the current database)
constraint_schema	sql_identifier	Name of the schema that contains the constraint
constraint_name	sql_identifier	Name of the constraint
table_catalog	sql_identifier	Name of the database that contains the table (always the current database)
table_schema	sql_identifier	Name of the schema that contains the table
table_name	sql_identifier	Name of the table
constraint_type	character_data	Type of the constraint: CHECK, FOREIGN KEY, PRIMARY KEY, or UNIQUE
is_deferrable	yes_or_no	YES if the constraint is deferrable, NO if not
initially_deferred	yes_or_no	YES if the constraint is deferrable and initially deferred, NO if not

35.51. `table_privileges`

The view `table_privileges` identifies all privileges granted on tables or views to a currently enabled role or by a currently enabled role. There is one row for each combination of table, grantor, and grantee.

Table 35-49. `table_privileges` Columns

Name	Data Type	Description
grantor	sql_identifier	Name of the role that granted the privilege
grantee	sql_identifier	Name of the role that the privilege was granted to
table_catalog	sql_identifier	Name of the database that contains the table (always the current database)

Name	Data Type	Description
table_schema	sql_identifier	Name of the schema that contains the table
table_name	sql_identifier	Name of the table
privilege_type	character_data	Type of the privilege: SELECT, INSERT, UPDATE, DELETE, TRUNCATE, REFERENCES, or TRIGGER
is_grantable	yes_or_no	YES if the privilege is grantable, NO if not
with_hierarchy	yes_or_no	In the SQL standard, WITH HIERARCHY OPTION is a separate (sub-)privilege allowing certain operations on table inheritance hierarchies. In PostgreSQL, this is included in the SELECT privilege, so this column shows YES if the privilege is SELECT, else NO.

35.52. `tables`

The view `tables` contains all tables and views defined in the current database. Only those tables and views are shown that the current user has access to (by way of being the owner or having some privilege).

Table 35-50. `tables` Columns

Name	Data Type	Description
table_catalog	sql_identifier	Name of the database that contains the table (always the current database)
table_schema	sql_identifier	Name of the schema that contains the table
table_name	sql_identifier	Name of the table
table_type	character_data	Type of the table: BASE TABLE for a persistent base table (the normal table type), VIEW for a view, FOREIGN TABLE for a foreign table, or LOCAL TEMPORARY for a temporary table
self_referencing_column_name	sql_identifier	Applies to a feature not available in PostgreSQL

Name	Data Type	Description
reference_generation	character_data	Applies to a feature not available in PostgreSQL
user_defined_type_catalog	sql_identifier	If the table is a typed table, the name of the database that contains the underlying data type (always the current database), else null.
user_defined_type_schema	sql_identifier	If the table is a typed table, the name of the schema that contains the underlying data type, else null.
user_defined_type_name	sql_identifier	If the table is a typed table, the name of the underlying data type, else null.
is_insertable_into	yes_or_no	YES if the table is insertable into, NO if not (Base tables are always insertable into, views not necessarily.)
is_typed	yes_or_no	YES if the table is a typed table, NO if not
commit_action	character_data	Not yet implemented

35.53. `transforms`

The view `transforms` contains information about the transforms defined in the current database. More precisely, it contains a row for each function contained in a transform (the "from SQL" or "to SQL" function).

Table 35-51. `transforms` Columns

Name	Data Type	Description
udt_catalog	sql_identifier	Name of the database that contains the type the transform is for (always the current database)
udt_schema	sql_identifier	Name of the schema that contains the type the transform is for
udt_name	sql_identifier	Name of the type the transform is for
specific_catalog	sql_identifier	Name of the database containing the function (always the current database)

Name	Data Type	Description
specific_schema	sql_identifier	Name of the schema containing the function
specific_name	sql_identifier	The "specific name" of the function. See Section 35.40 for more information.
group_name	sql_identifier	The SQL standard allows defining transforms in "groups", and selecting a group at run time. PostgreSQL does not support this. Instead, transforms are specific to a language. As a compromise, this field contains the language the transform is for.
transform_type	character_data	FROM SQL or TO SQL

35.54. `triggered_update_columns`

For triggers in the current database that specify a column list (like UPDATE OF column1, column2), the view triggered_update_columns identifies these columns. Triggers that do not specify a column list are not included in this view. Only those columns are shown that the current user owns or has some privilege other than SELECT on.

Table 35-52. `triggered_update_columns` Columns

Name	Data Type	Description
trigger_catalog	sql_identifier	Name of the database that contains the trigger (always the current database)
trigger_schema	sql_identifier	Name of the schema that contains the trigger
trigger_name	sql_identifier	Name of the trigger
event_object_catalog	sql_identifier	Name of the database that contains the table that the trigger is defined on (always the current database)
event_object_schema	sql_identifier	Name of the schema that contains the table that the trigger is defined on
event_object_table	sql_identifier	Name of the table that the trigger is defined on

Name	Data Type	Description
event_object_column	sql_identifier	Name of the column that the trigger is defined on

35.55. `triggers`

The view `triggers` contains all triggers defined in the current database on tables and views that the current user owns or has some privilege other than `SELECT` on.

Table 35-53. `triggers` Columns

Name	Data Type	Description
trigger_catalog	sql_identifier	Name of the database that contains the trigger (always the current database)
trigger_schema	sql_identifier	Name of the schema that contains the trigger
trigger_name	sql_identifier	Name of the trigger
event_manipulation	character_data	Event that fires the trigger (INSERT, UPDATE, or DELETE)
event_object_catalog	sql_identifier	Name of the database that contains the table that the trigger is defined on (always the current database)
event_object_schema	sql_identifier	Name of the schema that contains the table that the trigger is defined on
event_object_table	sql_identifier	Name of the table that the trigger is defined on
action_order	cardinal_number	Not yet implemented
action_condition	character_data	WHEN condition of the trigger, null if none (also null if the table is not owned by a currently enabled role)
action_statement	character_data	Statement that is executed by the trigger (currently always EXECUTE PROCEDURE function(...))
action_orientation	character_data	Identifies whether the trigger fires once for each processed row or once for each statement (ROW or STATEMENT)

Name	Data Type	Description
action_timing	character_data	Time at which the trigger fires (BEFORE, AFTER, or INSTEAD OF)
action_reference_old_table	sql_identifier	Applies to a feature not available in PostgreSQL
action_reference_new_table	sql_identifier	Applies to a feature not available in PostgreSQL
action_reference_old_row	sql_identifier	Applies to a feature not available in PostgreSQL
action_reference_new_row	sql_identifier	Applies to a feature not available in PostgreSQL
created	time_stamp	Applies to a feature not available in PostgreSQL

Triggers in PostgreSQL have two incompatibilities with the SQL standard that affect the representation in the information schema. First, trigger names are local to each table in PostgreSQL, rather than being independent schema objects. Therefore there can be duplicate trigger names defined in one schema, so long as they belong to different tables. (trigger_catalog and trigger_schema are really the values pertaining to the table that the trigger is defined on.) Second, triggers can be defined to fire on multiple events in PostgreSQL (e.g., ON INSERT OR UPDATE), whereas the SQL standard only allows one. If a trigger is defined to fire on multiple events, it is represented as multiple rows in the information schema, one for each type of event. As a consequence of these two issues, the primary key of the view triggers is really (trigger_catalog, trigger_schema, event_object_table, trigger_name, event_manipulation) instead of (trigger_catalog, trigger_schema, trigger_name), which is what the SQL standard specifies. Nonetheless, if you define your triggers in a manner that conforms with the SQL standard (trigger names unique in the schema and only one event type per trigger), this will not affect you.

> **Note:** Prior to PostgreSQL 9.1, this view's columns action_timing, action_reference_old_table, action_reference_new_table, action_reference_old_row, and action_reference_new_row were named condition_timing, condition_reference_old_table, condition_reference_new_table, condition_reference_old_row, and condition_reference_new_row respectively. That was how they were named in the SQL:1999 standard. The new naming conforms to SQL:2003 and later.

35.56. udt_privileges

The view udt_privileges identifies USAGE privileges granted on user-defined types to a currently enabled role or by a currently enabled role. There is one row for each combination of type, grantor, and grantee. This view shows only composite types (see under Section 35.58 for why); see Section 35.57 for domain privileges.

Table 35-54. `udt_privileges` Columns

Name	Data Type	Description
grantor	sql_identifier	Name of the role that granted the privilege
grantee	sql_identifier	Name of the role that the privilege was granted to
udt_catalog	sql_identifier	Name of the database containing the type (always the current database)
udt_schema	sql_identifier	Name of the schema containing the type
udt_name	sql_identifier	Name of the type
privilege_type	character_data	Always TYPE USAGE
is_grantable	yes_or_no	YES if the privilege is grantable, NO if not

35.57. `usage_privileges`

The view `usage_privileges` identifies USAGE privileges granted on various kinds of objects to a currently enabled role or by a currently enabled role. In PostgreSQL, this currently applies to collations, domains, foreign-data wrappers, foreign servers, and sequences. There is one row for each combination of object, grantor, and grantee.

Since collations do not have real privileges in PostgreSQL, this view shows implicit non-grantable USAGE privileges granted by the owner to PUBLIC for all collations. The other object types, however, show real privileges.

In PostgreSQL, sequences also support SELECT and UPDATE privileges in addition to the USAGE privilege. These are nonstandard and therefore not visible in the information schema.

Table 35-55. `usage_privileges` Columns

Name	Data Type	Description
grantor	sql_identifier	Name of the role that granted the privilege
grantee	sql_identifier	Name of the role that the privilege was granted to
object_catalog	sql_identifier	Name of the database containing the object (always the current database)
object_schema	sql_identifier	Name of the schema containing the object, if applicable, else an empty string
object_name	sql_identifier	Name of the object

Name	Data Type	Description
`object_type`	`character_data`	`COLLATION` or `DOMAIN` or `FOREIGN DATA WRAPPER` or `FOREIGN SERVER` or `SEQUENCE`
`privilege_type`	`character_data`	Always `USAGE`
`is_grantable`	`yes_or_no`	`YES` if the privilege is grantable, `NO` if not

35.58. `user_defined_types`

The view `user_defined_types` currently contains all composite types defined in the current database. Only those types are shown that the current user has access to (by way of being the owner or having some privilege).

SQL knows about two kinds of user-defined types: structured types (also known as composite types in PostgreSQL) and distinct types (not implemented in PostgreSQL). To be future-proof, use the column `user_defined_type_category` to differentiate between these. Other user-defined types such as base types and enums, which are PostgreSQL extensions, are not shown here. For domains, see Section 35.22 instead.

Table 35-56. `user_defined_types` Columns

Name	Data Type	Description
`user_defined_type_catalog`	`sql_identifier`	Name of the database that contains the type (always the current database)
`user_defined_type_schema`	`sql_identifier`	Name of the schema that contains the type
`user_defined_type_name`	`sql_identifier`	Name of the type
`user_defined_type_category`	`character_data`	Currently always `STRUCTURED`
`is_instantiable`	`yes_or_no`	Applies to a feature not available in PostgreSQL
`is_final`	`yes_or_no`	Applies to a feature not available in PostgreSQL
`ordering_form`	`character_data`	Applies to a feature not available in PostgreSQL
`ordering_category`	`character_data`	Applies to a feature not available in PostgreSQL
`ordering_routine_catalog`	`sql_identifier`	Applies to a feature not available in PostgreSQL
`ordering_routine_schema`	`sql_identifier`	Applies to a feature not available in PostgreSQL

Name	Data Type	Description
ordering_routine_name	sql_identifier	Applies to a feature not available in PostgreSQL
reference_type	character_data	Applies to a feature not available in PostgreSQL
data_type	character_data	Applies to a feature not available in PostgreSQL
character_maximum_length	cardinal_number	Applies to a feature not available in PostgreSQL
character_octet_length	cardinal_number	Applies to a feature not available in PostgreSQL
character_set_catalog	sql_identifier	Applies to a feature not available in PostgreSQL
character_set_schema	sql_identifier	Applies to a feature not available in PostgreSQL
character_set_name	sql_identifier	Applies to a feature not available in PostgreSQL
collation_catalog	sql_identifier	Applies to a feature not available in PostgreSQL
collation_schema	sql_identifier	Applies to a feature not available in PostgreSQL
collation_name	sql_identifier	Applies to a feature not available in PostgreSQL
numeric_precision	cardinal_number	Applies to a feature not available in PostgreSQL
numeric_precision_radix	cardinal_number	Applies to a feature not available in PostgreSQL
numeric_scale	cardinal_number	Applies to a feature not available in PostgreSQL
datetime_precision	cardinal_number	Applies to a feature not available in PostgreSQL
interval_type	character_data	Applies to a feature not available in PostgreSQL
interval_precision	cardinal_number	Applies to a feature not available in PostgreSQL
source_dtd_identifier	sql_identifier	Applies to a feature not available in PostgreSQL
ref_dtd_identifier	sql_identifier	Applies to a feature not available in PostgreSQL

35.59. `user_mapping_options`

The view `user_mapping_options` contains all the options defined for user mappings in the current database. Only those user mappings are shown where the current user has access to the corresponding foreign server (by way of being the owner or having some privilege).

Table 35-57. `user_mapping_options` Columns

Name	Data Type	Description
authorization_identifier	sql_identifier	Name of the user being mapped, or PUBLIC if the mapping is public
foreign_server_catalog	sql_identifier	Name of the database that the foreign server used by this mapping is defined in (always the current database)
foreign_server_name	sql_identifier	Name of the foreign server used by this mapping
option_name	sql_identifier	Name of an option
option_value	character_data	Value of the option. This column will show as null unless the current user is the user being mapped, or the mapping is for PUBLIC and the current user is the server owner, or the current user is a superuser. The intent is to protect password information stored as user mapping option.

35.60. `user_mappings`

The view `user_mappings` contains all user mappings defined in the current database. Only those user mappings are shown where the current user has access to the corresponding foreign server (by way of being the owner or having some privilege).

Table 35-58. `user_mappings` Columns

Name	Data Type	Description
authorization_identifier	sql_identifier	Name of the user being mapped, or PUBLIC if the mapping is public

Name	Data Type	Description
foreign_server_catalog	sql_identifier	Name of the database that the foreign server used by this mapping is defined in (always the current database)
foreign_server_name	sql_identifier	Name of the foreign server used by this mapping

35.61. `view_column_usage`

The view `view_column_usage` identifies all columns that are used in the query expression of a view (the `SELECT` statement that defines the view). A column is only included if the table that contains the column is owned by a currently enabled role.

Note: Columns of system tables are not included. This should be fixed sometime.

Table 35-59. `view_column_usage` Columns

Name	Data Type	Description
view_catalog	sql_identifier	Name of the database that contains the view (always the current database)
view_schema	sql_identifier	Name of the schema that contains the view
view_name	sql_identifier	Name of the view
table_catalog	sql_identifier	Name of the database that contains the table that contains the column that is used by the view (always the current database)
table_schema	sql_identifier	Name of the schema that contains the table that contains the column that is used by the view
table_name	sql_identifier	Name of the table that contains the column that is used by the view
column_name	sql_identifier	Name of the column that is used by the view

35.62. `view_routine_usage`

The view `view_routine_usage` identifies all routines (functions and procedures) that are used in the query expression of a view (the `SELECT` statement that defines the view). A routine is only included if that routine is owned by a currently enabled role.

Table 35-60. `view_routine_usage` Columns

Name	Data Type	Description
table_catalog	sql_identifier	Name of the database containing the view (always the current database)
table_schema	sql_identifier	Name of the schema containing the view
table_name	sql_identifier	Name of the view
specific_catalog	sql_identifier	Name of the database containing the function (always the current database)
specific_schema	sql_identifier	Name of the schema containing the function
specific_name	sql_identifier	The "specific name" of the function. See Section 35.40 for more information.

35.63. `view_table_usage`

The view `view_table_usage` identifies all tables that are used in the query expression of a view (the `SELECT` statement that defines the view). A table is only included if that table is owned by a currently enabled role.

Note: System tables are not included. This should be fixed sometime.

Table 35-61. `view_table_usage` Columns

Name	Data Type	Description
view_catalog	sql_identifier	Name of the database that contains the view (always the current database)
view_schema	sql_identifier	Name of the schema that contains the view
view_name	sql_identifier	Name of the view

Name	Data Type	Description
table_catalog	sql_identifier	Name of the database that contains the table that is used by the view (always the current database)
table_schema	sql_identifier	Name of the schema that contains the table that is used by the view
table_name	sql_identifier	Name of the table that is used by the view

35.64. `views`

The view `views` contains all views defined in the current database. Only those views are shown that the current user has access to (by way of being the owner or having some privilege).

Table 35-62. `views` Columns

Name	Data Type	Description
table_catalog	sql_identifier	Name of the database that contains the view (always the current database)
table_schema	sql_identifier	Name of the schema that contains the view
table_name	sql_identifier	Name of the view
view_definition	character_data	Query expression defining the view (null if the view is not owned by a currently enabled role)
check_option	character_data	Applies to a feature not available in PostgreSQL
is_updatable	yes_or_no	YES if the view is updatable (allows UPDATE and DELETE), NO if not
is_insertable_into	yes_or_no	YES if the view is insertable into (allows INSERT), NO if not
is_trigger_updatable	yes_or_no	YES if the view has an INSTEAD OF UPDATE trigger defined on it, NO if not
is_trigger_deletable	yes_or_no	YES if the view has an INSTEAD OF DELETE trigger defined on it, NO if not

Name	Data Type	Description
is_trigger_insertable_into	yes_or_no	YES if the view has an INSTEAD OF INSERT trigger defined on it, NO if not

www.ingramcontent.com/pod-product-compliance
Lightning Source LLC
Chambersburg PA
CBHW080153060326

40689CB00018B/3955